The Executive Politics and Governance series

The *Executive Politics and Governance* series focuses on central government, its organisation and its instruments. It is particularly concerned with how the changing conditions of contemporary governing affect perennial questions in political science and public administration. *Executive Politics and Governance* is therefore centrally interested in questions such as how politics interacts with bureaucracies, how issues rise and fall on political agendas, and how public organisations and services are designed and operated. This book series encourages a closer engagement with the role of politics in shaping executive structures, and how administration shapes politics and policy-making. In addition, this series also wishes to engage with the scholarship that focuses on the organisational aspects of politics, such as government formation and legislative institutions.

The series welcomes high quality research-led monographs with comparative appeal. Edited volumes that provide in-depth analysis and critical insights into the field of Executive Politics and Governance are also encouraged.

Titles include:

Simon Bastow
GOVERNANCE, PERFORMANCE, AND CAPACITY STRESS
The Chronic Case of Prison Crowding

Will Jennings
OLYMPIC RISKS

Martin Lodge and Kai Wegrich (*editors*)
EXECUTIVE POLITICS IN TIMES OF CRISIS

The Executive Politics and Governance series
Series standing order ISBN 978–0–230–30484–0
(outside North America only)

You can receive future titles in this series as they are published by placing a standing order. Please contact your bookseller or, in case of difficulty, write to us at the address below with your name and address, the title of the series and the ISBN quoted above.

Customer Services Department, Macmillan Distribution Ltd, Houndmills, Basingstoke, Hampshire RG21 6XS, England

Governance, Performance, and Capacity Stress

The Chronic Case of Prison Crowding

Simon Bastow
Senior Research Fellow, LSE Public Policy Group,
London School of Economics and Political Science, UK

palgrave
macmillan

First published 2013 by
PALGRAVE MACMILLAN

Palgrave Macmillan in the UK is an imprint of Macmillan Publishers Limited, registered in England, company number 785998, of Houndmills, Basingstoke, Hampshire RG21 6XS.

Palgrave Macmillan in the US is a division of St Martin's Press LLC, 175 Fifth Avenue, New York, NY 10010.

Palgrave Macmillan is the global academic imprint of the above companies and has companies and representatives throughout the world.

Palgrave® and Macmillan® are registered trademarks in the United States, the United Kingdom, Europe and other countries.

ISBN: 978–1–137–28915–5

This book is printed on paper suitable for recycling and made from fully managed and sustained forest sources. Logging, pulping and manufacturing processes are expected to conform to the environmental regulations of the country of origin.

A catalogue record for this book is available from the British Library.

A catalog record for this book is available from the Library of Congress.

To Dorothy Hicks Harrison

Contents

List of Figures ix

List of Tables xi

Acknowledgements xiii

Introduction 1

1 Traditional Explanations of Capacity Stress and Their Limitations 12

1.1 Capacity stress in a managerialist era 14
1.2 Strategic actors, rational choices, and alignment problems 19
1.3 Adding in institutions, shared values and cultures 24
1.4 Seeing the system as a dynamic whole 30
1.5 Why we need a more integrated approach 34

2 A More Holistic Governance-Style Approach 38

2.1 The perception of prison as an inherently failing system 40
2.2 A culture of coping and making the system work 47
2.3 Direct or benign resistance to reform 51
2.4 Obsolescence and redundancy sustained in the system 56
2.5 Integrating the four loops into one 59

3 Performance and Capacity in a Managerialist Era 65

3.1 Productivity analysis as a proxy for performance 67
3.2 Adjusting productivity to account for performance 71
3.3 Countervailing dynamics of managerialist change 82
3.4 Conclusions 94

4 Measuring and Setting Capacity Standards 97

4.1 *Ex ante* and *ex post* standards for prison capacity 98
4.2 Two capacity standards 101
4.3 Perceptions of how these two standards have performed 114
4.4 Control through counterbalance between standards 119
4.5 Conclusions 121

5	**Senior Ministers and the Limits of Their Influence to Resolve the Capacity Problem**	**124**
	5.1 The view of crowding from the top of the system	125
	5.2 Autonomy of ministers to shape and impact CCS	132
	5.3 Constraints on ministerial autonomy to reform the system	139
	5.4 Conclusions	150
6	**Top Officials and the Interface between Political and Operational**	**153**
	6.1 The shift towards managerial and operational cultures	154
	6.2 The managerial challenge of making the system work	158
	6.3 Autonomy of senior officials to influence capacity	164
	6.4 How senior officials are constrained by the system	169
	6.5 Conclusions	175
7	**Governors, Staff, and Strategies of Local Adaptation**	**178**
	7.1 Managing prisoners, cost savings, and renewing physical assets	179
	7.2 How governors are constrained by managers	184
	7.3 Autonomy of governors to influence capacity in their prisons	193
	7.4 Conclusions	198
8	**Privately Contracted Prisons: New Setting, Same Condition**	**201**
	8.1 Constraints on the autonomy of the private sector	202
	8.2 The 'contractualization' of crowding and capacity stress	210
	8.3 Operational autonomy and comparisons with the public sector	218
	8.4 Conclusions	223
9	**Chronic Capacity Stress: A Complex Condition**	**225**
	9.1 Individual actors, constrained autonomy, and adaptation	227
	9.2 Theoretical implications of the holistic approach	237
	9.3 The future of chronic capacity stress: in prisons and beyond	243
Notes		251
Bibliography		261
Index		273

List of Figures

A	Four relationships at the heart of CCS in the prison system	8
1.1	Key relationships between actors in the prison system	20
1.2	A whole system view and four potential misalignment problems	32
2.1	Collapse of the rehabilitative ideal	44
2.2	Number of receptions into custody of prisoners sentenced to immediate imprisonment, by length of sentence	45
2.3	Reoffending rates for adult males, within two years of discharge from custody	46
2.4	Adding in the 'coping and crisis culture' loop	49
2.5	Adding in the 'direct or benign resistance' loop	52
2.6	Expenditure at different levels of the prison system, 1979 to 2011	54
2.7	Adding in the 'sustained obsolescence and redundancy' loop	58
2.8	CCS – the overall schema	60
3.1	Total factor productivity in the prison system, 1979 to 2011	68
3.2	Trends in labour productivity in the prison system, 1979 to 2009	69
3.3	Average annual number of prisoner escapes, per 1000 prisoners	73
3.4	Index of disturbances and riots across the prison system	74
3.5	Percentage of prisoners 'tripled' or 'doubled' in cells designed for one, since 1945	75
3.6	Rate of self-inflicted deaths in custody, per 1000 prisoners	76
3.7	Indicators of effective capacity management in the prison system	79
3.8	Revised productivity tracks after adjustments for performance quality	80
3.9	Comparing indexed rates of change in crowding and quality-adjusted productivity	83
3.10	Rates of reoffending within two years after discharge from different types of prison, for sentences less than 12 months and more than 12 months	86

3.11 Unadjusted actual reconviction rates within 18 months of release, by length of sentence 87
3.12 Progress in reconviction rates adjusted for offending characteristics of those released, within 18 months of release, by length of sentence (baseline year 2000) 88
3.13 Reference to crowding made by HM Inspectorate reports, and specific focus of the reference, 1998 to 2011 93
4.1 Crowding in local prisons and remand centres, measured against CNA 106
4.2 Crowding in adult closed training prisons, measured against CNA 107
4.3 Crowding in all other types of prisons, measured against CNA 108
5.1 Number of spoken mentions of 'crowding' in parliament, by role of the person speaking 133
6.1 Number of new prisoner places, by type of accommodation 160
6.2 Number of new prisoner places, by type of prison 160
6.3 Estimated 'headroom' capacity in the prison system and rates of executive release under End of Custody Licence (ECL) 172
7.1 Flow of prisoners processed in and out of a local prison 181
7.2 Box plots showing average daily movement of prisoners processed in and out of Birmingham prison, from January to December 2008 182
7.3 Numbers of mentions of Prisoner Officers Association (POA) and Prison Governors Association (PGA) in national newspapers 192
8.1 Growth in market share for privately contracted prisons 203

List of Tables

1.1	Key features of new public management (NPM) and how they relate to CCS	16
1.2	Four cultural archetypes and their inherent risks	25
1.3	Three competing theoretical explanations and their inherent limitations	35
2.1	Four potential misalignments in the holistic schema and how they relate to prison crowding	41
2.2	Overview of references to rehabilitative goals in annual reports	43
3.1	Positive and negative interpretations of different capacity situations	66
3.2	Summary of performance-related data and performance targets	78
3.3	Scores for seven key quality indicators for the prison system, and calculations for quality-adjusted productivity, 1979 to 2011	81
3.4	Overcrowding drafts from region to region, July 2008 to July 2009	92
4.1	Formal targets for crowding in annuals reports of the Prison Service and NOMS	100
4.2	Certified Normal Accommodation and Operational Capacity	104
4.3	Percentage crowding in major urban local prisons, 1979 to 2009	110
4.4	Estimated stretch of Op Cap away from CNA, 2004 to 2011	112
5.1	Overview of thirty years of Secretaries of State and prison capacity	127
5.2	The range of options available to ministers for balancing demand and supply in the prison system	131
5.3	How different ministers have emphasized different options for dealing with capacity stress, 1979 to 2012	135
5.4	Percentage of references implying supply- or demand-side interpretations of crowding: under Conservative governments, 1979 to 1997	137

5.5 Percentage of references implying supply- or demand-side interpretations of crowding: under Labour governments, 1997 to 2010 138
6.1 Summary of key senior officials in the prison system, 1979 to 2012 157
6.2 New additional prison capacity built by region, 1979 to 2012 162
6.3 Type of new additional prison capacity by region, 1979 to 2012 163
8.1 Privately contracted prisons, since 1992 204
8.2 Percentage crowding in private prisons, 1992 to 2012 216
9.1 Constrained autonomy of four groups of actors 230

Acknowledgements

I would like to thank the National Offender Management Service (NOMS) for agreeing to grant approval for this research in June 2009. I am particularly grateful to Dr Susan Wishart, Chair of the NOMS National Research Committee, for overseeing this process. Without this approval, it would not have been possible to produce this book in its current form. I would like to thank all the 120 or so persons who gave up their time to be interviewed, plus the many others who took part in focus groups. Research trips to twenty-nine prisons were undoubtedly the most enjoyable and fulfilling aspects of the research, and I met many interesting, kind, and thoughtful officials who, in their own different ways, greatly enriched and improved the quality of the work. I would also like to thank some key people who have contributed in important ways. Jane Tinkler and Patrick Dunleavy, at the LSE Public Policy Group, have both been endlessly supportive and have inspired me along the way. Martin Lodge, co-editor of this Executive Politics and Governance book series and professor in the LSE Government department, has been vital in helping the book to take shape. I would also like to thank Ed Page and Oliver James for their valuable comments on an earlier draft of the book which also happened to be my doctoral thesis (Bastow, 2012). My thanks also go to Andrew Baird and Amber Stone-Galilee at Palgrave Macmillan for their help in getting this book ready for publication; and Kai Wegrich, the other co-editor of this Palgrave Executive Politics and Governance series. It is also important to mention other important people who have supported and inspired me over the years. These include Klaus Goetz, Helen Margetts, David Rowland, Ian Hawkesworth, Oyvind Rekstad, Leandro Carrera, and all the great people that I have worked with at the LSE Public Policy Group. Finally, I would like to thank my mum and dad, and Belinda, for all their love and support.

Introduction

> There is a curious unanimity, just a failure to make it happen. There is nobody who thinks that crowding doesn't matter, nobody who thinks you shouldn't provide a prison estate to deal with the adequate numbers, nobody who disagrees with the view that there are significant numbers of people [in prison] who shouldn't be there. And there is nobody who disagrees with the idea of providing appropriate alternatives to imprisonment if possible. (Former Conservative Home Secretary)

On a normal Friday in the autumn of 2009 I spent the day as a London School of Economics researcher in the reception of Brixton prison, observing the work done by prison officers to process prisoners in and out of the jail. As a local prison, Brixton holds prisoners on remand, on trial, or awaiting sentencing at courts across south-east London. Managing the constant movement of prisoners in and out is therefore a major part of the daily routine. On a busy day, the reception can process anything up to eighty prisoners in and roughly the same number out (equivalent to one tenth of the prison's capacity). The modern-looking vans of the prisoner-escort contractors inch their way through the narrow Georgian gatehouse, and perform five- or six-point turns in order to manoeuvre around the cramped space of the prison courtyard. It is one of many visible manifestations of the way in which ancient and modern interact to keep the system continually moving.

For each of the thirty-five prisoners going out to court that morning, staff carried out a full strip-search, bagged up the prisoner's case files and personal effects, prepared a prisoner-escort record, and all of this went with the prisoner onto the Serco van waiting in the yard. Of those thirty-five prisoners leaving Brixton in the morning, twenty returned to the prison in the evening. On their return, staff performed pretty much exactly the same procedure in reverse – a full strip-search, re-opening the bags of case files and personal property, returning essential items to the prisoner, and packing away the remaining property into black boxes and into the storerooms. For these twenty prisoners, officers were spending much of their morning packing up the files and property only to have to unpack the same files and property in the evening.

Why was this necessary, I wondered, when there was a relatively strong likelihood that most of those prisoners would return to the prison in the evening? Staff explained that the pressure on capacity in London local prisons, and the movement of prisoners around the London system, meant they could not guarantee that those leaving Brixton in the morning would return to Brixton in the evening. Court sessions may run late and vans may have to wait for the last prisoner in the group. In the meantime, available spaces at Brixton fill up with new prisoner intake, displacing the morning's prisoners elsewhere. Also, prisoner-escort contractors design their routes to be as cost-efficient as possible, and hence prisoners may be inadvertently displaced as part of the need to fill up vans on pre-set routes. The behaviour of other London local prisons also had an effect. If Wandsworth decides to shut its gates for the evening, Brixton reception may have to take those prisoners that would have gone into Wandsworth, again displacing other Brixton prisoners who had not yet returned. In short, the risk of a prisoner not returning to Brixton in the evening meant that their files and property were bagged up and sent along with them, in order to avoid the stresses of having to reunite them with their property once they had left the prison.

The difficulty of locating prisoners once they had left Brixton compounded this problem. At that time there was no prisoner database that would allow staff an instant overview of where individuals had gone once they had left Brixton. This complicated the task of sending their property after them. Furthermore, the logistical systems involved were largely free of what we might expect as modern technology to aid the process of linking prisoners, their files, and their property. Prisoner-property boxes were not electronically tagged. There were no van-compatible boxes which could be slotted into the vans without having to decant things back and forth between black boxes and plastic bags. Prisoner case files were moved around in often sizeable piles of cardboard folders and loose-leaf, bagged up in a plastic sack with a tie around the neck. Indeed, staff relied largely on manual and handwritten registration techniques, with prisoner-property information written longhand in a large bound ledger. None of this was what one might expect from a modern logistical operation in the late 2000s – even if it was a prison.

At the end of my day in reception, the duty manager came to say good-bye and good luck with the research. He said he hoped that I'd got a good insight into the kinds of pressures which reception staff in a large London local prison have to cope with on a daily basis. I felt that I had got an insight into a system which is expected to operate continually at high levels of capacity, and in a context which is inherently uncertain, emotionally charged, and often hazardous. Yet it was clear also that, despite this, here was a system that had managed to sustain and, to a large extent, normalize striking levels of obsolescence, inefficiency, and redundancy.

Staff on duty that day were well aware of these limitations, yet also fatalistic about the possibilities of change. The patterns of prisoner movement in London were beyond the control of Brixton prison, they pointed out, and redesigning the process in Brixton would require redesign of the process across other prisons. The lack of the modern technology was down to funding and decisions made way above their pay-grade. They just worked with what they had. I suggested that changing the system would allow staff to be redeployed in more fulfilling ways around the prison, rather than (needlessly) packing and unpacking property all day. Even if this argument could be made, they explained, it would be difficult to get it past the union. They would see it as a threat. This would make the issue political, yet for ministers it would be seen as such a small operational issue that it would be unlikely ever to figure prominently on a minister's to-do list. From all angles, perceptions on the constraints of modernizing, even this small technical aspect of the system, made the problem appear beyond the gift of any one actor in the system to solve.

Even in this short vignette, it is possible to see how pulling on a seemingly innocuous thread can unravel a potentially complex tapestry of governance considerations, all of which seem to implicate much wider questions about the way the prison system works as a whole. Indeed, this vignette illustrates the key themes at the heart of this book and its analysis of prison crowding. Three themes are worth mentioning from the outset.

First, it illustrates a potentially complex relationship between the performance and capacity of public-policy systems. It may, for example, be possible for systems to perform well, or simply continue to function in one way or another, with or despite limited capacity and resources. Indeed, in a managerialist world this may even be desirable. Yet, it is also likely that limited capacity and resources will constrain the ability of the system to perform well. Hence, we must view this relationship as incorporating essential (albeit ever-changing) equilibria between the two. The central concept developed in this book – 'chronic capacity stress' (CCS) – is one that helps us to understand the dynamics of this balance in public policy systems that appear to operate under continual pressure. CCS can be defined as follows:

a) a significant stress on the capacity of a policy system to respond to expectations and demands made on it;
b) one that is sustainable over time, and can be managed as such, and therefore becomes chronic in the system;
c) one that is a function of the way in which the system itself is governed and operates;
d) one that is simultaneously both cause and symptom of dysfunction in the overall governance of the system.

Related to this is the second major theme of the book. A large public-policy system, such as prisons, incorporates a great range of different types of actors and stakeholders – from senior politicians, through the ranks of bureaucrats and managers, to prison officers and prisoners – often with shared, conflicting, or just diverse values and goals and interests. The system is the entirety of these actors, and its outcomes are the cumulative affect of their priorities, efforts, decisions and actions. As we have seen in the Brixton vignette, the individuals who make the system work can only do so from their position in it. They may recognize the problems and see the sense in solving them. They may be able to go some way in mitigating or compensating for them, and on occasion, they may have some degree of success in alleviating them. However, in many other important ways, they are constrained – by dint of their position in the system – in how far they are able to go in doing this.

The third major theme of the book, one that is already strongly apparent in the Brixton vignette, is the need for a sufficiently expansive explanation, analytical and theoretical, for how and why CCS sustains. As mentioned, pulling on a single thread unravels a much wider nexus of considerations and constraints, and hence in diagnosing the problem of CCS, we must, it seems, give our lens width and depth enough to encompass not only the dynamics of individual stakeholders in the system, but also how all of those dynamics fit together to contribute to sustaining the chronic condition. In such circumstances, it is clearly not enough to identify one group of actors or one set of processes as the sole causal mechanism for sustaining CCS. These actors or processes may be an important part of the picture, but we must also take into account that they are determined or shaped by the reality and predicaments they face as part of a larger system.

So what are the main intentions of this book? First and foremost, it is a study of how a large public-policy system has coped with and sustained CCS over a long period of time. Prison crowding provides a familiar and, in many ways, archetypal case of CCS, and I look at it in the context of the last thirty-two years in the England and Wales prison system. As discussed already, the decision to look at the one system in one jurisdiction over an extended period of time provides the opportunity to explore in a fine-grained way the dynamics that underpin CCS, the perspectives and predicaments of individual stakeholders in the system, and the way in which the whole system fits together to sustain the CCS syndrome.

There is much in this book for those with interest in prisons generally, as well as the specific development of the England and Wales system throughout a managerialist era. The England and Wales system is one of the larger and more developed in comparative terms, and there will be much of relevance to readers from other countries, even if it is not explicitly a formal comparative analysis across prison systems. The empirical focus on the England and Wales system is detailed and in-depth, based on a mix of time-series data analysis, extensive interviewing with former ministers, top officials, managers and governors, prison staff, and the private sector. It is a thirty-two-year picture of complex change in a large and core public-policy system – still a relatively rare phenomenon in general public-policy literatures.

It is also important to say that this is a book about the dynamics within the prison system that contribute to sustaining crowding and CCS. This does not mean to suggest that the prison system itself is the *only* determining factor in the size of the prison population and crowding. Clearly, there are other factors that come into play. I have, however, chosen to scope the book in such a way that it is possible to focus on important dynamics within the prison system itself that contribute to and allow the system to sustain crowding in ways which have seemed chronic over the years. I have not covered wider issues of crime and punishment in UK society. Neither have I covered the intricacies of the legislative behaviour relating to crime and punishment, laws on sentencing, or judicial behaviour.

For many readers, this will seem like a far too narrow scope for a book about prison crowding and what to do about it. In more recent years, particularly as the UK prison population has climbed to around 85,000, conventional wisdom has tended to support the view that the root cause of crowding is an excessively high prison population, and that the secret to resolving crowding and problems of prison more widely lies in finding ways to reduce the size of the prison population. It is easy to have sympathy with this view; however, this should not preclude the question of whether there are also dynamics within the prison system itself that contribute to sustaining crowding and CCS. The basic argument of this book is that there are, and that they are complex. Controversial though this may be in certain camps, it is an argument well worth pursuing, as I hope this book will bear out.

It is also important to mention that this book is part of wider series on executive politics and governance (Lodge and Wegrich, 2012). Both themes run to the heart of what the book is about. Looking at prison crowding and CCS as 'whole-system' phenomena, the book encompasses the wide range of dynamics in play from high politics and ministers, through the work of bureaucratic officials at the interface of political and operational, to the frontline work of prison staff and other services provided to prisoners. In this sense, the book has much to offer scholars and practitioners interested in the interface between politics and bureaucracy. Similarly, the 'whole-system' approach draws directly upon governance paradigms, and ultimately the thrust of the analytical and theoretical work is towards a more 'holistic' governance-style approach to understanding CCS.

Although themes of executive politics and governance shape the approach in the book, its findings also arguably do much to reshape how we look at these themes in future – particularly in relation to large and complex public-policy systems. A main aim of the book is to show how their characteristics – in this case, crowding and CCS – must be seen in the round, interpreted in ways which acknowledge constrained autonomy of actors, and understood in ways which take into account manageable and acceptable states of equilibrium through time. As we will see throughout the book, the story of CCS seems more complicated than just one of 'politics of bureaucracy', in which actors in the system selfishly follow their own interests and motives. Their position in the system, in all sorts of ways, constrains them from such pursuits. Similarly, the story of CCS seems more complicated than one of 'bureaucracy of politics', in which actors are unable to act autonomously or strategically at all due to the bureaucratic, institutional, and cultural world in which they operate. Clearly, actors in the system at all levels have certain levels of autonomy and influence over their bit of the wider problem. The challenge therefore is to understand how these two possibilities interact and, more specifically, how they interact dynamically over time to sustain the chronic condition. Understanding this in the context of prisons and crowding is where this book, I hope, has much to offer.

The structure of the book

Chapter 1 asks how traditional political science and management theory can help to explain how and why public-policy systems sustain CCS. I focus on three axiomatic groups of theoretical approach – rational choice, cultural theory, and systems theory. Each of these, respectively, place explanatory emphasis on different aspects: rational choice of strategic actors; cultural theory on prevailing values and cultures; and systems theory on the non-linear dynamics of systems generally. All three groups of theoretical orientation offer important insights for explaining potential aspects of CCS and how it sustains in a large public-policy system. However, each approach independently seems insufficient to capture the particular systemic nature of CCS. This leads us to conclude that a more holistic governance-style approach is required, one that integrates key aspects of these axiomatic theories, and in a way that helps us to understand how a system can function at acceptable level of performance despite CCS.

Chapter 2 begins the work of reorganizing these theoretical building blocks to form a possible hypothetical schema for understanding the dynamics of CCS in the prison system. I introduce four key interrelated aspects of CCS as follows:

1. systemic ambivalence towards rehabilitative goals of prison, further aggravated by perceptions that the prison population is ever too high for this situation to be reversed;
2. a coping culture allowing the prison system to function in response to ever higher prison population, yet in a way which feeds back into perceptions of the system inherently failing;
3. direct or benign resistance in response to political and policy interventions imposed on the system, themselves in response to perceptions of failure;
4. sustained obsolescence and redundancy in the system aggravated by resistance and coping cultures, which feeds back into perceptions of failure.

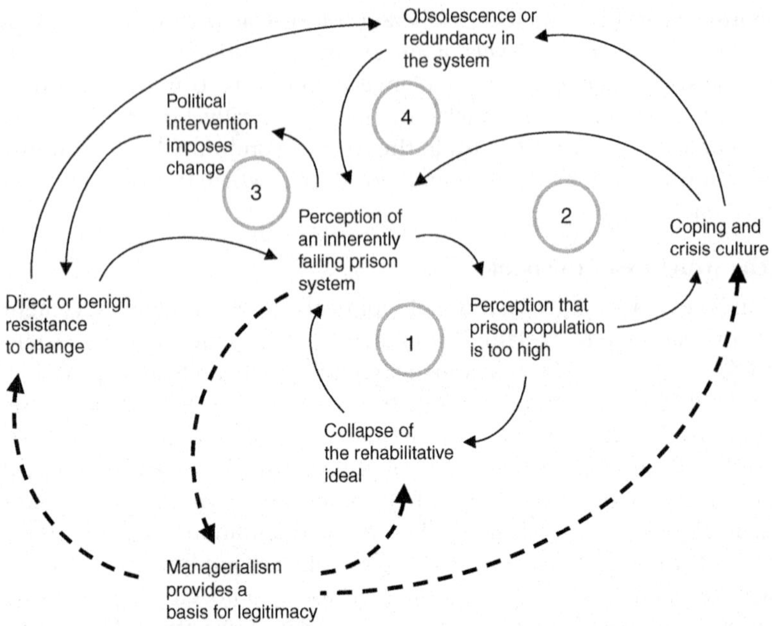

Figure A Four relationships at the heart of CCS in the prison system

Based on existing prisons literature, I discuss each of these aspects in turn, and show how each of them can be built into an overall schema depicting the dynamics of CCS. This schema consists of aggravating and compensating factors that together form a kind of performance equilibrium of which CCS is a necessary function. The schema is previewed here above.

Chapters 3 and 4 develop some important aspects relating to the impact of managerialist change in the prison system over three decades. Chapter 3 uses 'quality-adjusted productivity' as a proxy indicator for performance of the prison system. It argues that managerialist features have played an important role in bringing about performance improvements over three decades. Indeed, managerialism has had a 'tightening' effect on the system, allowing it to cope at close-to-tolerance levels of capacity and in a more ordered and disciplined way. Paradoxically, however, managerialism has also had countervailing effects on the ability of the system to address goals around rehabilitation, and has also contributed to sustaining inefficiencies and obsolescence in the system.

Chapter 4 looks at role of standards in protecting the prison system against crowding over the years. Two standards have been central in this respect, Certified Normal Accommodation (CNA) and Operational Capacity (Op Cap). CNA has long been an input-oriented standard defining what prisons *should* be expected to hold; however, for many years, most local prisons have operated well above CNA. Although it continues to serve as an 'ideal world' measure for an un-crowded prison system, it is also widely seen as obsolescent, and devalued by the reality of crowding in the system. Op Cap, on the other hand, is an outcome-oriented standard defining what prisons *can* hold safely and decently. As a managerialist device, this standard has provided a basis for rationalizing and justifying stretch in capacity of the system. Both have been important to the system in different ways to different actors, and in combination have provided a 'hybrid' means of control through counterbalance. This has been an important legitimating basis on which the system has sustained and coped with crowding.

The next three chapters look at the issue of crowding and CCS from the perspective of key groups of actors – senior ministers (Chapter 5), senior executive officials (Chapter 6), and prison governors and staff (Chapter 7). Up to this point, the book has talked in relatively abstract terms about 'the system', but clearly the system is constituted of 'real-life' actors who face dilemmas and choices, take decisions and actions, and do so in ways that are shaped by all sorts of forces and considerations. At the heart of each of these chapters is the concept of 'constrained autonomy', depicting a situation in which actors, in different ways, have a degree of autonomy to impact on issues of capacity, but at the same time are also inherently constrained by their position in the system. In each group of actors, we identify important questions about the extent to which any one individual group of theories, or indeed any one theory in particular, is able to encompass the broad variety of dynamics and considerations that each of these actors must face in finding ways to manage their own 'local' equilibrium positions in the system.

Constrained autonomy is also visible in the growth of markets for privately managed prisons since the early 1990s, and in the predicaments with which the firms providing prison services must contend. This challenges the conventional wisdom that private-sector firms are able to operate with high degrees of autonomy and engage in rent-seeking. In Chapter 8, I show how private-sector operators, as part of the national prison system, are subject to many of the same constraints which the public sector must face. Indeed, one can argue that they are more constrained than many public-sector prisons. Despite this, however, privately run prisons have much greater autonomy to do things to mitigate the effects of crowding, and to get more out of latent capacity, particularly in the way in which they deploy staff, use facilities, and encourage more 'normal' working cultures. This presents interesting countervailing dynamics, in which private-sector prisons show many of the same symptoms of CCS, yet at the same time have different kinds of autonomy with which to counteract these symptoms.

In the final chapter, I bring together the holistic concept of CCS and the analysis of constrained autonomy of actors at different levels in the system. Looking at the four aspects of CCS, it is possible to see how actors at all levels find themselves constrained by those above and below them in the system, and that much of their focus lies therefore in finding ways to keep their bit of the system in some kind of manageable and acceptable equilibria. In looking at the system and the actors within, it becomes clear that it is beyond the gift of any one actor in the system to resolve the problem. Although it may be tempting to blame senior politicians, even politicians are constrained in their ability to reform this large and complex system. They may have autonomy to shape and carry reform so far, but they are also at the mercy of wider and more uncontrollable constraints in terms of how far they can push reform through. At each level of the system, actors are able to recognize and acknowledge the problems. They also recognize the limits to what they can do to solve them, and the rationale behind what they have to do to sustain equilibrium in their part of the system. When seen in the context of the system and the predicaments they face, their choices seem rational and entirely reasonable. Collectively, however, their choices feed into sustaining the condition of CCS writ large.

The implication is therefore that traditional theoretical explanations have to be integrated into a more holistic approach to the problem. Actors can have interests, priorities, or strategies, and act on them. But these will only tell us so much about how particular outcomes evolve in a systemic context. Similarly, actors are likely to be influenced by prevailing cultures and conventional wisdoms but, again, these will only predict to a certain extent how they will act. Explanation of CCS must therefore find a way of integrating agency and culture to take into account how these things are shaped by the systemic context in which actors act. For the concept of managerialism, CCS and constrained autonomy also present quite fundamental questions. On the one hand, managerialism has done much to bring discipline and order to the prison system over the years. Yet, on the other hand, it is has done much to constrain the system from excelling in its performance. The analysis of CCS shows how these things can be complicated in a large and complex public-policy system. It shows how they can incorporate aggravating and compensating dynamics simultaneously. It also reveals that policy systems can incorporate simultaneously these countervailing characteristics – efficiency and inefficiency, success and failure, and, in economistic terms, relative under-supply and over-supply of capacity. This underscores the importance of the holistic approach to understand the dynamics of CCS as a function of performance equilibrium.

1
Traditional Explanations of Capacity Stress and Their Limitations

Take a snapshot of any public-policy system at a particular moment in time, and you will see a picture of equilibrium between the demands made upon that system by governments and society, and all the things that the system does (and does not do) to somehow meet those demands. Continually evolving values and expectations are balanced against resources, capabilities, and efforts of actors involved, all of which sustains an equilibrium that allows the system, in one way or another, to fulfil its purpose, do its job, add value to society – in short, perform.

Clearly, however, a snapshot of the system is insufficient to understand the dynamics which determine equilibria over time. The actors that constitute the system are continually in motion and, through their values, cultures, relationships, strategies, choices, and actions, they determine the dynamics of continually evolving equilibria. Characteristics of public-policy systems can be seen as outcomes of all this, properties of these equilibria and the dynamics which are contained within. This book is about one particular characteristic described as *chronic capacity stress* (CCS). It is examined through the lens of what seems like a classic and archetypal illustration – the familiar issue of prison crowding. Through this I ask some key questions:

- What is the nature of CCS?
- How and why does it sustain?
- And how can we develop ways to alleviate it?

For many core state services, prisons included, the systems that provide them may be seen as too important to be allowed to fail completely.

Whereas failure in the private sector often, although by no means always, can lead to firms going out of business, core public-sector systems of the kind which are vital to modern society often seem to go on and on. It is inconceivable that a prison system, for example, would be allowed to fold or go bust (though abolitionists may be in favour). A consequence is that these systems tend to incorporate any imbalance or shortfall (between things society demands of them and their capacity to supply those things) into their equilibria. If demands are too high, then actors find ways of doing the best they can to cope and make the system (or at least their bit of the system) work. If resources or capabilities are too low, then actors can find ways of recalibrating expectations accordingly. This recalibration may be entirely strategic and instrumental. It may on the other hand be a genuine response to the need to find ways of rationalizing why a system is having to under-perform in the face of seemingly impossible constraints.

It is interesting therefore that political science and public policy literature over the years has tended to focus on the extremes of public-sector performance, either failure or excellence.[1] Yet surprisingly little has been written about these positions in between, the tendency for public-policy systems to find ways of coping, getting by, managing without necessarily completely failing nor completely excelling in what they do. In the vignette in the opening pages of this book we have seen how a public-policy system can incorporate elements of success and failure simultaneously, and not only that, for these elements to be aggravating and compensating, linked and related to each other in often complex ways.

There are perhaps notable exceptions to this general blind spot. Rittel and Webber (1973) outlined the concept of 'wicked' public-policy problems, the kind which are intractable, complex, and never seem to get solved. Hogwood and Peters (1985) characterized 'chronic' problems as the kind which tend to 'go on and on, and never appear to be cured' (p. 10), and after long enough 'become a fact of life rather than a problem' (p. 11). Whether wicked or chronic, these problems are the kind that tend to get coped with, absorbed, and normalized. They may build up into acute problems every so often, or they may stay incubated in the system for long periods of time. They can behave in complex ways as both cause and symptom of dysfunction, and hence can seldom be reduced to simple causal factors. They may also get reified and given life of their own, and used to justify or excuse why characteristics of systems are as they are. Chronic problems in large policy systems, much like in humans in fact, tend therefore to be multi-faceted, and in need of holistic, all-round, and balanced diagnoses or interventions.

How then does public policy and political science literature help us to understand the dynamics of crowding and CCS? How do existing theories help us to shed light on why a large public-policy system may be able to sustain a situation of capacity stress over the long term? And how do existing theories help to capture the complexities and the multi-dimensionality of this as a chronic condition?

In this opening chapter, I turn to three well-established groups of theory for insights – rational choice theory, cultural theory, and system theory. Each in their own way offer insights into the dynamics of the problem. But independently they do not seem sufficient to capture the entirety of the chronic condition. As David Easton (1965) has pointed out:

> No one way of conceptualizing any major area of human behaviour will do full justice to all its variety and complexity. Each type of theoretical orientation brings to the surface a different set of problems, provides unique insights and emphases, and thereby makes it possible for alternative and even competing theories to be equally and simultaneously useful, although often for quite different purposes. (p. 23)

As the analysis in the book will show, these three approaches should not be seen as potential competing theories vying to be the best and only explanation of CCS. Rather they must be seen as necessarily complementary approaches, interrelated and dynamic. We cannot and should not reject them, but merely entertain the idea that in order to understand CCS in its entirety, they must be broken down and redeployed in a more integrative way.

1.1 Capacity stress in a managerialist era

Ideas relating to stress on the state and public sector have long permeated political science and public administration. From the late 1970s, political scientists drew attention to problems of 'ungovernability' and 'overload' on the UK state, arising from a combination of unchecked growth in the size of the public sector and an expansion of the functions that government should be expected to fulfil (King, 1975; Rose, 1979, 1980; Birch, 1984). Political scientists pointed out that such expansion and growth had in effect reduced the capacity of government to deal with problems effectively, and this encouraged a sense of pessimism about what big government had become and how it needed to slim down and shape up. Capacity stress, in this context, was linked to perceptions of excessive weight and expectation, a demand side that had become too large for supply.

Whereas critics had complained about overload and excessive demand during the 1970s and early 1980s, waves of managerialist change from then on took perceptions of capacity stress to the other extreme. New Right doctrines began to gain dominance at the heart of the UK state, and underpinned 'new public management' (NPM) reforms throughout the 1980s and 1990s. These reforms focused more directly on efficiency and effectiveness of government and the public sector (Jenkins, 2008), inculcation of private sector management principles into the public sector, and the integration of private sector markets and competition into traditional monopolistic state forms of delivery. Christensen and Lægraid (2002) describe this as 'one-dimensional economic-normative dominance' (p. 301), in which 'reform ideas are imbued with a common vision of a new orthodoxy with strong market and management orientation' (p. 303).

In many ways, NPM changes were a direct response and antidote to the kinds of problems associated with overload and ungovernability. Critics began to interpret the problem as one of supply-side stress, a 'hollowing out' (Rhodes, 1994, 1996; Foster and Plowden, 1996), and squeezing of resources and capacity within. Waves of privatization and outsourcing impacted on the public sector, and transferred generic administrative functions into private-sector management (Margetts, 1999; Walsh, 1995). Renewed emphasis on values of efficiency and effectiveness encouraged the need to think about maximizing impact from available resources and capacity, and systematic tightening or squeezing of resources over time (Chapman, 1982). Running a form of constructive under-supply of capacity provided a way of 'sweating' public-sector assets, 'keeping its feet to the fire', and heavy emphasis on performance targets and measurement sought to underpin 'value of money' in what the state and public services were providing. Table 1.1 summarizes key aspects of NPM change and links them to possible sources of capacity stress.

Clearly, however, such characterization of change from one extreme to the other seems far too simplistic. Critics have pointed out, for example, much of the pessimism associated with ideas of overload and ungovernability did not take into account the inherent resilience of the systems involved (Birch, 1984). As Goetz (2008) argues, the 'gloomy scenarios of ungovernability [...] have not materialized' (p. 273). Likewise we may

Table 1.1 Key features of new public management (NPM) and how they relate to capacity stress

	Three dimensions of governance		
	Ordering principles	**Levels of organization**	**Steering mechanisms**
General governance dimension	Boundaries of public and private, and the limits and instruments of state power.	Allocation of policy and implementation tasks across different tiers of government.	Means by which power, interests, rights, and obligations are mediated between actors.
Particular feature of new public management (NPM)	Strong emphasis on efficiency and effectiveness. Integration of private-sector markets and competition into public-service provision.	Fragmentation of traditional bureaucratic hierarchies into mission-specific agencies. Principle of separation of policy and implementation.	Incentivizing actors around outputs and outcomes. Widespread use of contracts, outsourcing, and performance management.
How this potentially contributes to capacity stress	'Hollowing out' of public sector and squeezing of resources.	Capacity leaks out of the system due to principal–agent and coordination problems.	Transaction costs and complexity of public-policy systems increase.
Developments associated with late NPM and possible new paradigms	Private-sector markets and competition still a major factor in public management.	Reintegration of government structures and systems. Emphasis on co-production of services with local and third-sector suppliers.	Radical disintermediation in delivery chains. Digitization is key in facilitating this.

Source: The three governance dimensions in this table are based on my own analysis of Gamble and Thomas (2010, p. 4). I have found them a useful basis for organizing key dimensions of 'new public management' (NPM), and showing the links between the specific paradigm of NPM and more general themes at the heart of governance.

have seen signs of 'hollowing out' and ongoing financial stress to the public sector from contracting and outsourcing throughout the 1980s and 1990s, but this has not translated pound-for-pound into large-scale reductions in the cost or size of the core public sector, or in striking improvements in productivity (Dunleavy and Carrera, 2013). The state has proven resilient in lots of different ways. So we are faced, on the one hand, with conceptual models or paradigms of public-management change and, on the other, a more complex and mixed picture of actual change through time. This inherent ambivalence has not been lost on critics. Focus in the last decade has turned to the 'paradoxes' of managerialism and modernization (Maor, 1999; Hood and Peters, 2004; Margetts et al., 2010), and these insights have highlighted the limitations of the paradigm in how much it can tell us about the way in which large and complex public-policy systems work in real life.

The rise and maturation of NPM will be a major theme of this book. In many ways, the prison system has been an archetypal adopter of NPM change, and it has also shown countervailing and indeed paradoxical dynamics in its relationship with system capacity and performance. As we will see, CCS appears to incorporate these dynamics simultaneously, on the one hand, squeezing and hollowing out (i.e. under-supply) and, on the other, aspects of overload and excessive expectation (i.e. over-demand). Similarly, as we will see, there is much about NPM that has helped the prison system to cope and indeed improve. But there is also much about it that has constrained and shaped the system in ways that have required it to cope in the first place.

Paradigms such as NPM provide useful tools with which to boil down complexity into manageable concepts, as well as help to explore the causal dynamics between them. The problem is, however, that once we begin to dig down into cases in more empirical detail, and understand these dynamics, it becomes apparent that these paradigms will only take us so far. In her stylish analysis of the problems facing the UK prison system, for example, Lacey (2008) uses 'varieties of capitalism' paradigms to argue that the political economic structures of liberal market economies, notably the UK and the US, create specific incentives for politicians and governments to allow prison populations to increase, while at the same time, deprioritize rehabilitative goals of prison and under-invest in non-custodial alternatives. It is a good example of how paradigmatic tools can be applied as explanatory or independent variables of change, and the neatness of the argument has much to recommend it. Nevertheless, as we will see throughout this book, to generalize about the dynamics of stress at a comparative-system level runs the risk that we normalize important forces within a system that seem to run counter to the predictions generated by the paradigm itself.

It seems necessary therefore to move away from specific paradigms, and formulate the theoretical schema for understanding CCS around the more general concept of 'governance'. We can of course understand and interpret NPM in terms of governance, as Table 1.1 does. Governance can be seen as a more general set of concepts, whereas NPM can be seen as a specific paradigmatic variation of these concepts. There are of course potentially interesting links and commonalities between the two that are worth mentioning. For example, a key feature of NPM has been a disaggregation and fragmentation of what we might call traditional hierarchical bureaucracies, as well as the introduction of new types of actors into the policy process, not least the private sector. Inherent in governance literatures also has been a sense that public-policy environments and the institutions that give them shape have somehow become more complex and variegated. The need to control this more fragmented universe has encouraged the governance metaphor of 'steering rather than rowing' to describe the strategic challenge facing governments in a governance era (Peters and Savoie, 2000; Pierre and Peters, 2005). In this sense, the rise of governance can be seen as a response or antidote to the pathologies of NPM.

It is an interesting paradox, however, that some of the key assumptions and prescriptions of governance as an antidote to NPM indeed share many of the same principles of NPM itself. For a start, the concept of 'steering' implies a self-sustaining paradigm of public management, based closely on principles of markets in which economic actors respond to structured incentives that have been instrumentally designed. As Dunsire explains in *Holistic Governance* (1990), the challenge for governments under such principles becomes one of finding ways to intervene sufficiently to keep this self-sustaining logic of incentives and sanctions working towards desired outcomes. As his book title suggests, this must be a holistic enterprise, one in which policy makers are able to keep the whole system working towards desired outcomes. The basic point is that this discourse of institutional design and getting the incentive structures right is also at the heart of NPM doctrines. It is the idea that it is possible to intervene in all-encompassing ways, to influence all actors in the system, in the right way, all of the time. As we see later in this chapter, there are limitations to this doctrine of instrumental agency.

As a general approach to understanding the problem of CCS, however, it seems that governance must be the way forward. Its general mood value, prescriptive outlook, and broad applicability may make it difficult to define, as critics have argued (Rhodes, 1996), but this may also be one of its conceptual strengths in that it is not a pre-defined theory or paradigm, but a more loosely defined set of principles that can be used to understand the dynamics of whole systems and how they sustain particular characteristics. In this sense, governance gives us a certain conceptual looseness and flexibility with which to scope and build from first principles.

If our overarching approach to understanding crowding and CCS in this book is one of governance, then we must be clear about what the main components of a governance approach should be. Even proponents of governance over the years have acknowledged that the concept is still in need of greater specificity and more integrated understanding of how individuals that make up the systems interact with the institutional and cultural structures in which they operate. Peters (2010), for example, casts a critical eye over governance literature, and suggests that they 'do not have any explicit mechanisms of integrating individuals and structures' (p. 17). In many ways this book is an integrative project along these lines. It is an attempt to use a holistic governance-style approach to understand the dynamics of CCS and performance.

In the rest of this chapter, I examine what I consider to be three key aspects of such an approach – strategic actors, institutions and culture, and the dynamics of systems. Each has much to contribute to understanding of the overall problem of CCS. Yet, independently, each has limitations that only the others can mitigate.

1.2 Strategic actors, rational choices, and alignment problems

A good place to start in understanding why policy systems sustain CCS is with the individual actors who constitute those systems, and the way in which their choices and the decisions perpetuate the condition. From a rational-choice perspective, chronicity can be explained as a recurring outcome of the entirety of the decisions and actions taken by actors in the system over time. What is 'rational' in rational choice, however, is determined intrinsically by the structure of incentives that individual actors face (Coleman and Fararo, 1992; Scharpf, 1997; Besley, 2006). The underlying assumption here is that actors are able to assess the range of options available to them, and make calculated decisions about which options best suit their own interest. Rationality is also 'optimizing' in that it assumes that actors choose the option that gives them what looks like the best prospective outcome in terms of their own self-interest (however that may be defined). Broadly speaking, therefore, we can interpret CCS as a recurring state of capacity stress sustained by the particular structure of incentives that individual actors face.

It is probably important here to outline briefly what is meant by 'system' in the context of a prison system. As Figure 1.1 shows, it incorporates a broad range of different groups of actors from senior government ministers, through top officials and managers, to prison officers and prisoners. We can think about this system as a chain of relationships involving 'principals' and 'agents', running from voters at the top down through the parliamentary, political, executive, management echelons, to prisoners at the bottom (consumers, as it were, of prison services). Prisoners, of course, once released from prison, become voters again (at least in the England and Wales system), and thus complete the principal–agent chain. We can also conceptualize the system as a set of coordination relationships, and again some important ones in the prison system are illustrated in Figure 1.1. Let us assume that misalignments or problems with either of these relationships may be at the heart of CCS. To what extent therefore can we explain CCS as either a principal–agent problem or a coordination problem?

Thinking first about the principal–agent relationship, we might start at the top of the chain with the relationship between voters and elected

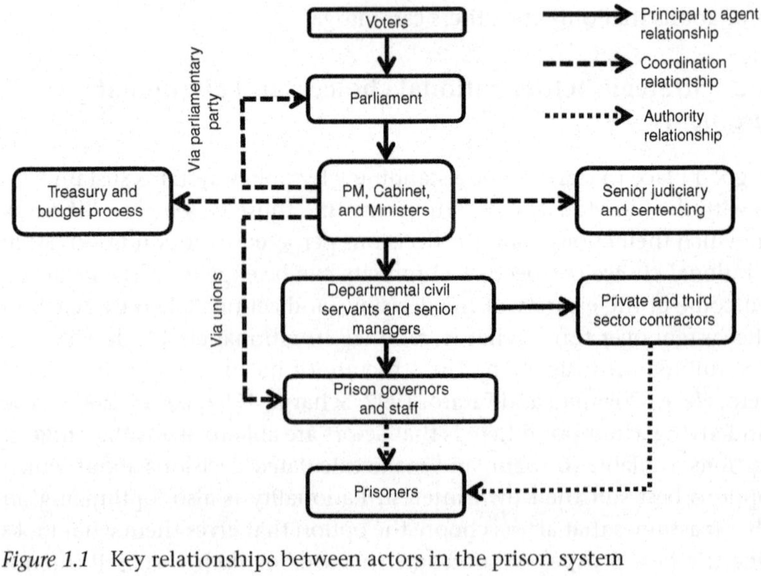

Figure 1.1 Key relationships between actors in the prison system

governments. Median-voter theory (Downs, 1957) predicts that the views and interests of elected officials will inherently reflect the views and interests of the median voter, particularly in polities with majoritarian electoral systems. We should not be surprised therefore if the issue of prison crowding ranks relatively lowly in the wider scheme of voters' and therefore politicians' priorities. Although we might find this kind of argument quite compelling, it does raise questions to suggest that things may be more complicated. For example, how might we explain significant increases in funding in prisons or surges in political or policy prioritization? Also, how might we explain signs of CCS in other policy areas that do figure highly in the priorities of the median voter, say for example health or education? In short, it may not be enough to put prison crowding down to prevailing views of a theoretical median voter.

Other principal–agent theories help us to understand the potential for CCS to be sustained in large bureaucratic systems due to various types of 'capacity-extracting' behaviour by actors within. Whereas in the example of median-voter theory above, capacity stress is likely to be caused by capacity in the system *ex ante*, in the case of principal–agent explanations, capacity leaks out of the system due to the self-interested behaviour of actors. Rent-seeking theory (Tullock, 1967) would explain CCS as the sustained outcome of self-interested behaviour by actors in the system powerful enough to extract capacity for their own ends. For it to be extensive enough to sustain CCS however, it would either have to involve collusion or complicity throughout large parts of the system, or the ability for one group or other to be in a position of such power that they are able to extract capacity with relative impunity. Similarly, bureau-shaping theory (Dunleavy, 1991; James, 2003) offers another, more nuanced explanation for how capacity could be extracted out of the system at all levels. Here, the strategy for actors is to attempt to shape their organization, budget, priorities, and workloads in such a way that it brings selective benefits to those actors concerned, and pushes the costs of doing so downwards to actors below them in the system. CCS would therefore be explained as the cumulative effect of this continual shaping and squeezing of the system, and pushing the costs of shaping down through the system.

Applied to prisons, there may be any number of ways in which shaping behaviour can aggravate CCS. Governments or ministers, for example, may espouse tough stances on crime and punishment, and 'talk up' the deterrent effects of prison. If this behaviour feeds through into an increase in the prison population, then the budget of the prison system should in theory expand to reflect this increase. However, the opportunity costs of securing or reallocating money to expand prison capacity are likely to be high, and hence governments or ministers may opt for a strategy of absorbing increased population by seeing how far they can stretch or squeeze the system with crowding and other cutbacks in service provision. Costs of shaping activity are therefore pushed downwards to senior officials who are expected to make the system work at incrementally higher levels of capacity stress. In principle, actors at all levels of the system in Figure 1.1 may engage in shaping activity, with the consequence that prisoners at the end of the chain must absorb the impacts of this 'stress' (with the risk that voters must absorb the costs of a continually stressed prison system).

There may be good reason to believe that both rent-seeking or shaping behaviour would provide credible explanation for CCS. Traditionally, prison has been an area in which a strong staff union, the Prison Officers Association, has been able to wield considerable influence over politicians and senior officials. Also, the general 'total institutional'[2] characteristics of prisons has tended to encourage rent-seeking syndromes by managers and staff, particularly during eras in which media and public rarely had the opportunity to glimpse inside prisons. Similarly, shaping behaviours at all levels have been closely associated with managerialist or NPM principles, involving a continual squeezing or paring down of capacity and resources through the system. Despite the intuitive attractions of these principal–agent explanations for CCS, however, there may be limitations to which they actually explain the entirety of the condition. Indeed, it is unlikely that individual actors will have such degrees of autonomy that they will be able to successfully maintain self-interested rent-seeking or shaping without sanction, penalty or costs. To explain CCS by simply putting it down to cumulative rent-seeking or shaping seems too reductionist in a modern public-policy setting.

A second way to conceptualize CCS may be as the cumulative outcome of continual coordination problems. Such problems at 'high' political level may involve build-up of pressure or stress being tolerated or even overlooked, until that is, crisis occurs. Game-theoretical scenarios of 'poker' or 'chicken' are relevant here for thinking about how governments handle this risk. In prisons, ministers face inherent uncertainty about fluctuations in demand for prison during their terms in office and, in this sense, they play poker with their environment in making decisions about how to prepare the system for potential fluctuations. Some ministers may be lucky in that prisons remain relatively quiet and free of crisis. Others may be less lucky, and have to contend with major disturbances or extreme population pressure which has been allowed to build up incrementally (often before their term in office has even started). In this sense, ministers must play the hand they are dealt. They must make a whole series of imperfect and 'boundedly rational' calculations about sufficiency of latent capacity in the system, probability of severe failure, and the likelihood that they will be in office and have to suffer its political consequences.

Even if a senior minister is inclined to tackle CCS, incentives must be continuously renewed for key actors to remain supportive and engaged. As Miller (1992) points out, collective-action problems inherent in the prisoner's dilemma (of the theoretical not literal kind) can be dissolved by 'repeated games' between key actors which build up trust and incentive that further cooperation is the best possible option. 'Cooperation', Miller argues, 'is only rational when each player has a great deal of confidence that others are cooperating' (p. 186). Ensuring institutional and inter-personal opportunities for successful repeated interactions between key actors is not easy however. Even with the best intentions, ministers and top officials may be inclined to make policy promises that cannot be kept for reasons entirely beyond their control. We will see in later chapters how ministers have seen goodwill and trust with senior judiciary dissipate over time on matters of prison and sentencing reform. As Riker and others illustrate, political manipulation towards desired reform may be possible for highly skilled politicians; but it is not straightforward and failure rates can be high (Riker, 1986; McLean, 2001, 2002). CCS may therefore be the result of valiant yet ultimately unsuccessful attempts to solve coordination problems, and manipulate and sustain reform.

CCS may be sustained by the inability of actors in the system to optimize full capacity inherent in the system. One key aspect here is the quality of coordination between centralizing and decentralizing measures. CCS may result if there is excessive movement in either direction, in that the system may be too centralized to empower actors within or too decentralized to coordinate effectively. Horn (1995) argues that principals face dilemmas in deciding to what extent to intervene in the activities of bureaucratic administrators; an inherent trade-off between costs and risks of doing too much or doing too little. CCS is likely therefore to be sustained by these syndromes in public bureaucratic systems.

A strong theme of Horn's approach, and others such as Moe (1995), is the tendency for political actors to engineer their institutional environment in such a way that it brings selective benefits to their own group (and costs to others). Horn argues that legislators seek to maximize long-term commitment to their own goals by passing legislative and institutional reforms which are difficult for their opponents to reverse in the future. In a similar way, Moe points out that public bureaucratic systems are unavoidably about politics and political organization (p. 122), and that the 'fundamental task for political actors is to find and institute a governance structure that can protect their public organizations from control by opponents' (p. 125). This, says Moe, tends to produce incoherent and ineffectual public policy systems. As he puts it, 'winning groups, losing groups, legislators and presidents combine to produce bureaucratic arrangements that, by economic standards, appear to make no sense at all' (p. 149). CCS may therefore be partly the outcome of ineffectual and incoherent institutional design.

Finally, those running the system may actually see benefits in supporting a strategy of maintaining a manageable degree of capacity stress. Running prisons at close-to-tolerance levels may be associated with political toughness, hardship, punishment, and deterrence. Actors at all levels may also feel that there is latent capacity already in the system, and that some degree of stress is a constructive way of 'keeping its feet to the fire'. In both senses, stress may be engineered by design, either unspoken or formalized through government policy. The dynamics of instrumental rationality here may be subtle and nuanced. Indeed, senior ministers and officials may have much to gain from maintaining a state of constructive under-supply in the system, both to elicit greater value, but also to orchestrate some kind of supply-side pressure on the judiciary to keep rates of custodial sentencing under control. Constructive squeezing or under-supply of prison capacity may also bring political benefits to actors at all levels by sustaining a widespread impression of a system constantly over-stretched and under-resourced.

1.3 Adding in institutions, shared values and cultures

Social scientists often talk about an axiomatic distinction between strategic actor and cultural explanations for social phenomena (Douglas, 1986; Barnett and Finnemore, 1999). Whereas economistic explanations conceptualize CCS as an outcome of structured incentives between actors, cultural-theory explanations suggest that the problem is a function of shared values and beliefs amongst groups of individuals in institutional settings, and contestation between them (Thompson et al., 1999). In saying that CCS is 'cultural', we are saying that there is something about the mix of shared values and beliefs that causes individuals in their institutional settings to think and behave in ways which sustain the basic condition. We are saying that CCS is part of the culture of the system and, in this sense, there is something much bigger than individual actors that determines the way in which these actors think and behave.

For Douglas (1986), it is individuals' 'demand for order and coherence and control of uncertainty' (p. 18) which explains how they shape their institutional setting. And it is the institutional setting which provides them with a 'set of analogies' with which to 'justify the naturalness and reasonableness of the instituted rules' (p. 112). Inherent in such analogies is a prevailing outlook on how the world is and an associated set of prescriptions about what must be done to maintain its order and coherence. Drawing on cultural-theory 'grid-group' analysis (Thompson et al., 1990; Hood, 1998), Table 1.2 sets out possible explanations for CCS. The

Table 1.2 Four cultural archetypes and their inherent risks

		Importance of GROUP norms	
		High	**Low**
Importance of GRID norms	**High**	WORLD is generally forgiving but can sometimes tip over into instability and crisis. RESPONSE is **HIERARCHIST** consisting of strong social and rule-based control structures. RISK of excessive rigidity and inward-focus, perverse effects of 'bossism', stifling command-and-control, and normalization of deviance.	WORLD is capricious, erratic, and impossible to predict. RESPSONSE is **FATALIST**, i.e. there is little point in trying to control anything, although randomized control techniques can work. RISK of excessively pessimistic or passive attitudes amongst actors in the system, and normalization of coping.
	Low	WORLD is inherently unstable and unforgiving, and crisis is imminent. RESPONSE is **EGALITARIAN** in that the group identity is all-important and provides the main basis for action. RISK of resistant professional bodies, territorial attitudes amongst different types of actors, and 'them and us' attitudes to punishment and prison.	WORLD is inherently stable and forgiving. RESPONSE is **INDIVIDUALIST** in which boundaries are subject to negotiation, and control is mediated through open competition. RISK of excessive opportunism or rent-seeking behaviour.

grid dimension (high/low) is determined by the extent to which institutionalized rules and classifications regulate the interactions of individuals. The group dimension (high/low) is determined by the extent to which the individual is absorbed in and sustained by group membership. Four cultural archetypes are generated – hierarchical, individualist, egalitarian, and fatalist.[3] For each, I highlight the particular prevailing worldview ('WORLD'), the prescribed response in terms of how to organize public policy systems ('RESPONSE'), and the inherent risk of this corresponding strategy ('RISK'). Each cultural archetype contains the seeds of its own demise, and it is these respective weaknesses which give clues as to how culture may contribute to CCS.

The relationship between *fatalism* and CCS is an interesting one. If individual actors in the system, from senior politicians through to prisoners, see themselves as continually at the mercy of external forces beyond their control, it is not surprising that fatalistic cultures persist. In the England and Wales prison system, there is no queuing or waiting list for prison, no formal rationing of capacity beyond the pragmatic limitations of space available, and hence, by and large, the system and those working in it are expected to accommodate whatever the courts send their way. In this fundamental sense, fatalism may be strong. Furthermore, if fatalistic cultures exist in wider society about the role of a public-sector system, then it may not be surprising if those working in the system absorb and reflect these perceptions in the way they calibrate their own values (Barnett and Finnemore, 1999).

We see clear strands of fatalism in already established concepts for understanding ongoing dysfunction in organizations. Meyer and Zucker's (1989) concept of 'permanently failing organizations', for example, argues that the reason why many organizations appear to survive in a state of permanent failure is that groups dependent on their survival (e.g. workers, unions, suppliers) exert pressure enough to maintain status-quo practices despite continual sub-optimal performance. Resistant behaviour may seek to maintain inefficient status-quo positions, or increase inefficient practices to the detriment of the overall performance of the organization. Critics have often looked to policy areas such as prisons and social welfare for examples of organizations existing in states of permanent crisis (Bottoms, 1980; Tropman, 1981; Tournier, 1994). It is easy to see how fatalism may persist in organizations labelled as 'permanently failing'.

Hargrove and Glidewell's (1990) concept of 'impossible jobs' has similar fatalistic mood. Here, four dimensions combine to create the concept: low legitimacy of the agency's clientele; high intensity of conflict among the agency's constituencies; low public confidence in the authority of the agency's profession; and what they refer to as a persistently weak agency myth (p. 5). It is interesting here that, in cultural-theory terms, the general concept of 'impossible jobs' seems strongly fatalistic, yet these four component aspects combine other cultural archetypes which are constituent in the dominant culture. Low legitimacy of the agency's clientele and low public confidence, for example, both imply strong egalitarian strands of 'us and them'. And high intensity of conflict implies strong individualistic strands. The point here is that cultural archetypes are not straightforward and, indeed, imply balance and competing tensions within the grid. Again, particular policy areas can be strongly associated with 'impossible jobs', such as running welfare services or correctional institutions (Dilulio, 1990).

As Hargrove and Glidewell point out, organizational coping becomes an important mode of response for organizations doing 'impossible jobs'. They suggest that elected officials have very little incentive to grapple with 'no-win dilemmas' experienced by public managers, because most of the time 'the political benefit is too uncertain and contentious' (p. 32). Professional-political entrepreneurship becomes the most significant mode of coping, and unless the danger is seen as 'real and pressing' enacting any change usually requires more than scarce resources will allow. Hargrove and Glidewell say that 'although embarrassing, some low-frequency, high-cost, high-visibility, but inevitable tragic events may provide opportunities for resource mobilisation for reform' (p. 35). As later chapters will show, we have seen signs of this dynamic in the prison system over the years.

The relationship between *hierarchist* cultures and CCS is similarly provocative. Indeed, it is particularly key for prisons, which at least in formal terms tend to rely on discipline through rules and authority-based chains of accountability. The potential for rule-making can lead to rigidity and lack of ability in the system to respond to changes in the external environment (Crozier, 1964). For Crozier, crisis is seen, somewhat paradoxically, as a 'distinctive and necessary element of a bureaucratic system', enabling it to 'develop, and indirectly [...] to grow' (p. 196). Without crisis, bureaucratic systems may be 'too rigid to adjust to the transformations that the accelerated evolution of industrial society makes more and more imperative' (p. 198). The chronic aspect here is that the response to crisis is that 'new pressure is generated for impersonality and centralization' (p. 194), leading once again to more rigidly defined tasks, thus perpetuating the syndrome. In a similar vein, Wildavsky (1988) argues that in seeking to design public-policy systems in such a way as to eliminate all but infinitesimal sources of risk, policy makers actually increase risks of major failure or crisis. He advocates building 'resilience' into organizations to be able to cope more effectively with uncertainty, rather than over-designing rules, regulations, planning and other systems in the misplaced hope that risk can be nullified. Wildavsky views this process of 'anticipation over resilience' as part of the pathology of modern bureaucracies (p. 12).[4]

This links neatly to what some critics have called the perverse effects of 'bossism' (Dunleavy and Hood, 1994; Hood, 1998). Bossism may be viewed as strong orientation in public-policy systems towards the importance, indeed 'fetishization', of the top officials. In hierarchical cultures, such as prisons, emphasis on the importance of top officials tends to be supported by strong hierarchical discipline throughout the ranks. Indeed, command-and-control hierarchy is likely in itself to sustain CCS if the order coming down from on high is to find ways of coping and making things work (and not questioning it). Excessive hierarchalism may also encourage what Hogwood and Peters (1985) refer to as 'iatrogenic' control problems, whereby attempts from the top to impose greater control simply have counteractive effects and produce less control (p. 42).

A third general risk of excessive hierarchalism is that it offers scope for 'normalizing deviance' in high-risk public-policy systems (Vaughan, 1996, 2005). As long as bureaucratic procedural targets are being met, potentially serious build-up of stress can be normalized within the bureaucratic culture of the system. In large and complex systems, the actual process of normalization takes place at the margins and is barely visible. It is the cumulative effect of lots of small incremental decisions to find ways round problems or to push the capacity of the system slightly further in order to absorb increments of pressure. Barnett and Finnemore (1999) characterize this as 'bureaucrats making small, calculated deviations from established rules because of new environmental or institutional developments, explicitly calculating that bending the rules in this instance does not create excessive risk of policy failure' (p. 271). Systems can therefore continue to absorb pressure invisibly and chronically until, at some point, acute crisis is triggered.

The maintenance of strong *egalitarian* cultures in and around a public-policy system can also have important implications for CCS. In the egalitarian worldview, it is the social group which is the all-important reference point for prescriptive action. Again, staff unions or professional bodies may have strong group influence on the deployment of capacity in a public-policy system, both in terms of resistance to, and facilitation of, change. In 'total institutions', of which prisons are one strong archetype, group identities define the community inside the walls (i.e. staff and inmates) in opposition to those outside. On the one hand, actors may be able to hide rent-seeking activities more easily in these closed environments, while those on the outside may be disinclined to worry too much about a world out-of-sight and out-of-mind.[5] On the other hand, the scope for flexibility between the formal and informal 'how things really work in practice' life of the prison (to use Goffman's terminology, the 'primary' and 'secondary adjustments') is an important factor in allowing the institution to cope with and sustain CCS.

Egalitarian emphasis is also prominent in Foucault's (1991) argument that 'carceral' state institutions, particularly prisons, reflect latent class divisions and power relations in society. For Foucault, the mechanisms and the dynamics are deeply structural and embedded in operation of state institutions, yet they perpetuate 'two distinct classes of men, one of which always meets on the seats of accusers and judges, the other on the benches of the accused' (p. 276). In this way, 'law and justice do not hesitate to proclaim their class dissymmetry' (p. 276). Indeed, the institutions of state demarcate and reproduce a 'delinquent' class, which itself functions as a 'political observatory' for the judging and monitoring classes (p. 281). For Foucault, 'so successful has the prison been that after a century and a half of failures, then prison still exists, producing the same results, and there is the greatest reluctance to dispense with it' (p. 277). CCS may be interpreted as reflecting deeply entrenched power relations in society, as an artefact of one class's ability to engineer institutions of dominance over another class by means of, what Foucault calls, a 'political and economic less dangerous illegality' (p. 277).

Inherent in all these kinds of cultural explanations is a functionalist logic that would explain CCS in terms of the function they serve in the system. As Merton (1957) explains, 'functions are those observed consequences which make for the adaptation or adjustment of a given system' (p. 51). 'Functional analysis', he claims, 'calls for a concrete and detailed account of the mechanisms which operate to perform a designated function' (p. 51). In this section, we have therefore added a further layer of complexity to our theoretical understanding of CCS. Whereas the previous section envisaged CCS as an outcome of the interplay between individual choices and actions, this kind of functionalist explanation attributes the condition to the role it plays in keeping the prison system stable and in some kind of manageable equilibrium. In other words, perhaps paradoxically, the implication is that the prevailing cultures and the necessary balance between them require that there is a degree of something called CCS.

1.4 Seeing the system as a dynamic whole

The third broad theoretical perspective on CCS sets the analytical aperture wider to focus on the system as a whole. Holistic strands of theory have long been a part of political science, economics, and sociology (Phillips, 1976). Indeed, both rational choice and cultural theory perspectives incorporate elements of holism, in the sense that they are based on different kinds of internally structured logic, which encompass a whole and within which individual actors *cannot but* act. In rational choice, holism is inherent in the particular equilibrium of structured incentives. In cultural theory, it is inherent in the fact that the matrix encompasses a universe of all cultural possibilities (unless one is hermitic). This third perspective is holistic in the sense that it attributes explanatory power to the dynamics of the system as a whole. Phillips outlines five general characteristics of holistic analysis:

1. the analytic approach is inadequate when applied to organic wholes;
2. the whole is more than the sum of its parts;
3. the whole determines the nature of its parts;
4. parts cannot be understood in isolation from the whole;
5. parts are dynamically interrelated or interdependent. (p. 6)

At the heart of many holistic approaches to public policy is a distinction and a relationship between three aspects: the values and goals of public policies; the way in which institutions are designed to achieve these goals; and finally, the way in which both of these aspects interact with their environment. In 1947, Robert Dahl wrote as much in an article entitled *The Science of Public Administration: Three Problems*. Throughout the 1960s, political scientists, notably David Easton, applied systems theory to political analysis, conceiving of the political process as a system consisting of defined inputs, transferred into outputs, which interact with the external environment, resulting in feedback loops defining inputs once again. For Easton, the answers to why political phenomena were as they were lay in understanding the whole system and its inherently dynamic equilibria. His contribution was to show how political life could be understood as a 'system of behaviour imbedded in an environment to the influences of which the political system itself is exposed and in turn reacts' (1967, p. 17). Key to Easton's argument is the observation that political systems by nature are able to find ways of being resilient to stresses from their environment and from within the system itself.

We see similar strands of thinking in subsequent systems-oriented theory. Luhmann's concept of autopoiesis, for example, has been interpreted by some to imply that a social system 'selectively transforms problems it finds in its environment into internal – systemic – problems' (Brans and Rossbach, 1997, p. 421). 'These problems', they point out, 'are not solved but reformulated, simplified, limited, distributed so that the system can deal with them. The system builds defensive internal complexity against the pressure of an environment which is always too complex' (p. 421). Again, we see that social systems by definition and by necessity find ways of equilibrating with environment. In the dynamics of aggravation and compensation involved, we must look for tell-tale symptoms or signs of this continual process. CCS, in this sense, can be seen as symptom or sign of such equilibrating resilience in a public-policy system.

Management economists writing on governance and performance in commercial firms have also drawn heavily on holistic explanations. John Roberts (2004) argues that high performance in a firm results from 'establishing and maintaining alignment across three elements: the strategy of the firm, organizational design, and the environment in which it operates' (p. 12) (Figure 1.2). The challenge 'becomes one of selecting the (long run) value-maximizing strategy for the particular environment and then creating the organization that will best realize it' (p. 22). The economistic drive towards optimization is explicit in such formulations. Roberts is however mindful of the inherent limitations involved in continually seeking perfect alignment. For he points out that the difficulties 'imply that there is value in an organizational design that will perform reasonably well in a variety of environments even if it is not perfectly suited to the current context' (p. 67). As Figure 1.2 suggests, potential misalignments in the system (four possible misalignments are indicated) will tend to aggravate in this sense, and hence there must also be compensating or adaptive mechanisms to keep the whole thing in some kind manageable balance. Cyert and March (2001) sum this up nicely in the context of firms, yet there is little reason why we should not replace 'the firm' in the following quote with 'public-policy system'.

> The [firm] is constrained by the uncertainty of its environment, the problems of maintaining viable coalition, and the limitations on its capacity as a system for assembling, storing, and utilizing information.

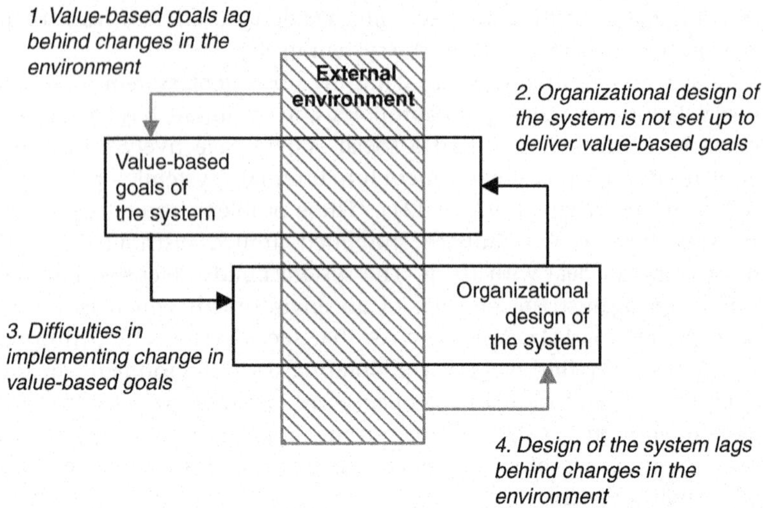

Figure 1.2 A whole system view and four potential misalignment problems

> As a result, the firm is an 'adaptively rational' system rather than an 'omnisciently rational' system'. (p. 117)

As public-policy systems grow in scale and complexity, so too do the difficulties of system-wide steering. In his 'problem of many hands', Bovens (1990), for example, reminds us that it becomes almost impossible to attribute instrumental causality across individual actors in the organization (let alone successfully plan steering in advance). He points out that causes and attribution of failure can be 'institutionalizable' and hence cleansed of individual accountability. He writes:

> Something which started as rational and deliberate human conduct can get transformed by the structure of complex organizations into a kind of 'act of god' with its own dynamics, which seem independent of any specific individual activity. The attribution of responsibility, secondly goes hand in hand with prevention. The fact that no-one can meaningfully be held accountable *ex post* for organizational misbehaviour, implies that no one needs to behave responsibly *ex ante*. (1990, p. 115)

The potential for accurate modelling of whole public-sector systems must therefore be seen in a more complex light. As this quote suggests, individuals are well aware that they are constrained by their position in the system but, at the same, well aware that they have a certain degree of influence in shaping their position. The quote perhaps overstates the degree to which individuals are tempted to misbehave or make gratuitously self-interested decisions. It nonetheless captures an important aspect of adaptiveness inherent in individuals and systems, both of which make it somewhat more problematic to think in terms of neat paradigms and linear models of change.

In recent decades, public administration has looked to theoretical biology for new models of understanding this kind of inherent complexity.[6] Complexity theory accentuates inherent unpredictability of outcomes in complex systems, and explains this uncertainty through adaptation of human actors involved (very much echoing Dahl's observations 60 years earlier!). As Teisman et al. (2009) argue, 'actors in social systems are reflexive: they respond, anticipate, plan, think, forecast, etc. [...] In the domain of public administration this means that actors can choose, within certain degrees of freedom, a certain response to a certain situation but also contradictory to the intention of the intervention' (p. 7). Adaptation in systems therefore undermines an assumption of *ceteris paribus,* that component parts of systems will act consistently and predictively in response to particular interventions. A capacity of the system to 'self-organize' means that new structures are enforced by local interaction, but they come about 'without the imposition of any external or internal actors' (Teisman et al., 2009, p. 9). Hence, complexity theorists tend to reject the idea that systems can be controlled or steered or manipulated by political elites, or for that matter, any other actor (Klijn and Snellen, 2009, p. 34).

Actual empirical application of complexity theory to public-policy problems is still relatively thin on the ground, and some critics have expressed doubt on the extent to which complexity theory brings anything new to political science that it did not already have (Pollitt, 2009). It is probably the case that we do not necessarily need a ready-made 'theory' of complexity in order to understand public-policy complexity itself. For this runs the risk of putting the theoretical cart before the empirical horse. Nevertheless, these themes of inherent adaptation by actors and the limitations on their ability to influence the system are important aspects in a concept of 'constrained autonomy' that is examined empirically in later chapters. For these chapters make clear that it is individual actors, in the abstract sense, who animate the system and make it work. It is their ability to adapt and be resilient, and make their bit of the system work,[7] that must be a key consideration in understanding how systems change and do not change, and how problems like capacity stress can become chronic.

1.5 Why we need a more integrated approach

If each of these three groups of explanations have useful things to say about CCS, then by definition, there must be limits to how far each one independently can bring us in understanding its dynamics in entirety. Logically, it is possible to criticize each of the three approaches from the perspective of the other two.

Rational-choice explanations may be seen as reductionist from a cultural-theory perspective, in that the assumption of rational self-interest limits the scope of explaining social or organizational phenomena to the 'individualist' quadrant of the cultural matrix. They may also be open to criticism from cultural perspectives for seeing the world in narrow terms of optimal alignment of incentives and utilities, while downplaying the *realpolitikal* implications of political power broking and the use of political power for its own sake. From a whole-system perspective also, rational-choice approaches can be criticized for conceptualising and ultimately explaining behaviour of actors by narrow claims to self-interest rather than recognizing inherently adaptive and reflexive tendencies of individuals depending on the situations they face. The rise of behavioural economics in recent years reflects a recognition amongst economists that rational-choice theories must be able to incorporate bounded rationality of actors in system contexts into their modelling. As Low (2012) puts it, 'behavioural economists argue that economics theory should consider the social context that informs and shapes individual decisions, such as social and cultural norms' (p. 26). And rightly so.

Cultural-theory explanations of CCS are no less immune to criticism. For rational choicers, the idea that organizational culture could be a sufficient independent variable explaining behaviour of individual actors in a public-policy system underestimates the instrumental ability of these actors to act independently of culture – either to ignore culture or actively attempt to change culture. Governments and ministers, after all, should have considerable degree of autonomy to wield policy-making power and executive authority to shape and reshape the system by their own design – again, regardless of its cultural characteristics. Such criticism may be writ large from a system theory perspective, in that dynamics in complex systems may be non-linear, and we should not always expect that behavioural outcomes should be directly contingent on prevailing cultural archetypes. Cultural orientations will

Table 1.3 Three competing theoretical explanations and their inherent limitations

	Three types of explanation for capacity stress		
	Rational choice theory (RC)	**Cultural theory (CT)**	**Systems theory (SYS)**
Methodological point of focus	Individual actors and the incentives they face, rational self-interest of these actors, and alignment of incentives.	Cultures defined by shared values and beliefs held by groups of individuals. Focus on inherent tension between cultures.	Architecture of the system as a whole and how system-wide dynamics influence outcomes of its individual parts.
Main reason for capacity stress	Misalignment in the structure of incentives amongst individual actors.	Function of prevailing cultural norms and contestation between them.	Inherent complexity and adaptivness of systems, actors are constrained by systems.
Limits of the explanation from the perspective of the other two standpoints	**CT** Culturally reductionist, i.e. discounts competing cultural factors in explaining individual behaviour. **SYS** Overlooks adaptive capacity of individual actors, and the fact that they are influenced by dynamic constraints of the system.	**RC** Assigns too much importance to culture as an independent variable, and is vague about the causes of individual action. **SYS** Downplays instrumental capacity of individuals, and the possibility for culture to be defined by system context.	**CT** Downplays the strength of the causal relationship between institutional cultures and individual behaviour. **RC** Does not provide a strong enough explanation of causality, due to systems effects being too unpredictable and inherent adaptivity.

Note: In row 3, I summarize likely criticisms of each theoretical approach from the perspective of the other two theoretical approaches. These are indicated by respective letters RC, CT, or SYS.

vary by issue – if one is fatalistic about one aspect of life, it is entirely possible to be individualistic about another. Similarly, it is possible to give the impression of being fatalistic for strategic purposes, perhaps for example to elicit individualistic benefits. As we have mentioned already, culturally specific models or paradigms can help to explain outcomes, but they can also help to conceal important dynamics in the system.

Finally, holistic explanations can help us to reflect on the architecture of the system as a whole, but they are also open to criticism. From the rational-choice perspective, systems theoretical approaches tend to be too pessimistic about the possibilities of getting to concrete models of strategic behaviour. As political or social scientists, we need something to grasp onto, a set of principles or dynamics that help us to understand the nature of causality in one way or another. To insist that inherent non-linearity and self-organization in complex systems undermines this possibility of finding concreteness makes these basic objectives continually and slightly out of reach. Similarly, cultural theory can state plainly that public-sector systems do have strong cultural norms and values, which, in one way or other, shape and condition the behaviour of its parts, regardless of non-linearity, self-organization, and so on.

Inherently therefore, each of these explanations has limitations from the perspective of the other two. It is, however, the limitations inherent in the specific application of these explanations to understanding CCS in large and complex public-policy systems, which are of particular interest here. How do these explanations fall short in helping us to understand chronic conditions in a large and complex public-policy system such as prisons? For a start, chronic problems tend to resist single-factor or reductionist causal dynamics, and rather consist of multi-factor and deeply interrelated dynamics, which are aggravating and compensating rather than unilinear and causal. Any theoretical approach to a chronic problem is therefore likely to require hypotheses in the form of a 'problematique',[8] able to integrate aspects of agency, culture, and the system as a whole.

The deployment of different theoretical approaches should therefore involve a non-zero-sum game in which all have something useful to contribute to a more integrated appreciation of the problem. This need not aspire to a tightly coupled 'grand theory' of CCS. Nevertheless, it should be a theory-based approach which leaves scope for this non-zero-sum characteristic. Social behaviour and institutional life of public-policy systems are complicated. The narrower one scopes a problem, the more tractable it appears. Yet the wider one scopes the same problem, the more uncertain this sense of tractability becomes.

The challenge is to set the focal length appropriately in order to understand the 'whole', as well as the atomized dynamics which make it add up to a whole in the first place. Each of the three explanations discussed in this chapter must undoubtedly play a part in lending substance to any overarching and integrated approach.

This is where the next chapter heads. I examine how this non-zero-sum theoretical approach might be constructed from the modular parts discussed in this chapter. As I will argue, the fundamental problem of CCS must still be seen as a holistic governance-style problem, but it must incorporate a systematic account of agency and culture, and the way in these factors interact dynamically to sustain CCS. I hope to persuade the reader that the condition of CCS in the prison system, as well as in other public-policy systems, requires this kind of integrative approach. We have thrown nothing away in our evaluation of competing theoretical approaches in this chapter. The landscape has not been cleared by any means. It has merely been cautiously and constructively dismantled, ready for reconstruction in the next chapter.

2
A More Holistic Governance-Style Approach

We left off at the end of the last chapter with the idea that we had prepared some building blocks of possible theoretical explanations for chronic capacity stress (CCS), and laid them ready for reconstruction. Each of the three groups of theory has helped to shed light on different dimensions of CCS, yet have also shown certain limitations. The challenge in this chapter is to start to build them back up again into a schema that incorporates characteristics of each these theoretical approaches, but which builds them into a more integrated picture of a public-policy system operating dynamically. Rather than looking for meaningful distinctions and cleavages along theoretical lines, we are looking for them along analytical lines, and building these theoretical approaches into the process.

How then might we begin to reconstitute these theoretical building blocks into something more integrated in order to help understand CCS in its entirety? Perhaps the best place to start is with the 'whole-system' view already discussed in the previous chapter and depicted in Figure 1.2. This presents a holistic schema incorporating four key relationships (or potential mis-relationships) between three factors – value-based goals, organizational design, and environment.[1] 'Value-based goals' refer specifically to the range of desirable outcomes that the system seeks to achieve, and the prevailing and competing values that underpin these goals. 'Organizational design' refers to the institutional structures and capacity that make the system work, including the range of incentives and sanctions that shape the behaviours of actors within. Finally, 'environment' refers to the great many factors outside the system – political, legal, technological, cultural, and so on – which put pressure on it to adapt and change.

From these three aspects, we can postulate four potential sources of 'misalignment' or dysfunction that provide a foundation for a holistic approach to help us explain how and why the prison system sustains CCS. As Figure 1.2 has already set out, these four potential misalignments are as follows:

1. value-based goals of the system lag behind changes in the wider environment;
2. organizational design of the system is not set up to deliver on prevailing value-based goals;
3. difficulties in implementing reform or change in value-based goals throughout the system;
4. organizational design of the system lags behind broader changes in the environment.

These four potential misalignments may arguably be applied to any system of governance as a first-principles foundation for understanding how dysfunction or imbalance creeps in. Indeed this schema provides a potentially useful foundation for understanding how the prison system is able to sustain crowding and capacity stress over long periods, while throughout also being able to function or operate in one way or another.

It is important to remember, however, that Figure 1.2 depicts these four relationships as systemically related. Thinking about the relationships in this systemic way reminds us that for the system to function it must to some degree be able to sustain manageable equilibria. In order for continual equilibria, it is necessary that aggravating dynamics resulting from misalignments are countered by compensating adjustments in other relationships. Say, for example, that value-based goals may be under pressure to respond to new environmental changes (1). This will be, to a large degree, dependent on the extent to which system design itself is able to cope with the new requirements from these changes (2). If deficiencies in system design constrain this ability to respond, then this will perpetuate misalignment with the environment, and a feedback effect whereby those responsible for setting the value-based goals of the system blame bad design of the system itself. Similarly, system design is likely to be subject to imposed change from above in response to new value-based goals (3). However, the fact that the system may be lagging in terms of its ability to keep pace with modern cultures and working practices (4) is also likely to constrain the extent to which it is actually able to implement changes. Again, this is likely to feed back into coping, and fatalistic views about the extent to which value-based reform is actually possible in a system which is inherently constrained by being out of kilter with its environment.

We have to this point discussed these governance misalignments in quite generalizable terms, and this has been intentionally so in order introduce the concept as applicable to public-policy areas other than prisons. These four potential misalignments now form the basis for a more detailed empirical look at the development of crowding and CCS in the England and Wales prison system during the last thirty years or so. Table 2.1 transposes the four misalignments into more specific potential risks and applications in the prison system.

We now move on to examine each of these four misalignments and their inter-relationships with specific reference to prison crowding. I draw on a large body of academic and practitioner literature on prisons in general and the English and Welsh system in particular. By the end of the chapter, I hope to have sketched out a more evolved picture of CCS and, based on these literatures, provided a more holistic overview of how it can be applied in the context of a prison system.

2.1 The perception of prison as an inherently failing system

Society changes and with it what we expect or demand from our public services. With advancements in knowledge and developments in the way we understand social problems, expectations and ambitions increase about what is possible by instrumental design and intervention. New pressures in society also emerge that test the prevailing values and goals of public-sector systems. If important changes occur, we might expect value-based goals upon which the system acts to be responsive enough to change with them. If value-based goals of the system lag or are out of kilter with changes in environment, then this may aggravate capacity stress. For example, value-based goals may be too ambiguous or not robust enough to maintain clarity in terms of what the system seeks to achieve. Or some value-based goals may be too dominant or comparatively more dominant than others, and hence become out of kilter with the environment in which it operates.

Since the Victorian era, value-based goals of prison have involved inherent trade-offs and tensions. Thickset historical accounts of the prison system have captured shifts in norms and expectations around the purpose of prison over the decades and centuries, and there is insufficient space to replay here the details of this complex story.[2] From this

Table 2.1 Four potential misalignments in the holistic schema and how they relate to prison crowding

Four potential misalignments in the holistic schema (see Figure 1.2)	General risk emanating from this misalignment	Specific risk in terms of the prison system, crowding and CCS
1. Value-based goals lag behind changes in the environment	Society changes while the policy orientation does not change with it.	Prison is seen as a continually failing system, unable to respond to prevailing challenges.
2. Design of the system is not set up to deliver value-based goals	The system is not able to deliver fully against policy expectations.	Culture of coping prevails in efforts to make the system work – actors behave fatalistically.
3. Difficulties in implementing change in value-based goals	Resistance from within the system in response to reform efforts.	Direct opposition or subtler forms of benign resistance in response to modernization of the prison system.
4. Design of the system lags behind broader changes in the environment	Obsolescence and redundant capacity is sustained throughout the system.	Prisons lack sufficiently modern assets and practices, constraining their ability to operate efficiently or effectively.

early era, historical accounts capture an inherent tension between two goals of prison – deterrence and reform – which have retained their resonance throughout the modern era. As Ruggles-Brise wrote in 1921, these two principal features began to 'assume a definite shape' from the mid-nineteenth century onwards, one which 'has been retained, subject to modification, until the present day' (p. 66) ('present day' in this sense referring to the early 1920s). Critics have argued that reformative principles tended to be secondary to deterrence throughout the nineteenth century. McConville (1981) describes 'an almost total collapse' of the reformative principle after 1850' (p. 349). And as the prison population began to grow from 1945 onwards, the pressures on the reformative role of prison grew ever greater. The picture is complicated, however. Official documentation of the prison system from the 1960s onwards has systematically referenced (albeit tentatively) its rehabilitative goals. Table 2.2 gives an overview of relevant specific statements in annual reports since 1979. Clearly, the rehabilitative goal has been very much part of the 'official' approach. Indeed, since the creation of the National Offender Management Service from 2004 onwards, and the policy commitment in 2010 by the new Conservative–Liberal Democrat coalition government to bringing about a 'rehabilitation revolution', one can argue that the rehabilitative ideal is very much alive and well – in the rhetoric, at least – at the top of government.

Despite this official line, however, the view that the rehabilitative goal has lost credibility has been pervasive in academic writing for at least the last thirty years (Bottoms, 1980; Garland, 2001; Cavadino and Dignan, 2003, 2006). In 1980, Bottoms wrote pessimistically that the 'abandonment of the rehabilitative ethic has led to a widespread abandonment of hope' (p. 20).[3] And as prison populations and crowding have risen in the UK and in other developed countries, scepticism on rehabilitative goals has intensified. Garland (2001) argues that this weakening has been characteristic of many modern penal systems in that they 'focus more and more upon their ability to hold offenders securely in custody and are much more circumspect in claiming the capacity to produce rehabilitative effects' (p. 119). Cavadino and Dignan (2003) have written specifically about a 'crisis of legitimacy' in the British prison system, which they argue, has its roots in what they call the 'collapse of rehabilitative ideal' (p. 21).

Such putative weakening of the rehabilitative ideal is closely linked to fatalistic views that cast prison as a kind of permanently or inherently failing system. Figure 2.1 depicts this aggravating relationship in simple looped form. First, the perception of an inherently failing system

Table 2.2 Overview of references to rehabilitative goals in annual reports

	Specific text in the annual report relating to rehabilitative goals
1980	'Positive custody' would be based on the '**admirable things being done in the name of treatment and training**' but it would also reflect what the May Committee saw as society's diminished expectation of the potential of the Prison Service to rehabilitate the majority of offenders committed to its charge.
1983 to 1989	*First working definition of the Prison Service*. 7(iv) to enable prisoners to retain links with the community and, where possible, prepare them for their return to it. (Note from 1984, text changed to '**assist them to prepare for their return to it**').
1990 to 1998	*As statement of purpose*. Our duty is to look after (prisoners) with humanity and **help them to lead law-abiding and useful lives** in custody and after release.
1992 to 1997	*More detailed expression of goals six stated goals which include*: To provide positive regimes which help prisoners address their offending behaviour and allow them as full and responsible life as possible. To **help prisoners prepare for their return to the community**.
1994 onwards	*Move to reporting performance against targets relating to rehabilitative programmes*. For example, Key Performance Indicator 7 'the number of prisoners completing programmes **accredited in reducing reoffending**'.
1998 to 2003	*Statement of purpose*. Prison Service is an Executive Agency of the Home Office working with others in the criminal-justice system to deliver the Home Office aim (4) of effective execution of the sentences of the courts so as to **reduce reoffending and protect the public**. *Objectives*. To reduce crime by providing constructive regimes which address offending behaviour, improve educational and work skills, and **promote law abiding behaviour in custody and after release**.
2004 to 2005	*Statement of Priorities as part of NOMS*. **Reducing reoffending and improving prisoners' prospects on release**. This was central to our agenda and efforts were made to direct extra resources to this work.
2006	The agreed priorities for the Service were as follows. Number 1 in the list was **Reducing Reoffending**.
2007 onwards	*NOMS Statement of Purpose*. We work to **protect the public and reduce reoffending** by delivering the punishment and orders of the courts and by helping offenders to reform their lives. *NOMS Vision*. As part of the wider justice service we will give the public confidence in our ability to protect the public and **reduce reoffending**.

Source: Prison Department, Prison Service, and National Offender Management Service (NOMS) annual reports.

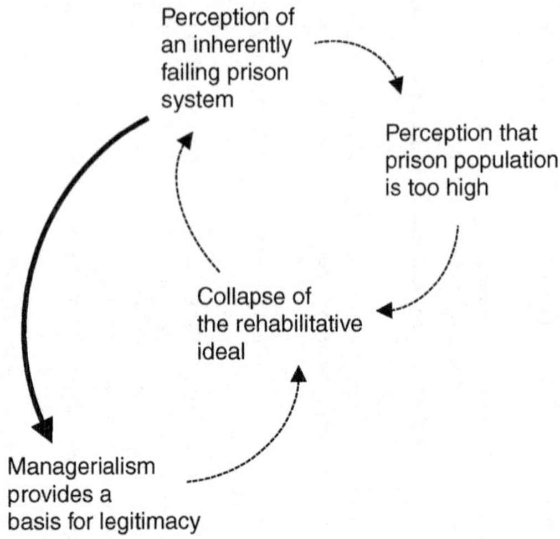

Figure 2.1 Collapse of the rehabilitative ideal

feeds into the perception that the prison population is ever too high. Reviewing prisons literature over the decades, it is striking how many academics and prison professionals have argued this point, namely that governments send too many people to prison, and that they have presided over excessive increases in the prison population.[4] Such demand-side interpretations of CCS have been prevalent throughout the last three decades in disciplines of criminology and penal studies.[5] King et al. (1980), for example, wrote the following about the system in England and Wales, at a time when the prison population was half the size of the prison population in 2012.

> We know of no statement of informed opinion suggesting anything other than our prison population is unnecessarily large and that a substantial number of persons currently receiving custodial sentences could be adequately controlled or better treated in the community. Indeed this view has been expressed by successive Home Secretaries, by both major political parties, by the all-party House of Commons Expenditure Committee, by the Home Office, by prison governors and officers, by penal reform groups and by academic specialists. (p.60)

We can reflect here on the relativized relationship between actual increase in the size of the prison population and more ideologically based perceptions about the optimal size of the prison population. As Figure 2.2 shows, since the early 1990s the system has had to respond to a rapid rise in the number of receptions of short-sentence prisoners (sentenced to less than six months), and this very striking increase has done much to fuel this perception about excessively large prison populations. The increase in the short-sentence prison population since the mid-1990s and continued argumentation around the failure of prison and the collapse of the rehabilitative ideal seem closely related over the years.

Perceptions of an excessively high prison population have tended to feed back into fatalistic views about what can be done in terms of rehabilitation. Garland (2001) argues that such pessimism has been prevalent in criminal-justice systems generally during the last quarter of a century, 'the period in which the criminal justice system came to be viewed primarily in terms of its limitations and propensity for failure rather than its prospects for future success' (p. 107). Looking at rates of reoffending amongst male adult prisoners (within two years of release) in Figure 2.3, it is striking how little variation there has been in the

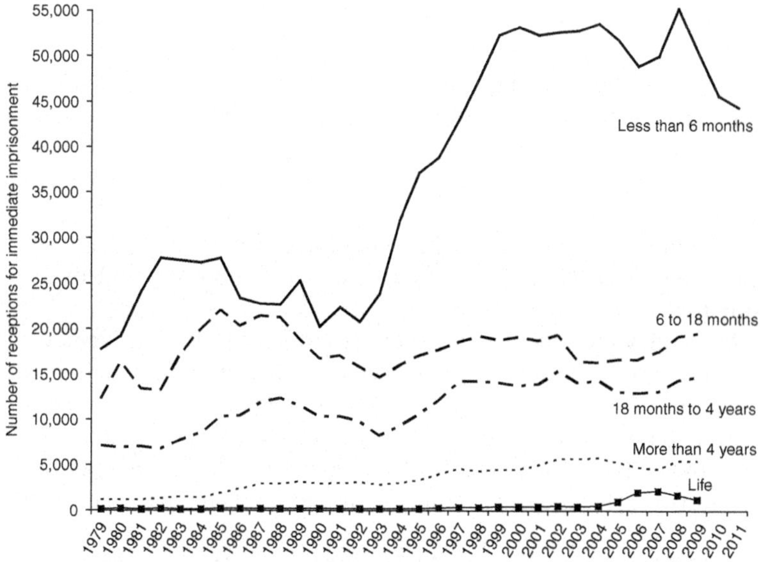

Figure 2.2 Number of receptions into custody of prisoners sentenced to immediate imprisonment, by length of sentence

Source: Home Office and Ministry of Justice prison population statistics, 1979 to 2011.

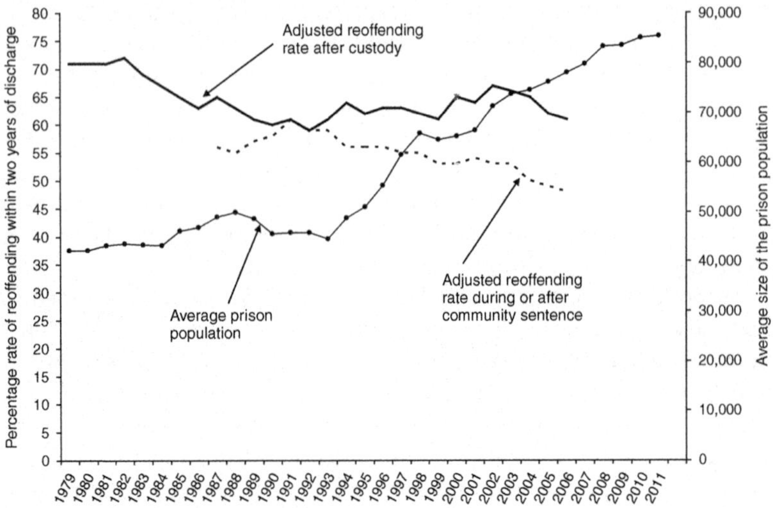

Figure 2.3 Reoffending rates for adult males, within two years of discharge from custody

Source: Ministry of Justice statistics on reoffending rates, 2010.

basic rate over thirty years. One may point out that reoffending rates have gradually dropped throughout the 2000s as the National Offender Management Service (NOMS) has focused directly on more integrated approaches to reducing reoffending, particular more joined-up working between prisons, probation, and local social services. More recent data from the Ministry of Justice suggests gradual improvements in this respect, but it is still the case that rates have only reduced to the levels they were at in the early 1990s. This is hardly improvement over the long term.

Academics and practitioners over the years have also put forward the view that prisons should not be expected to rehabilitate prisoners, particularly those who are in custody for short periods of time. This general view is reflected in the reference to 'diminished expectation' in the first row of Table 2.2 above. Similar scepticism is found in practitioner accounts. Coyle (1994), for example, implies fundamental scepticism.

> The first prison reformers had started out with the simple aim of improving prison conditions for their own sake, of making prisons places which were clean, well-ordered and where prisoners were treated decently. Where this later went wrong was that the humane

> and decent treatment of people in prison was linked to some vague principle of what became known as reform or rehabilitation. (p. 19)

In the last chapter, we touched briefly on how the paradigm of NPM has spread across the public sector during the last three decades or so. NPM has brought with it a certain kind of legitimacy, one that has been based in concepts of performance management, strong centralized policy coordination and devolution of operational tasks, and use of target regimes, which essentially set the parameters of success and failure of the system. In this sense, NPM has been the programmed response to perceived failure in the system, and it has provided a particular kind of basis for its legitimacy. For many critics, however, NPM has also, paradoxically, perpetuated failure (Parker, 2003; Cavadino and Dignan, 2003 and 2006). Cavadino and Dignan identify a 'penal crisis' which, they argue, has emerged from a form of 'penological pragmatism', in other words, 'attempting to manage the resources crisis with no clear or coherent philosophical or other theoretical basis' (2003, p. 30). For these critics, excessive managerialism has been a major part of the problem in prisons, targeting a material crisis of resources rather than a deeper 'crisis of legitimacy' about the use of prison and principles which underpin it.

Figure 2.1 depicts this potentially countervailing influence of NPM. First, it can be seen as a compensating response to perceptions of failure. Yet, according to its critics, managerialism has also played an aggravating role in the sense that it has constrained the system from addressing more ambitious goals and outcomes, particularly, it seems, the rehabilitative one. The argument here is that by providing a certain kind of legitimacy for the system, NPM has allowed politicians and senior officials to construct a discourse of success, one which has, in some senses, crowded out questions about rehabilitative outcomes. Paradoxically, NPM may be seen as the basis for demonstrating legitimacy of performance, but, according to the literature, for weakening the focus on the rehabilitative ideal. I return to these countervailing characteristics of NPM in the next chapter.

2.2 A culture of coping and making the system work

Whatever the value-based goals of prison, we might assume that the system itself will have to be set up appropriately to have a chance of fulfilling them. This basic ability to respond to and realize value-based goals, and cope with the demands involved, is the second aspect of the holistic schema. Misalignment emerges from the inability of the system to meet fully the demands made on it. This may be the result of any number of factors. Financial or human resources may be inadequate. Design of the structures and institutions may be incoherent or ineffective, or mechanisms in place to motivate, incentivize or control actors may be dysfunctional. Any of these factors, and others, may contribute to the system having to struggle to cope with the expectations and goals set for it.

Over the decades, there has been a strong theme of coping and crisis in the prisons literature (Weiler, 1992). Numerous accounts throughout the 1970s and 1980s, and indeed much of the 1990s, are scathingly critical about the state of British prisons, levels of under-investment, generally indecent conditions, and dysfunctional industrial relations.[6] These factors severely constrained the ability of the system to achieve even basic goals of decency and order. King and McDermott's (1989) article on the 'ever-deepening crisis' in British prisons from 1970 to 1987 found severe inadequacies in crowding and accommodation, as well as evidence that prisoners were locked up in their cells for long periods of time despite relative increase in the numbers of prison staff (p. 126). Indeed, at the start of the 1980s, King et al. (1980) argued that government should scale down its ambitions for prison to a kind of back-to-basics concept of 'humane containment', that would at least establish some of kind minimum standard of decency before it even began to think about its more ambitious goals (p. 25).

Some critics have pointed out that the emphasis on coping and crisis has been hardwired into the culture of criticism of prisons over the decades. Dunbar and Langdon (1998) remind us that 'writers on prisons customarily engage in a dialogue with themselves about whether the prisons can be said to be in a state of crisis, and if so, what kind of crisis'. They point out that 'in the 1980s, it was easy to diagnose a crisis on many dimensions, since the system was quite evidently near breakdown and many of the shortcomings identified in the Woolf report[7] were glaringly obvious. It would be untrue and unhelpful to say that the present situation is just the same' (p. 149). Again, managerialism has played its part here despite its critics. As Hood et al. (2004) show, the combination of management through hierarchical 'oversight' and egalitarian 'control through mutuality' have been important cultural factors in the way in which control over the system has been maintained throughout the 1990s and early 2000s.

Figure 2.4 develops the schema by adding this new dimension of 'coping and crisis' into the existing relationship. As this new dimension

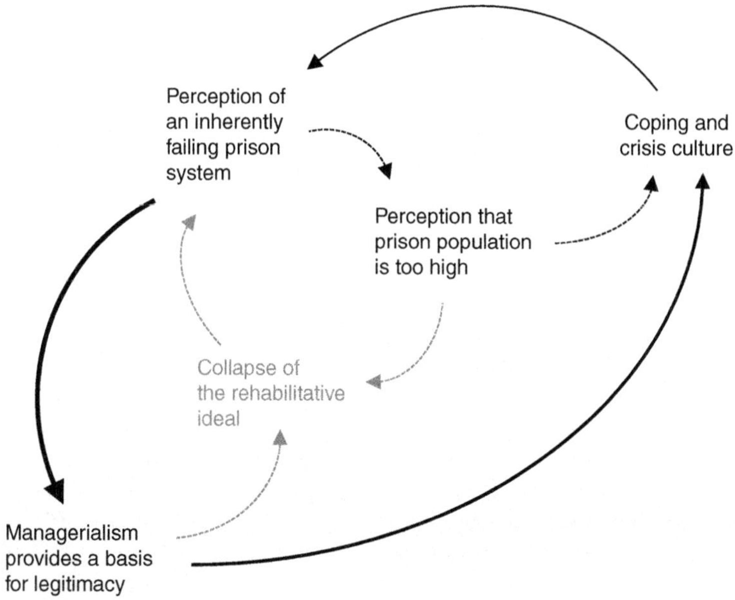

Figure 2.4 Adding in the 'coping and crisis culture' loop

shows, coping and crisis is an important cultural response to perceptions that the prison population is too high. As long as the prison population is perceived as being excessively high, the system itself will be seen as having to cope and occasionally having to deal with capacity crisis beyond its control. As mentioned, NPM can be seen as a strong facilitating factor in allowing the prison system to cope, both with its own internal inadequacies and external pressures exerted on it from having to deal with ever-increasing prison population and other changes in the policy-relevant environment

Another aspect of managerialist legitimacy has been the way in which measures and standards for prison capacity have been continually flexible over the years. Earlier discussion around 'normalizing deviance' is relevant here, particularly the tendency for incremental stretching to be rationalizable in complex chains of bureaucratic and managerialist relationships. The inherently stretchable nature of prison capacity and definitions for what constitutes crowding make it possible for heroic acts of redefinition and re-rationalization, both of which are self-justified largely on the grounds of pragmatism and necessity in order to make the system work. Throughout the 1980s and 1990s, critics have highlighted the resistance in the system to set in place hard-and-fast limits on physical capacity and crowding in British prisons, particularly in light of growing pressure from European regulations on acceptable levels of capacity (Casale, 1994; King and McDermott, 1995). Sylvia Casale's series of studies have continually emphasized inadequacies in the strength of *a priori* standards for prison capacity and prisoner conditions, and the tendency for governments to ignore input standards for maximum prison capacities (Casale, 1984, 1994; Casale and Plotnikoff, 1989, 1990).

The corollary to this, however, is that managerialism may also be seen as having detrimental effects on the ability of the system to respond to complex problems. Matthews and Young (2003) argue that the increase in the prison population is related to an inherent logic of managerialism, which involves target-based government, institutional fragmentation, and a push for cost-efficiency. They point out that 'part of the shift towards a greater punitiveness in the penal system and elsewhere is a consequence not so much of an inherent desire to get 'tough' but a product of attempts to develop and enforce more stringent procedures' (p. 228). The implication here is that excessive managerialism has constrained the capacity for coordinated response to complex issues such as intervening effectively in the chaotic or dysfunctional lives of offenders. Matthews and Young coin the term 'transcarceration' to capture the way in managerialist systems have the effect of 'churning' short-term offenders through the system, with the consequence that that 'system' is collectively unable to intervene effectively in the lives of those offenders. This implicates criminal-justice processes outside of the prison system also. For example, more than eleven thousand receptions into prison in 2009 were for breach of community orders, in order words a failure of non-custodial measures to deal effectively with offenders.

Coping can be a very real necessity. But, as we have already discussed in the previous chapter, actors in public-policy systems are adaptive, and have the ability to behave strategically based on how they perceive their predicament. Coping may therefore be used instrumentally as a kind of strategic option, an excuse, an alibi, a justification, or a way of demonstrating to the outside world how valiantly actors are working to keep the system operational. It is of course difficult to find hard evidence of this counterfactual dynamic. Adaptive actors are likely to be very much aware of the coping and crisis cultures in the system, and hence may be inclined, intentionally or necessarily, to employ these arguments for their own local gains. In the context of US prisons, for example, Bleich

(1989) argues that maintaining a perception of crowding has instrumental value to all actors in the system:

> It appears that no-one in the crowding debate has an interest in dispelling the perception of crowding. Legislators on both sides of the aisle see crowding as a way to achieve their political objectives. Administrators view crowding as an opportunity to increase control over prisoners, gain access to scarce resources, and shift blame for problems in correctional institutions. Prisoners and prison reformers value crowding as a means to obtain early release, improve prison conditions, and gain advantage in bargaining with prison administrators. (p. 1174)

This may be an excessively cynical view, and one which perhaps exaggerates the extent to which actors can or want to behave strategically. It is, however, a viewpoint which merits attention under conditions of coping in a system which, to borrow a term from Hargrove and Glidewell (1990), has a continually weak 'agency myth'. Actors in such a system may be inclined to use every available resource or tool to enhance their own standing or credibility, and one might reasonably suggest that it is their prerogative to do so. Coping behaviours can therefore have both intrinsic and instrumental significance in a public-policy system.

2.3 Direct or benign resistance to reform

Even if senior ministers and their officials are able to agree on value-based goals for the prison system, and formulate policy programmes based on them, they still have to be able to change or reform the system so as to realize these goals. We have discussed already the limitations of instrumental intervention and 'steering' from above, largely due to the adaptive and strategic responses of affected actors, the cumulative effect of which can distort or scupper desired outcomes. As principals attempt to impose value-based change on agents beneath them, these agents may be likely to respond in ways which resist this change – either directly and explicitly, or in more subtle and benign ways. Matthews (1999) writes as much:

> Various agencies involved in the criminal justice system are capable of resisting and even blocking policies with which they do not agree. They have historically demonstrated their capacity to change the direction of policy, although this has not always been in the direction

> of greater tolerance or leniency. If these factors are not taken into consideration, there is a danger of developing an over-politicised account of social change, and of seeing developments in penal policy as primarily the result of individual decision-making rather than as a social process. (p. 138)

We can add this new layer to the ever-growing schema. This involves capturing dynamics in the system which resist, either directly or benignly, the efforts of other actors to impose change. As Figure 2.5 shows, direct or benign resistance can have debilitating effects, and can feed into perceptions of an inherently failing system. For political leaders and top officials, the inclination may be to keep challenging status quo positions in order to reform the way in which the system works, or at least give the impression that they are trying to reform it for the better.

The imposition of managerialist change from above has been one important dynamic in this respect. Continual political intervention by ministers is likely to be another. Political elites may seek to impose their own value-based goals on the system, and these are likely to be met with direct or benign resistance by actors within. For experienced officials, political uncertainty and change is a professional hazard of working in a public-sector system, and the inclination is therefore to find ways of reducing the costs of this uncertainty. This is likely to involve a balance

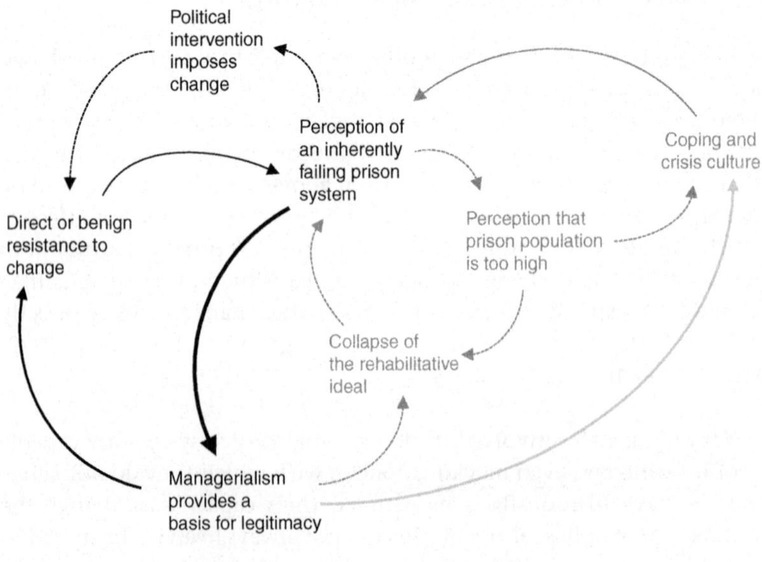

Figure 2.5 Adding in the 'direct or benign resistance' loop

between doing as much as is necessary to be seen to be responding to change, while at the same time keeping in mind that political priorities may change as ministers come and go, with the result that previous changes become defunct or part of an old order. Agents at all levels in the system cannot help but factor these considerations into the degree of urgency or diligence with which they respond to reformist measures from above.

As mentioned already, the prison system has been a strong archetype of NPM change over the decades, incorporating many of the characteristics of NPM discussed in the previous chapter.[8] Amongst the major managerialist reforms has been the creation of the Prison Service as executive agency in 1993 and the situation of management responsibility of the prison system in this agency under its own corporate governance structures, the growth of private-sector prison markets from the early 1990s onwards, and the intensification of output and outcome-based performance regimes. Figure 2.6 shows change on the profile of prison expenditure at different levels of the system throughout this period of emergence of NPM reform. Focusing on the relationship between the top lines in the graph, (1) total expenditure on prisons and (2) expenditure by prison establishments, this provides a proxy for the extent to which centralized control and coordination infrastructure has grown relative to prison establishments. Whereas in 1979, just over 90 per cent of total expenditure on prisons was spent by prison establishments, by 2009 this proportion had dropped to around 64 per cent. This ratio indicates the considerable bolstering of centralized control mechanisms which have been a function of more intensive managerialism over thirty years. We see also in this graph the (estimated) severe reduction in net operating expenditure on prisons since 2009, as the Ministry of Justice responds to government austerity measures and requirements to cut its budgets by 25 per cent (Bastow, 2010).

Managerialism has elicited many different types of directly or benignly resistant behaviour by actors in the system. Benign resistance is often likely to involve quite complex or nuanced combinations of factors, which aggravate or which put actors in unacceptable or unsatisfactory situations. As Harding (2001) illustrates, attempts by managers or officials to reform working arrangements or cultures of service have often been met with this kind of resistance, and sequential attempts and failures can have quite debilitating effects on a system:

> In a closed institutional structure, it is extremely difficult to maintain a culture that stresses programs and prisoner development rather than custody and control. There are myriad reasons for this, all interacting

with each other: low recruitment qualifications of officers; inadequate training resources; poor pay; senior management's poor appreciation of the role of the custodial officer, with consequential indifference or hostility to the workplace situation; thus, the use of union power to change or control conditions in the workplace, and so on. It can, and frequently does, become a downward spiral, with uniformed staff ultimately coming to stand in the way of the official correctional objectives. (Harding, 2001, p. 329)

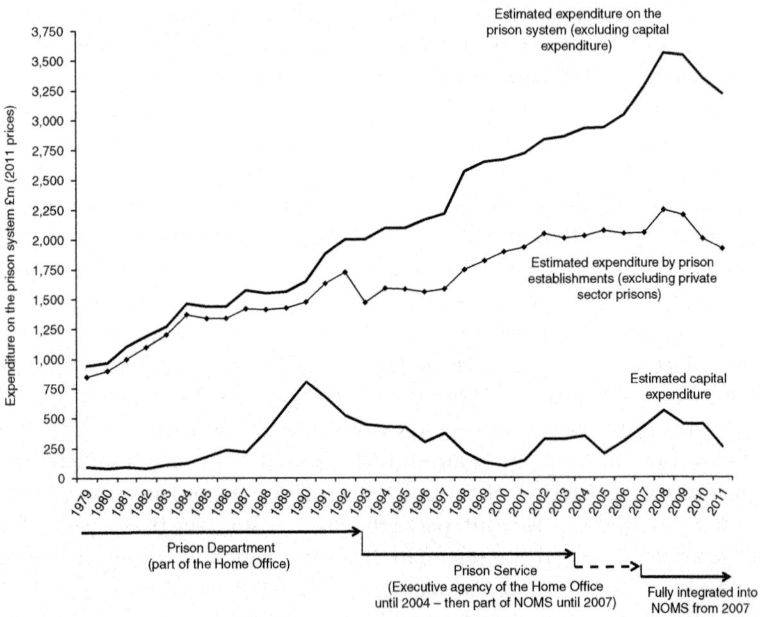

Figure 2.6 Expenditure at different levels of the prison system, 1979 to 2011

Note: Expenditure figures are deflated at 2011 prices. All data were sourced from Prison Department, Prison Service, and NOMS annual reports. Due to inconsistencies in the way data have reported over 32 years, it has been necessary to estimate total expenditures, while carefully cross-checking these estimates against other sources such as departmental expenditure reports. In the years since the National Offender Management Service has existed, it has not been possible to get exact figures on the expenditure on prisons by NOMS headquarters, and so I have estimated that two-thirds of total NOMS headquarters expenditure has been on prisons. NOMS officials interviewed confirmed that this is a reasonable rule of thumb. It has also been difficult to get exact data on prisons expenditure for 2010 and 2011. I have done my best to cross-check and confirm these figures as they are presented. Figures for 2010 and 2011 for expenditure by prison establishments have been estimated as they are not publicly available.

Source: My own analysis of data from Prison Department, Prison Service, and NOMS annual reports.

The introduction of competition into the provision of prison services is a good example of how attempts to orchestrate value-based change may be directly or benignly resisted. Critics have identified the power of the Prison Officers Association (POA) to resist attempts by ministers and officials to grow competition in the system (Black, 1995; Bennett and Wahidin, 2008). The threat (and execution) of widespread industrial action by the POA over the decades has been an obvious sign of more direct resistance to imposed change. More subtle resistance to modernization may also come from inside the bureaucracy of the prison system. As public-choice approaches have emphasized, senior officials may have considerable autonomy to shape the nature of their work, and employ 'dark arts' to resist or delay political projects, which threaten their position or interests. In his account of his time as the first chief executive of the new Prison Service agency, Derek Lewis (1997) reflects on the ability of senior prison bureaucrats to 'pursue their own agendas – supposedly hidden but conspicuously obvious' (p. 41).

Resistance to change may also come from senior ministers who are reluctant to take political risks with innovations or experiment in the system. Political pressures on ministers may come from fear of reactions from press and media, their own party, or the Prime Minister. Again, Lewis identifies resistance from senior ministers as a source of uncertainty and a constraint over actual operational freedoms. He reports the outcome of a meeting with former Home Secretary Kenneth Clarke on the political decision to reverse some of the reforms in the 1991 Criminal Justice Act which would have introduced more liberal approaches to parole and more expansive non-custodial punishment options:

> I left the meeting depressed. It had rammed home how little control the Prison Service had over its destiny. A large part of the 1991 Criminal Justice Act carefully crafted by Home Office civil servants to correct major failures in the system was being cast aside on the basis of short term backbench pressure and a few minutes of superficial consideration. (1997, p. 95)

Response to institutional disaggregation of the penal system as a result of NPM change has also led to the imposition of major re-integrative reforms to the machinery of government of the penal system. Again, the impact of resistance to desired change is implicit in much of the literature critical of this imposed reorganization. The creation of NOMS from 2004 is a good example of imposition of value-based goals onto the structures and institutions of the penal system. Through NOMS, officials aimed to reintegrate the administration of prison, probation, and youth justice, and tie this together under the label of offender management and a more joined-up approach to tackling the rehabilitative goal and reducing reoffending.

As mentioned earlier, the story of the creation (and re-creation) of NOMS has illustrated a more systematic and formalized approach to strengthening rehabilitative goals in the system. But as critics have argued, it has also shown what happens when reforms are imposed on systems, and actors are disposed to resist or influence those reforms to their own ends. Early incarnations of NOMS (from 2004 to 2007) were widely regarded by critics and practitioners as ineffective,[9] largely due to the difficulties which the new model had in integrating different cultures of prisons and probation systems. Experts have been critical of the way in which reform plans were imposed top-down without the involvement of key prisons and probation communities. Widespread criticism of organizational dysfunction in the first iteration of NOMS from 2004 provides perhaps good illustration of Moe's argument about inherently sub-optimal outcomes of structural choice.

2.4 Obsolescence and redundancy sustained in the system

The fourth potential source of misalignment involves the extent to which the design and operation of the prison system has kept pace with major changes in its external environment. We have seen already from the Brixton vignette at the very start of the book how it is possible for a system to be perceived as working at high rates of capacity, yet for it also at the same time to incorporate considerable obsolescence, inefficiency or redundancy. An important aspect of CCS therefore is the extent to which systems are able to incorporate and sustain outdated or badly designed systems that do not reflect wider practices in other modern organizations or arenas. This is an important final aspect in the overall holistic model. For it illustrates how systems can appear to incorporate aspects of success and failure simultaneously.

As we have seen in the previous chapter, systems can generate conventions or artefacts that can be seen as symptomatic of deeper cultural dynamics. Say, for example, an organization or system is operating with chronically out-of-date information systems, or a set of quality standards which are from a bygone era, then we can regard these as artefacts of obsolescence. If these artefacts play an important role in the day-to-day running of the system, then it becomes difficult to modernize them. And hence there is a risk that they become institutionalized in the system for long periods of time.

This relationship between system and environment, however, must factor in considerations about how societal norms change over time. For example, as Weiler (1992) points out, the practice of crowding three prisoners in a cell for one throughout the 1940s and 1950s was determined by cultural resistance in government to putting two prisoners in a cell together and risking homosexual activity. As society became more tolerant to homosexuality during the 1960s, and as the need for prison capacity increased, prisoners were doubled in single cells. During the last thirty years, we have seen fundamental changes in the technological, legal, and commercial environment, not least the expansion of computing and digital technology, revolutions in social and technological applications of wireless communication, growth of private-sector markets in public services, emergence of human-rights cultures and legislation, intensification of complex social problems such as drug addiction, new waves of immigration, and more specifically relating to the prison system, the sudden and sustained increase in the size of the short-term prison population. All of these environment changes have posed major challenges for the ability of the prison system to adapt and continually modernize its operational and organizational design.

As discussed in the previous chapter, bureaucratic cultures may be prone to internalizing and bureaucratizing responses to environmental complexity, while the world outside changes. For example, a series of reports by the UK National Audit Office showed how the Treasury was caught unawares by the first major refinancing of a private-sector prison by Group 4, and over subsequent years developed an elaborate set of rules and conditions to ensure that it received a fair share of financial dividends from future refinancing deals (NAO, 2000, 2006). In the meantime, interest rates for private finance reduced considerably as the private market developed and risk reduced, meaning that there was less scope for very large refinancing gains. Also, secondary markets in equity for public-sector contracts grew, thus changing the nature of the risk for government anyway. In short, Treasury had responded with a new set of rules to a problem which, broadly speaking, had changed fundamentally in nature by the time the response came.

It is likely that lags in keeping up with more complex and deep-seated features of modern society will build up gradually over long periods of time. Waves of social and cultural change may be hard for large public-sector systems to integrate into the way they operate. Hence, new pressures can accrete slowly while systems continue to operate in standardized ways. Often it will take cases of large upheaval of disturbance (i.e. crisis) to shake the system into modernizing. One former senior prison official reflected on how fundamental changes in UK society throughout the 1980s under Conservative governments underlay a period of severe disturbances in the prison system throughout the late 1980s and early 1990s:

> I think those changes in society, changes in background, people, changes in our view about revolutionary activity, all played into prisons and expectations about what prisoners were entitled to. And prisons weren't changing very much. Still dishing out much of what they had in the late 1960s. We continued to dish out the same things, which had worked with a post-war generation, rationing, overcrowded bedrooms, military discipline, and a fair amount of brutality at home.

We can add this final aspect to the schema in Figure 2.7. Here two potential factors can be seen as aggravating obsolescence or redundancy. First, 'coping and crisis' cultures may sustain perceptions that

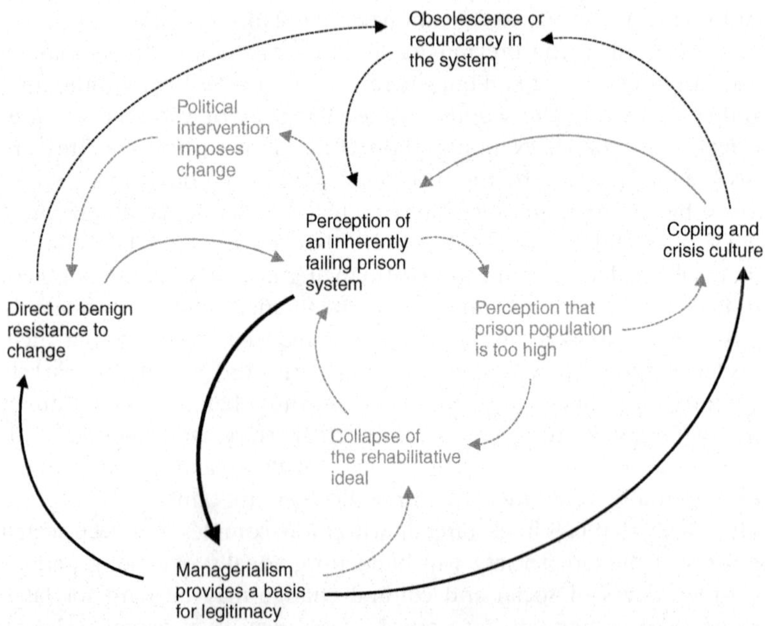

Figure 2.7 Adding in the 'sustained obsolescence and redundancy' loop

there is neither time nor opportunity to modernize the system or think strategically about the long term. In not investing intellectual or financial resources into continual modernization of systems and processes, there is a danger that public-sector organizations develop and, to a large extent, normalize obsolescence in the way they operate. Sustained reliance on obsolescent processes can come with strong feedback effects and constructed rationalization about the difficulties of changing things and the benefits inherent in maintaining these obsolescent ways. Obsolescence in the physical infrastructure of the estate may be caused by the need for continual short-term coping. For example, during times of prison population increase throughout the late 1990s, capital was made available for procurement of 'emergency' accommodation (NAO, 2005). Although this provided value for money in the short term, it also led to another variation of sustained obsolescence in the physical estate as these short-term units became an indispensable part of the long-term supply of accommodation.

Direct or benign resistance by actors in the system may also lead to lags in the ability of the system to keep up to date with major changes in environment. Actors in the system may be able to resist modernization, which in turn may be likely to have considerable impact on the way in which available capacity in the system is deployed. As discussed, resistance may not necessarily be direct, such as a staff union threatening industrial action. It may also be benign and systemic, not attributable to any one particular actor, and largely invisible to the human eye. It may also be the product of a combination of many different types of nuanced strategic or adaptive behaviour by actors in the system. As the schema suggests, whether obsolescence and redundancy in the system is caused by the imperatives of coping, or by different forms of resistant behaviour, the result is likely to feed back into perceptions of a permanently failing system.

I return to the many aspects of obsolescence and redundancy in subsequent chapters. It is a key part of the overall system approach, as it is both an artefact of dysfunction in governance arrangements in the system, and a cause of further dysfunction. In the final section, I discuss where we have got to with the development of this visual schema and its four interrelated loops.

2.5 Integrating the four loops into one

I have set out a more holistic governance-style framework for organizing and understanding how different theoretical perspectives discussed in

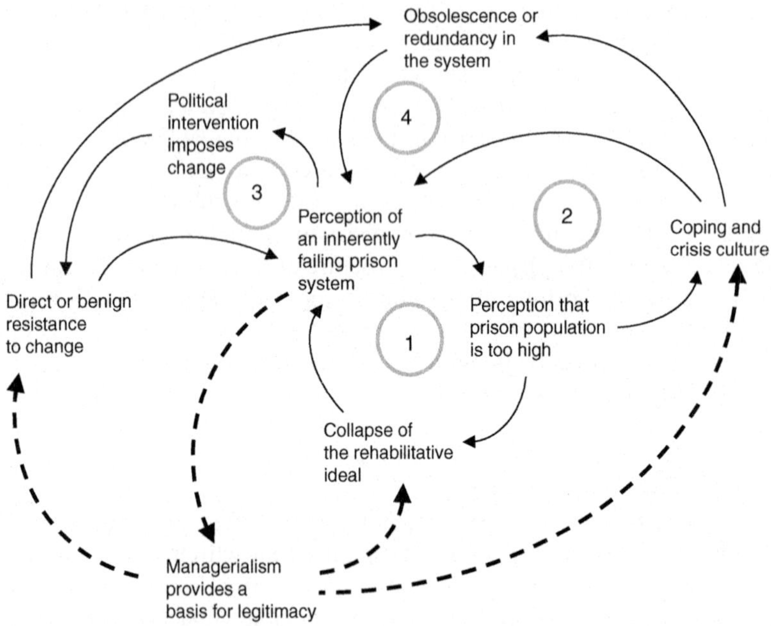

Figure 2.8 CCS – the overall schema

the first chapter might fit together to explain CCS in the prison system. As the incrementally layered and integrated schema has illustrated, some factors can play different types of roles in different loops (even though they are part of the same). Indeed, some factors appear in more than one loop and are therefore important nodal factors for thinking how each of the loops fit together in one whole-system view. Figure 2.8 summarizes this hypothetical problematique. It is an attempt to look at the various aspects of CCS in the round, and integrate existing and authoritative literature on the subject.

Looking at crowding throughout this period raises questions around how we reconcile universal and specific dynamics. Three decades is a long time for any public-policy system, and explanations must be flexible enough to incorporate universal and specific. One important specific change has been the development of NPM. It has played a dual role as dependent and independent variable in the system. Clearly, crowding existed in prisons prior to the emergence and development of NPM, and in this sense NPM must be seen as an independent variable of change which has impacted on the prison system. At the same time, NPM has been the dominant paradigm through which the system has evolved, and therefore must also be seen as a dependent variable upon which environment factors impact. I have therefore drawn the schema so that it is internally coherent with or without this managerialism factor (i.e. 'managerialism provides a basis for legitimacy' and its appended arrows (dotted lines) could be removed from the problematique, and the flows would still be internally coherent).

Through this diagrammatic depiction, we can begin to conceptualize how prison crowding can be seen as an example of CCS and, furthermore, how CCS can be seen an outcome of prevailing states of equilibrium in a public-policy system. Crucially, we see signs of aggravating and compensating dynamics that are constituent in these states of equilibrium over time. Prison crowding can therefore be conceptualized as a function of this governance equilibrium, and the particular aggravating and compensating dynamics that sustain this equilibrium. It provides a basis for beginning to explain how a system can function at continually high levels of capacity, yet at the same time incorporate strikingly high levels of obsolescence, redundancy, and inefficiency. It also provides a basis for understanding how a prison system, and indeed any other large public-sector system, can appear to neither completely excel nor completely fail in the things it does.

The schema does not at this stage tell us much about the relative influence of different factors. Small changes in one factor may lead to disproportionately large changes across others. Similarly, large changes in one factor may not necessarily guarantee similar change across others. This is where understanding 'system effects' becomes important. For example, the 'collapse of the rehabilitative ideal' may seem relatively small in the overall schema, but small improvements in this factor may well lead to disproportionately larger effects across the system. A committed or charismatic Home Secretary (now Minister for Justice), for example, may be able to trigger system-wide change simply on the basis of a change of tone in policy statements about the rehabilitative goals of prison. In many respects, we have seen exactly this change in emphasis since May 2010 as part of the intended 'rehabilitation revolution'. But success will rely on other factors in the schema working to support this outcome. Let us say that this minister begins to 'talk positively' about the rehabilitative role of prison. This may have a positive effect to reduce perceptions of a failing system, and if the minister is serious she may be likely to intervene politically to impose change on the system. Political intervention may also be 'managerialized' in the form of output or outcome targets or other outcome-based mechanisms.

As discussed, however, this kind of top-down attempt at policy engineering is no guarantee that rehabilitative outcomes in prisons will actually improve. Direct or benign resistance to efforts at rehabilitative change may be triggered if these political and managerialist interventions are not steered or handled 'successfully'. If they are not, these attempts run the risk of unravelling, as resistance feeds back into perceptions of failure, and if perceptions of failure reach criticality this may well persuade this senior minister (assuming she is still in office) that there are more winnable or worthwhile battles to be fought elsewhere. Hence, the chronic condition is likely to remain chronic.

Rather than being the solution to the problem, this schema provides a hypothetical device or heuristic around which to structure our thinking about the dynamics of CCS, and on which to base the empirical work in subsequent chapters. With this heuristic in mind, therefore, we move to the empirical and methodological plan of attack. This has needed to be encompassing enough to support this kind of 'whole-system' approach. As Minkin (1997) suggests, political research of this kind is as much a 'creative art' as it is an exercise in scientific analysis. In characterizing the role of the social science researcher as simultaneously one of 'detective', 'juggler', and 'patternmaker', these combined roles imply a kind of dynamic mix of inductive and deductive styles of reasoning (p. 192). The methods for this research have therefore had to be mixed and flexible in their design and application. Practically all of the theoretical and empirical work for this book has been done during the last four years. It is important to mention at this point that I received official approval to carry out this research from the National Offender Management Service in June 2009. This greatly transformed the level of access and insight which I was allowed, and I can be fairly sure that without this approval I would not have been able to produce this book. I have relied greatly on the wide range of interviews and visits that I was allowed to do, and these are summarized here below.

- 120 in-depth interviews with former senior ministers, top officials, prison governors, staff groups, private-sector officials, senior probation officials, senior judiciary, and third-sector officials;
- focus groups with deputy governors, prison officers, and private-sector executives and prison directors;
- site visits to 29 prisons of different types and locations, including walk-rounds with senior governors;
- work shadowing in Brixton prison and in Prison Service and National Offender Management Service (NOMS) headquarters;

- extensive collection of 32-year time series data from public sources on performance and capacity in the prison system.

Most of the 120 interviews conducted for this research were structured to capture key analytical themes, and to do so in such as way as to probe the evolution and development of these key public-policy and management themes longitudinally over time. The majority of interviews have been with individuals who have had many years experience in or of the prison system in England and Wales, and therefore they have been able to calibrate their comments and views in terms of these broader change. The way in which individuals rationalize change or improvement in the prison system over a long period itself presents interesting methodological questions about how to control for perceptions of relative and absolute levels of performance.

I have tried to fill the book with as much quantitative data as possible. The overall approach has relied on an essential mix of methods, and the book incorporates the product of literally hundreds of hours of data gathering and analysis in order to create the 32-year time series. I do not think that it would be excessive to suggest that this book provides, if nothing else, one of the most comprehensive quantitative accounts of public-management change in the England and Wales prison system ever published.

The discussion so far has intentionally limited itself (bar one or two minor exceptions) to existing public-policy theory and existing prison literatures. Now, it is time to delve more deeply into the new empirical work, and begin to develop in more detail the four main relationships discussed in this chapter. Although the schema helps to organize many of the key factors in this research, it is still somewhat vague in terms of how actual individual actors make decisions and take actions in a real live working prison system. In this sense, individual agency still needs to be 'injected' into the picture. Chapters 5 to 8 therefore look at the chronic condition of capacity stress in the prison system from four specific actor perspectives – senior ministers (Chapter 5), top officials (Chapter 6), prison governors and staff (Chapter 7), and private-sector firms (Chapter 8). In these chapters I examine in more detail the concept and challenges of 'constrained autonomy' for these different groups of actors, and identify how the predicaments they face in a situation of constrained autonomy contributes to sustaining CCS. As the previous chapter has made clear, in order to understand characteristics of the whole system, it is necessary to atomize the approach as much as possible, and dig down to the impacts of real-life actors in real-life situations. The corollary to this, as I hope to show, is that in order to understand the choice and decisions these actors, we need to interpret them in the context of their position as part of the whole system.

Before doing this, however, I turn to two key dimensions of the schema, both of which look at different aspects of NPM and the particular type of legitimacy it brings. Chapter 3 looks at how NPM has provided a basis for legitimacy through improved performance. Chapter 4 examines the dynamics of definitions and standards for capacity.

3
Performance and Capacity in a Managerialist Era

> I've been round lots of prisons, and I've never once thought this prison is running at the very edge. You could clearly make them much more efficient.
>
> (Former senior NOMS official)

> Historically, we have been given these efficiency savings while we are sat round a table, and actually they've been realistic and we've been able to deliver. The ones we are asked to do now? There is a general sense that they are not realistic without serious damage to services and establishments.
>
> (Deputy prison governor)

Probably the essential idea at the heart of the heuristic in the previous chapter is one of equilibrium between aggravating and compensating dynamics, and how these dynamics appear to co-exist as part of chronic capacity stress (CCS). One implication of these countervailing dynamics is that the system appears to incorporate elements of success and failure simultaneously. As we have seen, the prison system has been cast, almost serially, as a failing system, yet at the same time it has shown strong elements of coping. Indeed, as we will see in this chapter, it has not just coped, but in many ways has shown considerable improvements in basic aspects of its work. Another implication of CCS is that systems are also able to incorporate elements of relative under-supply and over-supply simultaneously. There are signs that the prison system has been squeezed and pared down as part of NPM change over the years (i.e. under-supply). Yet at the same time, there are also signs that the same system has been able to sustain quite striking levels of obsolescence and redundancy, both of which imply a kind of relative over-supply of capacity.

Table 3.1 Positive and negative interpretations of different capacity situations

	Running surplus capacity in the system	Running with capacity shortage in the system
Positive interpretation	High resilience and flexibility	Lean and efficient systems
Negative interpretation	Obsolescence, redundancy and inefficiency	Inflexibility, tightening, and paring down of the system

This raises some fundamental questions about the relationship between performance and capacity. Clearly, both concepts can be treated as separate, yet they are also interrelated in important ways. Performance of the prison system must to some extent be shaped by the amount of capacity latent in the system. If there is insufficient capacity, we would expect performance to deteriorate. On the other hand, having sufficient or surplus capacity in the system may be no guarantee that performance will necessarily improve or remain high. The challenge therefore is to understand the qualitative nature of this relationship, where the balance lies and what it looks like. Table 3.1 conveys the potential ambiguity involved. In short, we can interpret relative over-supply or under-supply of capacity in both positive or negative light.

It appears therefore that we need to know something about performance of the system in order to be able to interpret variations in capacity positively or negatively. In a system that is performing well, we may see surplus capacity as an important factor in ensuring resilience and flexibility. Yet, that same surplus capacity in a system which is not performing so well may be interpreted as redundancy or inefficiency to be ironed out. Similarly, under-supply of capacity seems no less enigmatic and open to interpretation. In a managerialist system, under-supply of capacity may be an important factor in ensuring leaner and more efficient systems. Yet, the negative spin on this is that under-supply can lead to excessive tightening and indeed 'hollowing out' to dangerous levels.

The intention in this chapter is to look in more empirical detail at performance in the England and Wales prison system over three decades, in an attempt to understand some of the complexity involved in the relationship between performance and capacity. Central to this story during this period has been the emergence and maturation of NPM. As we have seen in the previous chapter, managerialism can potentially play aggravating or compensating roles in the system, and this chapter will help to put more flesh on the bones of this argument.

As a way of assessing performance of the prison system over thirty years, I use the proxy concept of 'quality-adjusted productivity'. We find that once we have adjusted basic productivity to take into account some key aspects of performance over the decades, there are quite strong grounds for seeing the system as anything but failing, but rather a much improved and better managed system. I base our assessment of performance on the development of previous work done by academics at Princeton University during the early 1990s (DiIulio, 1993; Logan, 1993). I will show that managerialism has clearly played an important part in this process of improvement, and in this sense provided a basis for legitimacy as the previous chapter has discussed. In the second half of the chapter, however, I discuss five important countervailing aspects of managerialism, which bring to light its paradoxical nature and show how its dynamics have been as much aggravating as they have been compensating. Managerialism has done much to help the system cope with CCS in the prison system, while at the same time it has done much to help sustain the very same condition. I start first of all, however, with the analysis of productivity.

3.1 Productivity analysis as a proxy for performance

Productivity analysis provides a useful way of evaluating performance of public-sector organizations over long periods (Dunleavy and Carrera, 2013). For public-sector systems which process or deal with caseloads or throughput, so to speak, it can provide a useful way of cutting through the 'fog' of politics, and establishing a baseline proxy for performance over extended periods of time.[1] A good starting point is 'total factor productivity', calculated by the ratio of total outputs to total inputs. For prisons, total outputs can be estimated by the average annual size of the prison population cost-weighted to take into account variations in cost of accommodating different types of prisoners. Inputs can be estimated by deflated current expenditure on prisons.[2]

Figure 3.1 shows a first assessment of total factor productivity indexed across thirty-two years. Cost-weighted outputs have nearly doubled from around 70 to 130, while estimated net expenditure on the prison system has increased by a factor of almost four (from around 40 to 160). As a ratio of outputs divided by inputs, total factor productivity therefore decreases quite strongly up to the early 1990s and then flattens out at just below the baseline level. The steady decline in productivity throughout

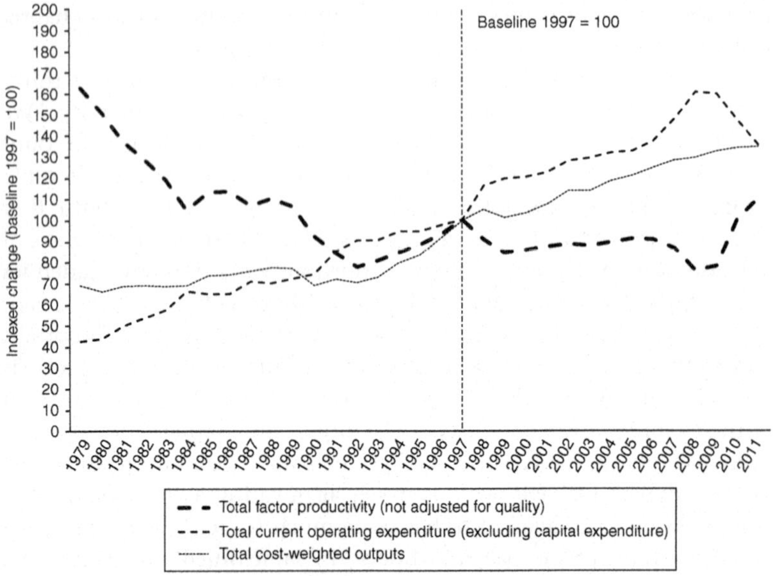

Figure 3.1 Total factor productivity in the prison system, 1979 to 2011

Source: My own analysis of data from Prison Department, Prison Service and NOMS annual reports, 1979 to 2011.

the 1980s and early 1990s can be explained by the considerable sums of new investment into the system which came from 1979 onwards, largely to compensate for chronic under-investment throughout the 1960s and 1970s.

On the demand side as well, the marginal reduction in the size of the prison population from the late 1980s to the early 1990s also led to downward trend in productivity. As we have seen in Figure 2.2, the rapid increase in the short-term prison population had the effect of reversing this steady decline in productivity from 1993 onwards. Indeed, productivity increase from this point reflects the system having to cope with much greater demand with little commensurate increase in supply of resources. With the new Labour government in 1997 came another injection of resources. Throughout the 2000s, rate of expenditure on the system climbed at roughly the same rate as cost-weighted outputs, sustaining relatively flat productivity. The sharp rise in productivity from 2009 onwards is explained by the sudden reduction in expenditure on prisons as part of government austerity measures.

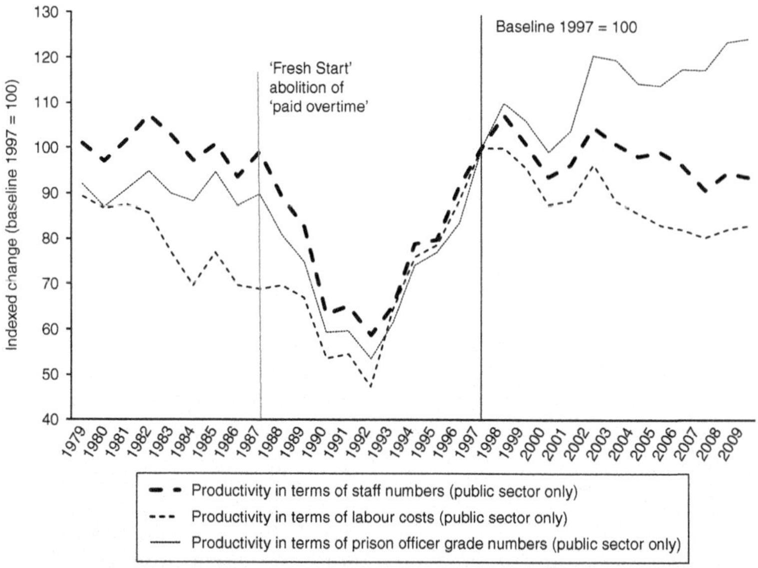

Figure 3.2 Trends in labour productivity in the prison system, 1979 to 2009

Note: All cost-weighted output data is as in Figure 3.1. Data on staff numbers and prison officers' grades were collated using Prison Department, Prison Service, and NOMS annual reports, and Hansard electronic archive of parliamentary written answers. Data in annual reports was often not reported consistently enough to ensure continuity over thirty years. Much of this data collation therefore had to be done forensically using data reported in parliamentary written answers. This involved many hours of systematic year-by-year searching in Hansard for all data on prison staffing, and then using triangulation techniques to give assurance that figures were internally coherent.

Source: My own analysis of data in Prison Department, Prison Service and NOMS annual reports, 1979 to 2009. Also Hansard archive of parliamentary written answers.

Trends in labour productivity show broadly similar trajectories (see Figure 3.2). Cost-weighted outputs are the same as above, but only including public-sector prisons. Instead of using total current expenditure as proxy for inputs, I use total full-time equivalent staff numbers.[3] Again, these data only cover public-sector prisons, as staff data on private-sector prisons (approximately 11 per cent of the market in 2009) are not publicly available. For labour inputs, I have used two separate measures, the total average number of staff employed in the prison system (including headquarters, regional and all prison staff), and the total amount of expenditure on staff in the public-sector system (deflated at 2009 prices). Figure 3.2 below shows the three productivity tracks for public-sector prisons only.

Looking first at labour productivity for all prison system staff (thick broken line), there is an initial increase above the baseline level, explained by a 16 per cent rise in the average prison population. From 1987, however, there is a rapid drop in labour productivity from around 100 to 60, the combined effect of a marginal reduction in the size of the prison population and an increase in the number of staff employed. This can be explained partly by the introduction of the 1987 'Fresh Start' reforms which 'bought out' the practice of prison-officer overtime and replaced it with a 38-hour working week. As a result, increased numbers of staff were employed in order to compensate for overtime that been worked by prison officers up to that point.

Interviews and literature confirmed the prevalence and power of this overtime culture.[4] Governors frequently reflected on the 'bad old days' of overtime and its associated detrimental practices. One governor explained a typical strategy on court-escort duty in the early 1980s, for example.

> You would go out for the day, prolong the day as long as possible, so you get over 5, 10, or 12 hours. Often the courts would finish, and principal officers would sit on the coach, the shutters of the vehicle were shut. And you would sit and sit and wait for the time to pass. Prisoners handcuffed. Then [he pauses] 'OK driver, thank you'. Shutters would go up, and the driver could drive out because you had gone over the 10 or 12 hours threshold.

The effect of overtime on productivity is shown by looking at labour productivity in terms of staff costs (thin broken line). This trend shows a steady decline throughout the 1980s, towards a convergence with the staff numbers trend into the early 1990s. The effect of overtime payments (i.e. paying more to relatively fewer staff) is likely to explain how productivity in terms of staff costs can be much lower than productivity in terms of staff numbers. Under overtime arrangements, the incentive for the POA was to keep actual staff numbers artificially low so that existing staff could maximize their gains from available overtime. This changed when overtime disappeared. As one former senior official explained:

> Say you need 100 prison officers to run a prison. Prior to Fresh Start, POA would not go for 100; they would go for 80, so that everybody got overtime. When they went onto salaries in 1987, they switched their argument to 'we need these 100 people [...] and, by the way, we need another five'.

From 1993 onwards, the productivity tracks show a radical change in a positive direction, and this can be explained by the rapid increase in the prison population. All three productivity tracks increase from mid-60s and low-70s back up towards the baseline level of 100. From 1997 onwards, there is an interesting divergence in the relationship between labour productivity in terms of all prison staff and prison-officer grades only (thin solid line). Throughout the 1980s these two tracks follow almost exactly the same trajectory; however, the lines diverge from the early 2000s. This divergence can be explained by two separate yet related factors. First, the number of headquarters and regional staff increased rapidly from the mid-1990s as the Prison Service grew as an executive agency and subsequently into NOMS. Hence, the number of prison-officer grades reduced compared with other staff in the system. Second, the cost of prison-officer grades has always been relatively expensive, once pensions and other benefits have been factored in, and over the years the Prison Service has sought to reduce these costs by introducing alternative lower-level grades into the system to take on much of the work done by officer grades.

This brief analysis suggests that throughout the 1980s, there was considerable latent capacity in the system. The abolition of overtime had a downward impact on productivity in that it increased the overall cost of staff in return for greater control and standardization over staffing arrangements across the Service. Since the mid-1990s, latent staff capacity has gradually been more efficiently deployed and costs have been taken out of the system by gradual streamlining of prison-officer grades, removal of layers of middle management, and introduction of non-graded, relatively cheaper prison staff. Nevertheless, as later sections will show, even as recently as the late 2000s there are still signs that there is latent staff capacity in the system.

3.2 Adjusting productivity to account for performance

The analysis so far has shown that despite a doubling in the prison population over thirty years, total factor productivity has been on a downward flat trend. This, however, is a narrow interpretation as it overlooks an almost universal view amongst interviewees that the system has improved many basic aspects of its performance during this timeframe. As one former senior prison official put it, 'the Prison Service I joined was an idle shambles, but it has improved enormously. It has got better every year. It is infinitely better managed that it was. People who say differently are just talking nonsense.' In key areas of performance, particularly security, decency and order, and general management of the system, it is possible to identify signs of major improvement. As another senior NOMS official put it:

> When I think back to 1983, conditions for staff are better, conditions for prisoners are better, and shock horror, managerialism has given some improvements. I can remember joining a Service where prisoners were treated with indifference; where public money was spent running prisons for the benefit of the staff, where 'reducing reoffending' was a word only; the concept of public protection was a fence and a wall; prisoners families didn't come into the equation; and as an organization, I think we were third rate.

We can work through some of these basic aspects of performance and think about how we might adjust our evaluation of overall 'total factor productivity' performance accordingly. A useful basis can be found in the work of the Princeton project,[5] a group of US-based academics who argued that prisons could and should be judged on a range of performance aspects other than recidivism rates. Their argument was it was inherently unfair to judge prisons on goals such as rehabilitation by dint of the fact that rehabilitation outcomes were partly or largely beyond the control of prisons. It was no wonder, they pointed out, that prisons were doomed to failure if these were the benchmarks against which they were continually being judged. The Princeton academics argued for a more scaled-down and realistic set of criteria for evaluation. As Logan (1993) writes:

> We do not want to set them up for failure, we must assign to prisons a function and a mission that we might reasonably expect them to fulfil. [...] This mission ought to be fairly narrow and consistent in scope, and it ought to be special to prisons, rather than conflated with the functions of other social institutions such as schools or welfare agencies. It also ought to be achievable and measurable mostly within the prison itself. (p. 23)

The framework for understanding performance of prisons was therefore re-couched more in terms of what prisons themselves were doing for prisoners, rather than what the outcomes of prisoners' behaviour would be upon leaving prisons. They highlighted eight key aspects of performance: security, safety, order, care, conditions, activity, management, and justice. In a more synthesized form, we look now at some of

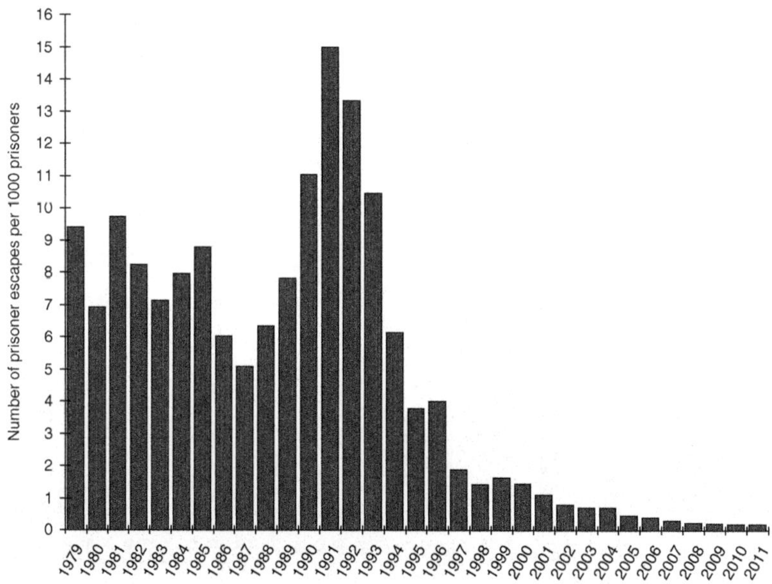

Figure 3.3 Average annual number of prisoner escapes, per 1000 prisoners

Source: Hansard electronic archive of written parliamentary answers and Prison Service annual reports.

these measures of performance applied to the England and Wales system over three decades.

We start with security and escapes. Since the mid-1990s, and the high-profile escapes of prisoners from high-security prisons Whitemoor (September 1994) and Parkhurst (January 1995), respectively, prison security has been a major area of priority and focus for ministers and top officials. This increased focus on security has been acknowledged by many interviewees and observers.[6] It is also supported by data on numbers of escapes in the system over thirty years (see Figure 3.3). The distribution is punctuated by a period of increase in escapes from the start of the 1990s and, as other indicators suggest, this reflects a period of upheaval and crisis in the system during those years. Without this punctuated increase, we discern a relatively continual decrease in escapes.

Analysis of major riots and disturbances suggests a more erratic picture of gradual improvements punctuated with bouts of unrest and violence. The index of riots and disturbances in Figure 3.4 reflects similar upheaval during the late 1980s and early 1990s, consisting of the series of disturbances leading up to the major and system-changing riots at

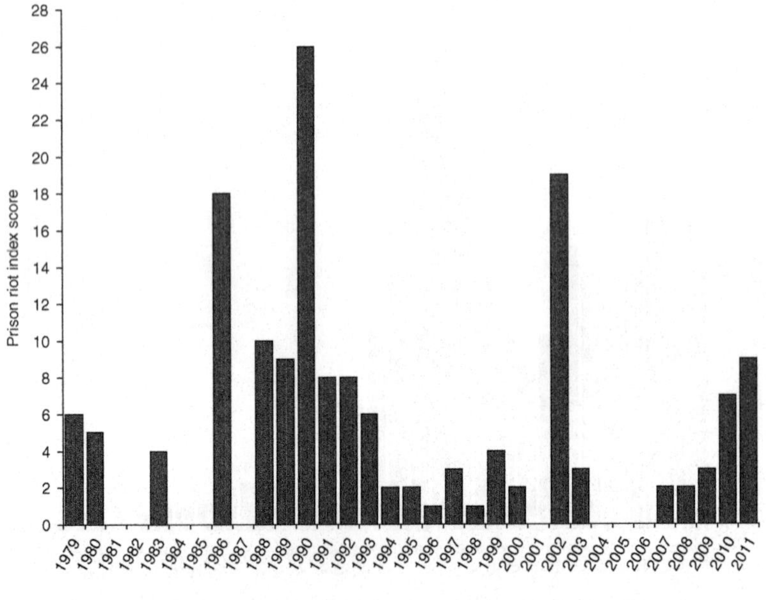

Figure 3.4 Index of disturbances and riots across the prison system

Note: Data in Figure 3.4 is compiled by systematic search of Hansard electronic archive and Nexis UK newspaper electronic archives for all references to riots or disturbances in prisons between 1979 and 2009. Information was collated about seventy-three major incidents, and they were coded 1 to 5 according to severity, where 1 = Very minor (rooftop), 2 = Minor (disturbance short-lived, minor injuries, low numbers), 3 = Moderate (more serious damage, fires, injuries, larger number, less than £500,000 damage), 4 = Major (more than £500,000 damage, days lost, accommodation lost, large fires), 5 = Very major. Scores were totalled for each year, and the figure shows the distribution of results.

Source: Hansard electronic archive of written parliamentary answers and Lexis UK electronic press archive.

Strangeways prison during a week in April 1990. Apart from a bad year in 2002,[7] on average the system has seen less major incidents since the mid-1990s, confirming perceptions of a safer and more ordered prison system. In Figure 3.4, however, we also see a revived increase in disturbances from 2007 and, as later graphs show, this is coterminous with increased pressure on prison capacity.

We also see improvement in standards of decency. Practices of 'tripling' prisoners in cells designed for one have all but ceased (Figure 3.5), and there has been much more systematic focus on maintaining the 'moral performance' of prisons since the early 2000s (Liebling, 2004). Figure 3.6 below shows how the rate of self-inflicted deaths in prisons have decreased gradually since the early 2000s, even though it had been

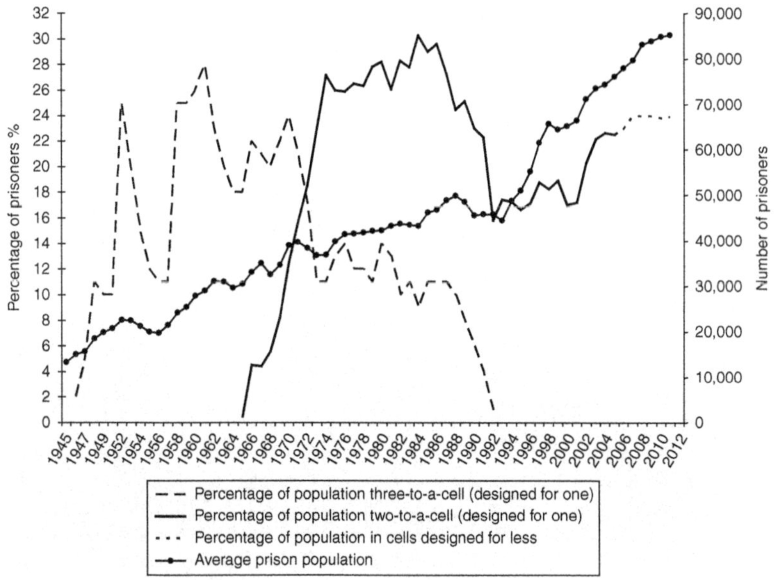

Figure 3.5 Percentage of prisoners 'tripled' or 'doubled' in cells designed for one, since 1945

Source: Hansard electronic archive of written parliamentary answers, and subsequently Ministry of Justice data 2011.

allowed to increase quite considerably throughout the 1980s and 1990s. Top officials have referenced this reduction as evidence of a more decent prison system during the last decade or so. Others have pointed out that, in the confined and highly controlled environment of prisons, the scope for monitoring and intervening to avoid self-inflicted deaths means that it should be possible to get much closer to near-zero levels of suicides

Since 1979 we have also seen expansion of services and programmes, and more intensive performance management. Table 3.2 shows the expansion of the performance regime across three decades.[8] Throughout the first half of the 1980s, Prison Department annual reports featured three indicators for performance in graphical tables, the rate of overcrowding, the cost per place of different types of prisoner, and the number of escapes from prison and prison escorts. From the mid-1980s, annual reports began to publish the number of hostage or violent incidents in the system, as well as data on the number of hours spent by prisoners in education and physical exercise. By the start of the 1990s, however, annual reports were publishing performance data on rates of

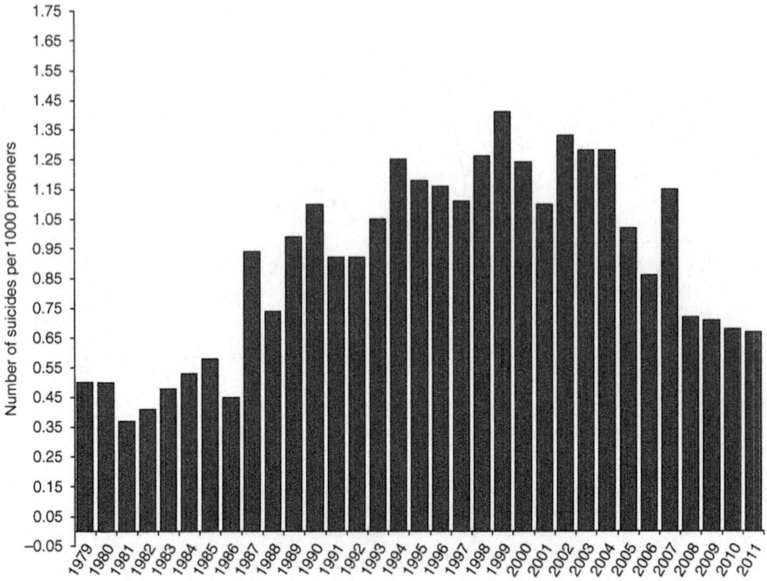

Figure 3.6 Rate of self-inflicted deaths in custody, per 1000 prisoners

Source: Hansard electronic archive of written parliamentary answers, and subsequently Ministry of Justice data 2011.

overcrowding, hours of education, hours spent on purposeful activity, numbers of assaults and incidents, escapes, and cost per prisoner place. From 1992, these data began to be reported against formal performance targets (Key Performance Targets or KPTs). Although some of these targets seem arbitrary, they did at least represent a much more systematic approach to defining and measuring performance.

An important expansion in prison programmes came with the introduction of targets for drug treatment and offender behaviour programmes. The problem of drug addiction amongst prisoners was not a new phenomenon, however; in 1995 the Prison Service began to report the percentage of positive random drug tests, and linked that to a target to reduce the proportion testing positive compared with the equivalent three months from the previous year. By 1998 this had changed into a target to keep the number of positive random tests to below 20 per cent, and by 2001 this target had decreased to 16 per cent and was met. In the subsequent years, the rate of positive detection was stable at around 11 per cent. From 2005, an additional target was introduced to complete 5,240 drug treatment programmes, increasing to 5,923 in 2006, and 6,595 in 2007. Again, it is impossible to tell to what extent these increases led to successful outcomes in reducing addiction.

From the mid-1990s the Prison Service also began to report its performance in delivering offender behaviour programmes. A performance target was introduced in 1996 which aimed to ensure that 'at least 1,300 prisoners completed programmes accredited as being effective in reducing re-offending', half of which should also complete a sex-offender treatment programme (HMPS, 1996). The completion target for offender behaviour programmes increased year-on-year up to the middle of the next decade, so that by 2000 the Prison Service aimed to complete 5,000 programmes, rising to nearly 8,500 by 2003 (HMPS, 2003). Even if it is difficult to assess the integrity of performance targets, they nonetheless suggest that the system has expanded its productive output in ways which are systematically geared towards achieving rehabilitative interventions. Say, for example, that each offender behaviour programme in 1996 involved the same amount of output as those in 2003. In 1996, completion of 1,300 offender behaviour programmes equated to around 1 in every 43 prisoners. In 2003, completion of 8,500 programmes equated to around 1 in every 9 prisoners. This represents a considerable beefing up of productive activity focused on rehabilitative outcomes – regardless of the actual effectiveness of these programmes.

There are signs that available capacity in the system has been much more efficiently used from the mid-1990s onwards. Figure 3.7 shows how throughout the 1980s, the system maintained relatively high levels of inefficient use of available capacity, while at the same time relatively high levels of use of police and court cells to deal with overflow of prisoners during times of acute capacity stress. A period of upheaval in the system around the early 1990s meant that inefficient use of capacity increased at the same time as use of the police and court cells. This can be explained by localized capacity shortages in prisons, despite the fact that the national system still has considerable free capacity in other types of accommodation. From the early 2000s, however, there are signs that available capacity in the system has been more efficiently used. The extent of 'inefficient' free capacity in the system has been managed down to consistently less than 5 per cent since 2008, and use of police or court cells has fallen to practically zero.

Using these indicators of performance, it is possible to create a composite multiplier which allows us to compensate for some important changes in quality over the years. We can use these seven variables

Table 3.2 Summary of performance-related data and performance targets

		Prison Department inside the Home Office							Prison Service Executive Agency of the Home Office					Prison Service in NOMS			NOMS	
		Data published in the annual report – not specifically performance targets							Key Performance Targets listed in the annual report (after 2010, targets are discontinued and changed to performance outcomes)									
Performance area		**1979**	**1981**	**1983**	**1985**	**1987**	**1989**	**1991**	**1993**	**1995**	**1997**	**1999**	**2001**	**2003**	**2005**	**2007**	**2009**	**2011**
1	Reoffending																	1
2	Escapes	1	1	1	1	1	1	1	1	2	2	3	3	3	2	2	3	6
3	Overcrowding	1	1	1	1	1	1	1	1	1	1	1	1	1	1	1	1	1
4	Offender behaviour										1	2	2	2	1	1	1	
5	Drugs										1	1	1	1	2	2	1	1
6	Cost per place	1	1	1		1			1	1	1	2	2					
7	Assaults								1	1	1	1	1	1	1	1	1	
7	Resettlement													1	2	2	2	2
8	Education					2	3	1					1	1	1	1		
9	Purposeful activity							1	1	1	1	1	1	1				
10	Staff sickness											1	1	1	1	1	1	1
11	Race equality												1	1	1	1	1	1
12	Time out of cell								1	1	1							
13	Suicides													1	1	1		1
14	Sanitation								1	1								
15	Visits								1	1								
16	Staff education										1							
17	Correspondence											1						
18	Incidents					1	1	1										
19	Prisoner escorts													1				
20	Farms	1																
	TOTAL SCORE	**4**	**3**	**3**	**2**	**6**	**6**	**5**	**8**	**9**	**10**	**13**	**14**	**15**	**13**	**13**	**11**	**14**

Note: *After 2007 NOMS was no longer responsible for provision of education in prisons.

Source: Prison Department, Prison Service, and NOMS annual reports, 1979 to 2011.

to adjust basic productivity so that it takes some assessment of quality and expansion of services into account. These can be organized into three general areas:

On security objectives:

- total escapes from prisons and escorts per 1000 prisoners (Figure 3.3);
- riots and disturbances index (Figure 3.4).

On decency objectives:

- percentage of prisoners sharing cells designed for less (Figure 3.5);
- number of self-inflicted deaths in custody per 1000 prisoners (Figure 3.6).

On management of the system and expansion of services:

- performance regime index (Table 3.1);
- total police cells used per 1000 prisoners (Figure 3.7);
- percentage of prisoners in prisons with more than 10 per cent free capacity (Figure 3.7).

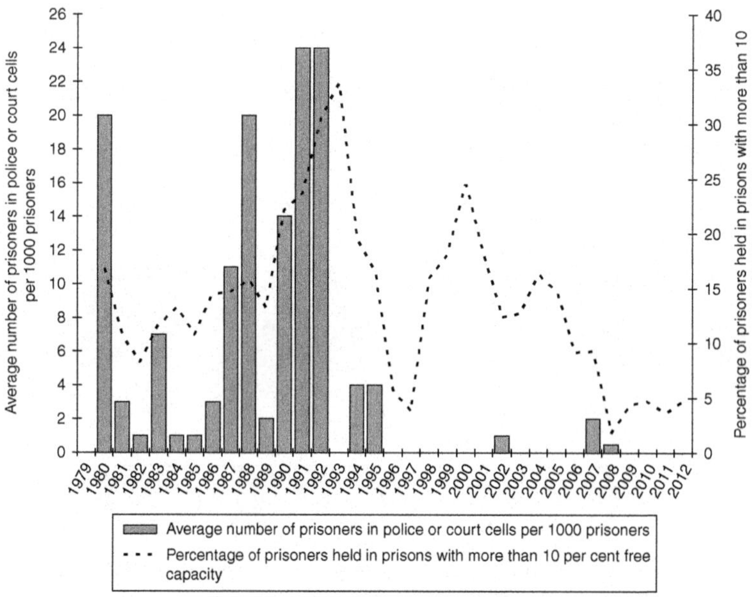

Figure 3.7 Indicators of effective capacity management in the prison system

Source: Prison Service and NOMS annual reports, and Hansard parliamentary written answers, 1995 to 2012.

Table 3.3 lists these seven indicators along with the appropriate steps in calculating 'quality-adjusted' productivity. In basic terms, the variations in each of the indicators have been coded into one of ten possible deciles, from 0.1 to 1, where 1 is the most desirable performance outcome and 0.1 is the least desirable. An overall adjustor score is calculated by multiplying all seven of these decile scores (row 8). These scores are then smoothed using two-year averages (row 9). I then multiply the adjustor score by cost-weighted outputs (row 10), to give a new quality-adjusted cost-weighted outputs (row 11). These are then divided by inputs (row 12) to give a new quality-adjusted total factor productivity index (row 13). The quality-adjusted productivity tracks are shown in Figure 3.8.

The impact of this quality adjustment on overall productivity is striking. As data in Table 3.2 shows, improvements in security, decency and order, and management quality in the system all impact on the outputs line to accentuate positive change over time. The impact of this on total factor productivity is something like a four-fold increase over thirty years, shown by the smoothed dotted line

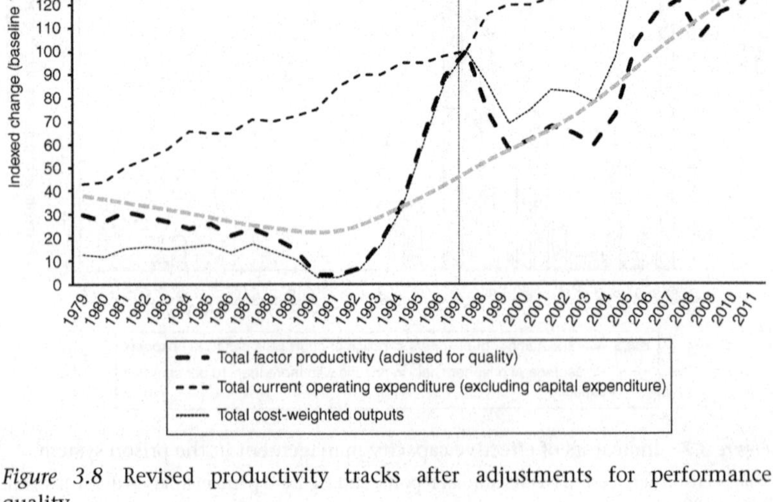

Figure 3.8 Revised productivity tracks after adjustments for performance quality

Table 3.3 Scores for seven key quality indicators for the prison system, and calculations for quality-adjusted total factor productivity, 1979 to 2011

		Prison Department inside the Home Office							Prison Service executive agency of the Home Office					Prison Service in NOMS			NOMS	
		1979	1981	1983	1985	1987	1989	1991	1993	1995	1997	1999	2001	2003	2005	2007	2009	2011
1	Total escapes from prisons and escorts per 1000 prisoners	0.6	0.6	0.8	0.7	0.8	0.7	0.3	0.6	0.9	0.9	0.9	1	1	1	1	1	1
2	Riots and disturbances index	0.8	0.9	1	0.8	0.6	0.3	0.3	0.8	0.9	0.9	0.9	0.8	0.8	1	1	0.9	0.7
3	Percentage of prisoners sharing cells designed for less	0.3	0.3	0.3	0.3	0.3	0.5	0.6	0.8	0.8	0.8	0.8	0.8	0.7	0.7	0.6	0.6	0.6
4	Self-inflicted deaths in custody per 1000 prisoners	0.8	0.9	0.8	0.8	0.6	0.6	0.6	0.5	0.4	0.5	0.3	0.5	0.3	0.5	0.5	0.7	0.8
5	Performance regime index	0.5	0.4	0.4	0.4	0.6	0.6	0.6	0.7	0.8	0.8	0.9	0.9	1	0.9	0.9	0.8	0.9
6	Total police cells used per 1000 prisoners	0.8	0.8	0.9	1	0.7	0.7	0.3	0.8	0.9	1	1	1	1	1	1	1	1
7	Percentage of prisoners in prisons with more than 10 per cent free capacity	0.8	0.8	0.8	0.8	0.8	0.8	0.5	0.3	0.8	0.9	0.7	0.7	0.8	0.8	0.9	0.9	0.9
8	Total multiplier for quality adjustment	0.04	0.04	0.06	0.04	0.03	0.02	0.003	0.03	0.15	0.23	0.12	0.20	0.13	0.25	0.24	0.27	0.27
9	Two-year average multiplier for quality adjustment	0.04	0.05	0.05	0.05	0.05	0.03	0.01	0.05	0.16	0.22	0.15	0.17	0.15	0.25	0.31	0.31	0.29
10	Cost-weighted outputs index (not yet adjusted for quality)(baseline 1997)	69	69	69	74	76	77	72	73	83	100	101	107	114	121	128	132	135
11	Quality-adjusted cost-weighted outputs index (baseline 1997)	2.8	3.4	3.4	3.7	3.8	2.3	0.7	3.7	13.3	22.0	15.2	18.3	17.1	30.3	39.7	41.0	39.1
12	Total current expenditure on prisons index (baseline 1997)	43	50	58	65	71	72	85	90	95	100	120	123	129	133	148	160	135
13	Quality-adjusted total factor productivity (baseline 1997)	30	31	27	26	24	15	4	18	64	100	58	68	60	104	122	117	131

Note: For presentation reasons, data in this table is presented for odd-number years only from 1979. All analysis in this chapter however is based on data for all years between 1979 and 2011.

Source: Bastow (2012)

in Figure 3.8 above. Quality adjustment has shown how the prison system, in some important ways, has made steady improvements over the long term.

3.3 Countervailing dynamics of managerialist change

Thirty years is a long timeframe for any public-policy system.[9] Relativization of change (or lack of it) can take place on different dimensions and suggest different ways of interpreting the same outcomes. For those who experienced the realities of working in local prisons throughout the 1970s and 1980s, for example, it may be difficult to look at the current day system as anything other than an improvement. As we have seen, managerialism has created a basis for legitimacy. It has underpinned a greater order and discipline. It has allowed the system to improve despite the rapid rise in the size of the short-term prison population since the early 1990s. It has, however, had aggravating influences. It may allow the system to cope, but it may also cause the system to have to cope. In the second half of the chapter, I discuss these aggravating dynamics, based on observations and insights from interviews with a wide range of prison officials.

In Figure 3.9, I have reproduced the quality-adjusted productivity line from Figure 3.8, and added a 'prison-crowding index' line which depicts an indexed scale of crowding in the system above 'normal' capacity.[10] As we see, the relationship between the two trends is one of convergence and co-development. Throughout the 1980s, crowding remains high and performance of the system shows relatively little change. By the start of the 1990s, however, crowding has reduced considerably and both trajectories thereafter, broadly speaking, move on an upward path together. By the end of the 2000s, crowding has risen once again to levels equivalent with the 1980s, while performance has risen gradually in comparison. Managerialism has tightened performance despite the ongoing pressures of crowding. But it has not done so without sustaining certain aggravating dynamics. I discuss five important aggravating dynamics below.

(i) Under and over-ambition in policy goals of prison

Looking first at change in general policy priorities, a major theme has been the increasing political emphasis put on reduction of escapes and security of the system since the mid-1990s. Senior officials acknowledged a general ambivalence towards escapes during 1970s and 1980s.

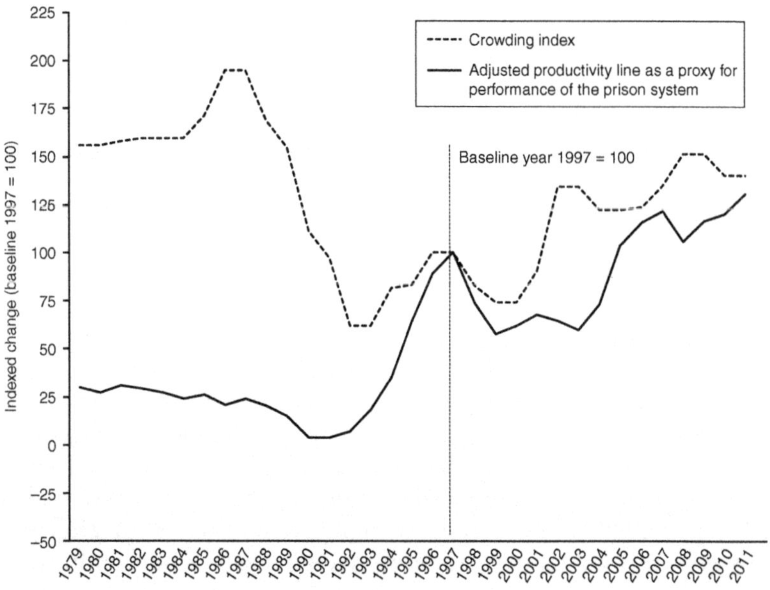

Figure 3.9 Comparing indexed rates of change in crowding and quality-adjusted productivity

Since the Whitemoor and Parkhurst escapes in the mid-1990s, however, policy priorities in this area appear to have intensified. For many, the political and financial investment in security has distracted from other more expansive objectives of prison. One experienced former governor captured this commonly expressed view.

> If the Service starts getting very proud about the fact that it has had very few escapes in 2009, I think it's wrong for them to be able to bask in that type of glory. I think they ought to be asked to be doing much riskier, more imaginative things, which extend staff more than I see happening now.

Indeed, interviewees frequently suggested that managerialist performance targets have allowed the prison system to sustain excessively narrow conceptions of success, based particularly around these security outcomes. As Table 3.2 shows, the number of targets focusing on reducing escapes has been far higher than any other priority. A current governor criticized the inherently constructed basis on which the prison system has judged its own performance.

> We are an organization which has hitherto been allowed to define what success is. That is a problem. You can tell how good the Prison Service is because we tell you how good we are. We have had three escapes and so on. But we have chosen to define success very narrowly in these terms. Security is everything [...] security, security, security.

While many interviewees criticized the perceived narrowing down of priorities towards security, others recognized exactly the opposite problem, one of excessively ambitious and unrealistic policy goals inherent in the move towards integrated offender management throughout the 2000s. At the heart of this policy shift has been a strong emphasis on rehabilitative goals, in which the prison system through NOMS has been directly implicated. For many interviewees, however, this policy shift has involved unrealistic ambition in what the system can be expected to achieve given the financial and infrastructural resources that have been made available. In this sense, the norms of managerialism underpin an idea that ambitious policy outcomes can be instrumentally willed, designed, and implemented. But the aggravating problem here has been perceived as disparity between the inherent ambition of offender management, and the reality of the system working at close-to-tolerance levels, and coping with continuous crowding and ever-tightening resources. As one former senior NOMS official put it, 'the mundane fact is that NOMS, ever since it was established, its scale of ambition has never been commensurate to its capacity'.

(ii) Constraining and distracting influence of performance targets

The impact of managerialism has been strong in the area of the prison regimes. We have seen above how the performance-management regime intensified from the early 1990s onwards. Performance targets, however, generate a particular type of legitimacy in the system, based on what those specific targets prioritize, and what they deprioritize. Governors frequently talked about the constraining effects of having to focus on meeting performance targets rather than on thinking more expansively about rehabilitative outcomes in their own prison. As one said, 'we can't make links between scale of ambition, reality of crowding, and entropy in the system. That's because everything is target-driven. Everyone spends all day looking at how you make a target rather than (how you) make a difference'.

Looking more closely at trends in rehabilitative outcomes of the prison system, the picture is again potentially complex. For a start, the impact of local prisons in 'making a difference' in reducing reoffending has seemed distinctly limited. Ministry of Justice data on average rates of reoffending by prisoners released from local prisons suggests that somewhere between 64 per cent and 67 per cent of prisoners sentenced to less than 12 months reoffend within two years (see box plot on the far left of Figure 3.10). It is interesting here that this distribution spans only 3 per cent. Indeed, the relative lack of variation in these figures suggests that there is little or no relationship between the quality of the regime inside a specific local prison and the likelihood that prisoners from that prison will reoffend. This suggests that reoffending amongst short-sentence prisoners is very much a structural problem, one that appears to exist regardless of the intervention of the local prison concerned.

The data therefore seems to bear out any structural inclination for those in the system to be fatalistic about the benefits of focusing on rehabilitative goals. On the strength of this aggregated picture, the performance of a local prison does not appear to influence propensity to reoffend. Hence, the inclination amongst many to be sceptical about the feasibility of evaluating prisons on their rehabilitative outcomes. It becomes difficult to make an argument for investing politically or financially in pursuing rehabilitative goals. A former Prisons Minister captures the syndrome involved:

> There is nothing sophisticated enough on the reoffending side of the argument to counter the managerialist approach to things. This is one of the huge weaknesses of the system. The success of the system is only judged by outcomes for security, or outputs for resettlement or trying to prevent reoffending. So it's a very loose argument that you can make [...] on reoffending.

Experienced officials also raised questions around the actual effectiveness of many of these programmes and treatments provided to prisoners over the years. This is particularly the case for short-sentence prisoners who are in custody for a matter of months. A former senior official reflected on the futility of providing short-sentence prisoners with education programmes, and the need to think more strategically

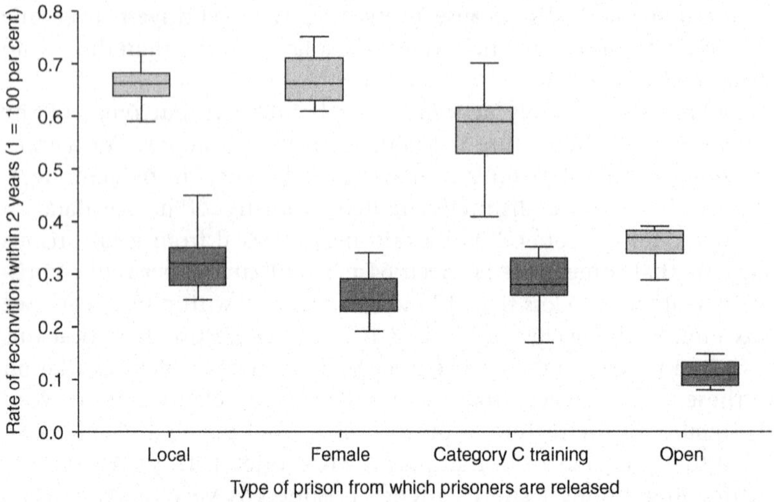

Figure 3.10 Rates of reoffending within two years after discharge from different types of prison, for sentences less than 12 months (light shaded on left side) and more than 12 months (dark shaded on right side).

Source: Ministry of Justice 2011 data. In this figure, the boxes show the interquartile range, and the black line inside the boxes shows the mean. The tails of the boxes show the distribution of the remaining data points outside the interquartile range, which are not considered statistical 'outliers'.

about the use of resources on programmes and treatments for this short-term population.

> I would have taken all rehabilitative activity out of local prisons other than detox. And I would have just concentrated on areas where you could make a difference. I was coming to the conclusion that throwing a few hours of education at someone for a few weeks where it wouldn't change their employability, was a waste of time. We should concentrate it where we could make an impact.

Looking in more detail at government data on actual reconviction rates over the last ten years, we see a similar lack of responsiveness to obvious improvements in performance of the system in general. Figure 3.11 shows the relatively flat trajectory of reconviction rates (within 18 months) amongst prisoners sentenced to less than six months – flat-lining at somewhere around 60 to 65 per cent. As senior officials have argued, however, this trajectory is potentially misleading. They point out that

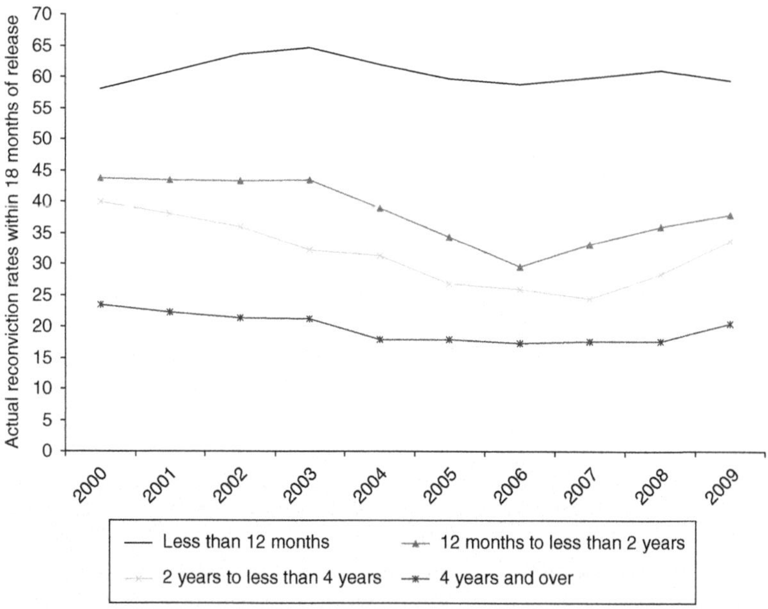

Figure 3.11 Unadjusted actual reconviction rates within 18 months of release, by length of sentence

Source: (MOJ, 2011), Table A5 p33.

it is necessary to take into account the changing characteristics of the prisoner population in any evaluation of reconviction outcomes. If the system is processing more intractable and more serious criminals, we must reflect this in our evaluation of intervention by the prison system. Figure 3.12 presents official data reported by the Ministry of Justice in 2010 that recasts the change in reconviction rates in such a way that it controls for such changes in the prisoner population profile (Ministry of Justice, 2011). As we see, for these short-sentence prisoners, the reconviction rate appears to have dropped by around 7 per cent throughout the course of the 2000s. This looks broadly comparable with the trajectory of decrease shown in Figure 2.3.

Again, there are interesting implications in terms of our understanding of the countervailing effects of managerialism. We have argued, on the one hand, that managerialism has provided a basis for legitimacy in the system that has deprioritized rehabilitative goals against more prison-specific activities. On the other hand, however, if we are to take this adjusted data at face value, and there is no apparent reason not to,

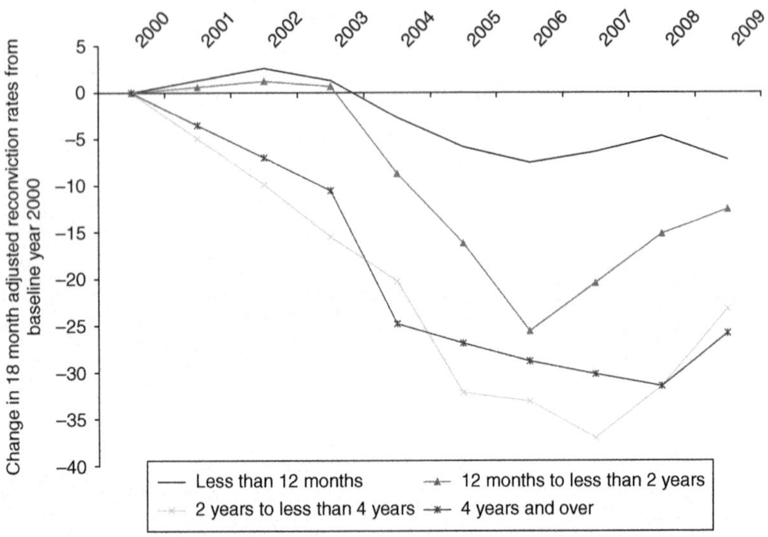

Figure 3.12 Progress in reconviction rates adjusted for offending characteristics of those released, within 18 months of release, by length of sentence (baseline year 2000)

Source: (MOJ, 2011), Table A5 p33.

it appears that managerialism has underpinned a degree of improvement in rehabilitation rates, particularly amongst longer-sentence prisoners. It is perhaps intuitive to think that this might be the case. A better organized and more disciplined system would presumably have some kind of discernible effect on reoffending or reconviction rates. Our data suggest that this 'management effect' appears to make a difference of somewhere between 10 and 30 per cent, depending on the length of sentence.

(iii) Command-and-control management and its stifling effects

The third dimension of managerialism has been the increasingly centralized control and line management, and the reported stifling effects that this has had on managerial autonomy. We have seen how the eradication of overtime in the late 1980s did much to systematize pay and conditions across the system. The establishment of area managers from the early 1990s also set the framework for centralized command-and-control across the system nationally. Interviewees talked about the constraining effects of centralized performance management coupled with these strong command-and-control cultures.

> Managerialism, if you are not careful, really means that you forget some of the fundamental things you are there to do. Because you will not get a good annual report if you say as a governor 'I've improved fifty prisoners this week but I've overspent on my budget'. You'd get shot. People are very focused on their targets and the next inspection. That's what you're thinking about. Have I done everything to meet my bit of the balance scorecard. Because that's what the governor will be asked by the area manager.

More centralized line management of the system throughout the late 1990s and 2000s also incorporated attempts at 'workforce modernization', involving reform to pay, working conditions, and pensions of prison staff, as well as delayering of operational and management staffing structures. We have partly seen the signs of this in Figure 3.2. Governors talked about the difficulties of finding cost savings year-on-year in a public-sector context in which there are considerable barriers to streamlining staff deployment. Cost savings must therefore be found by introducing more efficient ways of working, decommissioning services or facilities, or quite commonly by not refilling posts once staff retire or leave. Not refilling posts serves governors as a somewhat blunt instrument for responding to requests from headquarters to find requisite savings. One deputy governor characterized the wider problem:

> Usually, you'd be looking to reduce your staff headcount down, but there's no mechanism to reduce staff headcount with redundancy. So you are stuck with your staff, stuck with your costs, and the money is being taken out of your budget.

Often this can lead to perverse situations of staff obsolescence and inefficiency whereby facilities or services are shut down in the prisons in order to save costs, but the staff who operated those facilities remain in the system as 'surplus'. This allows the system to perpetuate the illusion of cost savings despite the fact that staff costs are still incurred. One governor characterized the peculiarities involved:

> If they say to me, you've got to save £100k, and I say well, I'll shut that workshop. And that four people are my £100k saving. I can't make them redundant, so I declare them as 'surplus'. I don't actually

save it, I save it on paper. So when a Minister stands up and says we've saved fifty million pounds in the Prison Service, we have saved it on paper, but the chances are that we are still spending £43k of it every month. We are still paying the wages. What it means is that if another job turns up somewhere else and they fit the criteria, then they are duty bound to move. There are so few jobs anywhere that people just remain. I've got people here who have been surplus for years.

(iv) Short- termism and an inherently imperfect prison estate

The fourth aspect has been increasing centralized coordination and management of the development of physical capacity in the estate. The aggravating dynamics of managerialism are potentially complex in this respect too. One major theme here has been the growth of private-sector markets for new prisons since the early 1990s. During this time, most new prisons have been built through Private Finance Initiative (PFI) contracts with private-sector consortia, and for much of the 1990s and early 2000s, government was able to limit its own exposure to the capital costs of these new assets by keeping the capital element off its balance sheets, and subsidizing new capacity through current expenditure payments to contractors. The consequence is that these private-sector solutions have offered quicker and cheaper (at least in the short term) prison capacity during times of increasing prison population. The knock-on effect is that government has been able to rely on these short- and medium-term solutions, and deprioritize any longer-term thinking about the design of the physical estate as a whole.

Linked to this is the role that the private sector has played in facilitating quick-fix 'emergency' accommodation in response to the increase of the short-term prison population from the mid-1990s onwards. Short-term accommodation has been added to existing prisons in the form of expansion programmes, new houseblocks, and pre-fabricated modular units. There is however a risk that in relying on such short-term measures, the system compounds the problem of sub-optimal distribution of capacity geographically. Short-term accommodation may well allow the system to cope, but it also runs the risk that obsolescence is built into the system if short-term measures become institutionalized as long-term solutions. In this sense, the pressure to cope in the short term undermines value for money in the long term. The managerialist response involves a paradox in that it is a necessary part of a short-term solution, yet at the same time, it is partly complicit in sustaining the need for such short-term solutions.

(v) Population management and running the system at close-to-tolerance

The final countervailing dynamic relates to the move towards more centralized management of the prison population. In order to compensate for an inherently imperfect geographical configuration of capacity, the system has had to move prisoners continually around the estate. The practice of moving prisoners has long been a central part of the system anyway. Prisoners enter through local prisons serving the courts and, depending on the length and requirements of their sentences, are then often (although not always) moved into training prisons or open prisons. Additional to this standard movement, however, has been the practice of moving prisoners between local prisons, particularly those on shorter sentences, in order to manage geographical disparity in demand and supply. The practice of moving prisoners from local to local prisons in order to maximize capacity and make room for new intakes is known as 'overcrowding drafts' and has become a vital centrally managed 'life-support' function in order to keep the prison system operational.[11] This systematic movement has been an absolutely key part in sustaining operational capacity levels consistently at more than 95 per cent (as shown in Figure 3.7). As one governor reflected, 'the efficiency with which the available capacity is used is phenomenal. I don't know how many hotel chains manage to operate at 98 per cent capacity. I suspect none. It's an extraordinary machine that moves prisoners round the country, all day, every day.' Table 3.4 illustrates the scale of continual movement of prisoners on overcrowding drafts.

The managerial paradox here is striking. It is widely acknowledged that centralized management of the prison population has been vital in keeping the system operational and allowing it to maximize available capacity and minimize the number of prisoners held in police cells. Yet it is has been short-sentence prisoners who have traditionally been moved in order to make room for new intakes. The act of the moving them away from their localities is seen by many as working directly against the objective of reducing reoffending. As many officials have pointed out, it is much harder to link these short-sentence prisoners with vital services in the community, and it is in building these links that the system is able to reduce the chances that prisoners will not reoffend. Interviews with local authorities, chief probation officers, and prisoner charities all agreed that there was a direct link between the extent to which short-sentence prisoners were moved and the extent to which they were able to establish strong links with them both in prison and on release. One experienced governor explained the potentialities

Table 3.4 Overcrowding drafts from region to region, July 2008 to July 2009

Most common prisoner movements from region to region		Number of prisoners sent	Number sent in reverse	Percentage of all prisoners sent by the sender
Sent from	**To**			
West Midlands	North West	3,900	200	90
London	West Midlands	2,110	80	66
South East	London	920	350	32
South East	West Midlands	480	60	17
London	Eastern	450	160	14
Eastern	East Midlands	450	100	32
London	South East	350	920	11
North West	Yorks & Humber	300	190	36
South East	Eastern	230	120	8
South East	East Midlands	210	100	7
South West	West Midlands	210	100	26
East Midlands	Yorks & Humber	190	180	28

Source: National Offender Management Service (NOMS) (2009).

of being able to keep these short-sentence prisoners relatively close to the services they would rely on after release:

> I had the regional Chief Officer for drugs and alcohol intervention in here last week. I said we are going to keep these prisoners. He said, 'What [...] you're not going to send them anywhere? So I can send my workers to you?' That becomes a serious conversation then. Two years ago I would have said yes but I can't guarantee that I'll be able to keep them here [...] what with the population pressures.

The disruptive effects and the risks of moving short-term prisoners around the system were acknowledged by many senior officials and governors. Figure 3.11 shows how references to crowding in the prison system made in HM Inspectorate reports since 1998 have predominantly been related to these disruptive effects on short-term prisoners.

We have seen already how the prison system has been run continually at levels of capacity close to 100 per cent, and the population-management function has been critical in allowing this to happen. For many officials, there are risks at running at close-to-tolerance levels. As one former senior NOMS official put it:

> When you've got a system that is that volatile, you shouldn't be trying to manage it within 1 per cent of capacity. It's a ludicrous thing

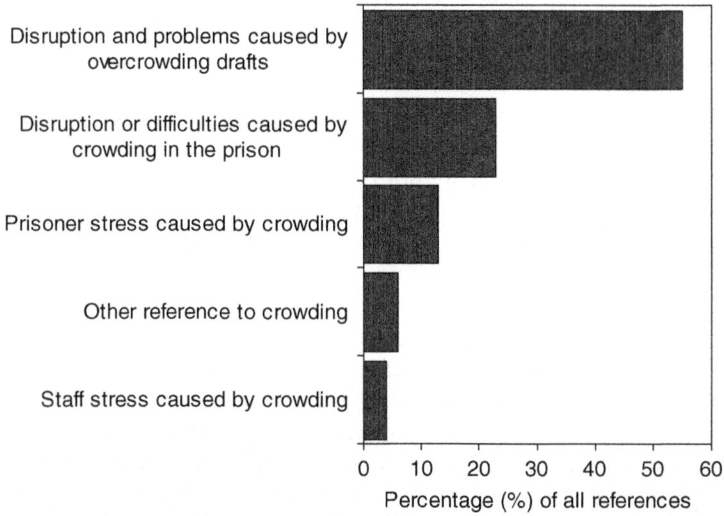

Figure 3.13 References to crowding made by HM Inspectorate reports, and specific focus of the reference, 1998 to 2011

Note: This figure is based on review of 224 Prisons Inspectorate reports on individual prisons, published between January 1998 and January 2011. Reports were searched electronically, and every mention of the term 'crowding' was coded, and categorized for its particular point of focus. In total, 369 references were coded.

Source: HM Prisons Inspectorate inspection reports.

> to try and do. I've had several ministers who have brought in their men who run hotels. And they just looked at me with utter amazement when I said we were running with 99.3 per cent capacity. How the bloody hell do you do that? They just sort of stagger away as ministers tell them to tell us how to do it more efficiently.

Not only does the system run at these continually close-to-tolerance levels, but it also does so despite incorporating striking obsolescence. For example, similar logistical operations in modern commercial settings in the late 2000s, such as hotels, would most likely involve sophisticated automated logistics systems. For population-management staff in headquarters, however, the process has relied predominantly on managers using pencil, paper, telephone and email, and up until mid-2010 there was no system-wide management system allowing real-time information about the whereabouts and case files of individual prisoners. Many officials recognize this obsolescence, and the operational risks involved.

Yet they also point out the inherent constraints involved in automating this process. As one former NOMS official explained:

> It's not unfamiliar to find the Prison Service lagging behind most areas of public life, never mind the public sector when it comes to the use of technology. You are not the first person to look at Pop Man[12] and say why? But no computer I've seen has got the flexibility in the 'black arts' that they demonstrate. It would be great to try. But the transition would be high risk.

In this quotation, we see how cultures and perceptions of coping in the system make the prospect of system modernization seem too difficult to risk. Frustratingly, complexity is both a product of sustained obsolescence and a rationale for why this obsolescence cannot be modernized. It is a form of benign resistance to such modernization that feeds into sustaining obsolescence.

3.4 Conclusions

We have seen some important countervailing dynamics at the heart of managerialism in the prison system over thirty years. Clearly, different aspects of managerialism have helped the system to achieve improvements in its performance. This supports an argument that the prison system over thirty years can be seen as *anything but* a permanently failing system. Indeed, resources flowing into the system have outpaced the rapid expansion in the number of prisoners, and these resources have translated into a considerable expansion of outputs provided. A former senior official in the Prisons Inspectorate characterizes this expansion.

> The reason that a lot more resources have gone into prisons is that they are doing a lot more. Twenty or thirty years ago, prison was a place where you were banged up and went out. We are expecting prisons to do work and expecting staff to do some work. Huge amounts of money for drug treatment, arguably far too much. We have put in healthcare to deal with mentally ill. Money for resettlement work. And security. And it's not just one guy anymore. I mean, sophisticated security machines. The difference is that prisons are actually doing something.

It may be difficult therefore to argue solely that managerialism has led to excessive paring down or hollowing out of the system. Quite the contrary in fact, as we have seen periods of extensive ramping up of resources compared at least with number of prisoners processed through the system.

Managerialism has played a central role in this expansion. We have seen how performance targets and incentives have shaped the logic of the system, and helped to move it towards running at ever higher levels of capacity. We have seen how managerialist logic can lead us to interpret capacity stress in a positive light, implying that as long as we can point to improvements in performance then capacity stress can be seen as a secondary issue. As one current governor put it:

> The currency of overcrowding gets devalued with every year that we are successful; we complete our KPTs, and show we can do it. Last year was our most successful year. Last year the Prison Service met all its KPTs. That's a successful business isn't it? Your headlines are down, not as many escapes, no riots, met all targets, how much more do you want?

Clearly, however, there is rhetorical inflection in these words which suggests that there may be much more that one *could* want from prisons. As the second half of this chapter has sought to show, managerialism has done much to feed into and sustain capacity stress, and in this sense, there is room for more negative interpretation (as the matrix at the start of this chapter depicts). Having provided a basis for improving the system, we have seen how it has simultaneously tightened the system. The process of tightening in this sense has various meanings. It refers to continual budgetary squeezing of prisons and staffing. It refers to efforts by managers and ministers to maximize the available and latent capacity in the system. It refers to centralized and command-and-control mechanisms which have allowed the system to run at increasingly close-to-tolerance levels. And it also refers to the logic of performance management and targets which has had the effect of focusing and constraining the actions of those subject to them. This senior Inspectorate official characterized the aggravating dynamics:

> It's a kind of [...] worst place. You are resourced to do a lot more than containment [of prisoners], but you are not resourced well enough to do the real rehabilitation work, that it says on the tin, and says in the aims of the Prison Service. That would require more space, fewer prisoners, more headroom. All the fancy stuff about offender management is positing the possibility of individualized planning for

> each prisoner. And you are moving people in industrial quantities around the place.

As we have seen, the need to focus on the pragmatic imperative of keeping the whole system upright – whether it is in being forced to use decrepit or inadequate premises to hold prisoners or in having to constantly focus on moving prisoners around the estate – has fed into sustaining a view that that there is considerable inefficiency and obsolescence throughout. This sustains a negative interpretation that there is latent capacity surplus in the system, and that this either has to be made less latent or taken out of the system altogether. Again, the logic of managerialism drives changes towards these ends.

The picture of the managerialist paradigm is therefore complex. The relationship between performance and capacity is far from straightforward. I have tried to show in this chapter some of these important countervailing dynamics, and to draw on the wealth of qualitative insight gained from interviews to raise some fundamental questions about the nature of these dynamics. I return to these themes in Chapters 5 to 8. Before moving to these individual actor perspectives however, I examine another fundamental aspect to CCS, and the relationship between performance and capacity. This relates to the way in which crowding has been defined and measured over the years, and how this has helped to sustain the problem.

4
Measuring and Setting Capacity Standards

> At what point does crowding start? What is 'normal' capacity? Who knows? It's only relatively recently that we had 'Operational Capacity'. Until then we had a 'Certified Normal Accommodation', which meant absolutely nothing at all. For years there was Certified Normal Accommodation, which was no real measure. It meant nothing. As far as your capacity was concerned, you had what you had. (Former prison governor and senior official)

To be able to say whether a prison or a prison system is crowded, one must have a set of standards in mind that demarcate a threshold between states of being 'too crowded' or 'not crowded enough', and what it means to be 'about right'. These subjective states are likely to involve policy and practical judgements which are complex and open to interpretation. On the one hand, standards give structural integrity to a system, and in theory provide some kind of protection against excessive overload. But the risk here is that standards are set at levels or in ways which are too rigid, and do not reflect the fact that systems and societies change, and expectations and pressures change along with them. Standards therefore must be flexible enough to move with the times. On the other hand, standards must not become so flexible that they provide insufficient protection to systems when pressures become acute.

Questions on how to define these standards and at what levels to set them therefore involve tricky policy and practical implications. We might decide that prison crowding should be measured and upheld against *ex ante* input-style standards, which set an acceptable level of crowdedness and restrict capacity stress from going beyond that point. Alternatively, we might opt for *ex post* outcome-style standards that base judgements about sufficiency of capacity on how well the system is performing. In the prison system during the last thirty years, we have seen use of both types of standard, one predominantly input-oriented known as Certified Normal Accommodation (CNA), and the other predominantly outcome-oriented known as Operational Capacity (Op Cap). In this chapter we examine both types and how they have performed in protecting against capacity stress.

This standards dilemma develops some central themes from the previous chapter. In particular, NPM has tended to emphasize a shift from input-oriented to output- and outcome-oriented standards. Looking at the relationship between CNA and Op Cap, we see some strong signs of this kind of shift. However, as I will discuss, the relationship between the two standards seems more complicated than one of simple transition from one to the other. We must see the two standards as having evolved independently *and* in relationship to each other. It is in this relationship that we find a complex standards ecosystem that relies on a kind of control through counterbalance between the two. This concept of 'control through counterbalance' incorporates some important dynamics that feed into sustaining chronic capacity stress (CCS) in the prison system. We focus first on the difference between *ex ante* and *ex post* standards.

4.1 *Ex ante* and *ex post* standards for prison capacity

An integral part of managerialist change has been a shift from input-oriented to output- or outcome-oriented legitimacy.[1] By input-oriented legitimacy, we mean that rules or principles which define standards in public services are framed in terms of *ex ante* requirements for acceptable or necessary levels of capacity. In terms of prison capacity, an input standard might for example stipulate that every prisoner should have a single cell or living accommodation above a certain minimum size. Outcome-oriented legitimacy, on the other hand, means that standards are based in inherently *ex post* judgement about how the system has performed. For example, if prisoners can be shown to be satisfied with their living accommodation, then actual input specifications may be seen as a secondary or subordinate concern.

There are strengths and weaknesses to both approaches. Input standards tend to provide structural integrity in that the system is protected by *ex ante* capacity limits beyond which it cannot be allowed to stretch. They may be formalized in some way, in legislation or legal provision, often in the form of basic rights, or they may just be deeply engrained in culture and operations of a system. Input standards have to be sufficiently strong to endure and be upheld to some meaningful extent. In the Victorian era, for example, the decision to build prisons with single cells was deemed part of the punishment and reform process, providing opportunity for solitary reflection by prisoners and a degree of lonely punishment. In this sense, it was a guiding principle around which capacity was allocated (McConville, 1995).

Implicit in any discussion about input standards for prison capacity is a set of assumptions about what it is the system is expected to do and what level of capacity is required to enable this. The problem here is that there is no easy algorithm which says that *X* amount of capacity translates into *Y* level of performance. Neither is there any easy algorithm which says that a certain of level of capacity is necessary or sufficient for the system to begin to address more ambitious goals or objectives. Setting input standards for capacity, i.e. prescribing minimum levels of space, human resources, or facilities for each prisoner, will not necessarily guarantee, for example, that prisons become more rehabilitative. There may be conventional (and indeed, plausible) wisdom that the more the system is put under strain, the less it can do for prisoners. For many, however, it does not necessarily follow that getting rid of crowding will automatically lead to more effective prisons. The danger is that rigid input standards may end up sustaining situations of inefficient surplus and redundancy.

As the previous chapter has discussed, the expansion in the performance regime in the prison system since the early 1990s has relied also on output and outcome targets. An important characteristic of such standards is the extent to which they are flexible and leave room for squeezing capacity already in the system. Outcome standards can also incorporate considerable ethical or normative significance, and be regarded by professionals as important 'moral limiters'. They may also provide strong basis for legitimacy to show that the system is operating successfully. Target discourse, as we have seen, is a constituent part of this. Yet, by their nature, these standards tend to leave room for interpretation, distortion, political manipulation, and 'dark arts' in the process of rationalizing whatever levels of capacity can be tolerated as long as the system can be shown to work in one way or another.

Looking at targets for crowding levels in the prison system since 1994, we see how input and output aspects intertwine in quite complex ways. As Table 4.1 shows, targets have been couched as a percentage of prisoners sharing a cell designed for fewer prisoners. At the heart of this is an input-oriented standard that stipulates *ex ante* how many prisoners

Table 4.1 Formal targets for crowding in annual reports of the Prison Service and NOMS

Year	Actual target as written in the annual report	Outturn
1994	Average number of prisoners held three to a cell in accommodation intended for one, to be fewer than in 1993–94, subject to ensuring no prisoner is held in police cells unless absolutely unavoidable.	
1995 1996 1997	To ensure that no prisoners are held three to a cell designed for one.	
1998	Percentage of the prison population above the uncrowded capacity of the estate is no more than 12%.	10.0
1999 2000 2001 2002 2003 2004	Prisoners held two to a cell designed for one, expressed as a percentage of the average prison population, does not exceed 18%.	18.9 17.2 17.0 20.4 21.7 21.7
2005 2006 2007	Percentage of the prison population held in accommodation units intended for fewer prisoners did not exceed 24% of the average population.	23.7 24.1 24.6
2008 2009 2010	Prisoners held in accommodation units intended for fewer prisoners does not exceed 26% of the average population.	25.0 24.0 23.8
2011	Percentage of prisoners held in overcrowded accommodation across the prison system.	23.9

Source: Prison Service and NOMS annual reports 1994 to 2011. Figures for 2011 are not specific targets but are performance outcomes.

each cell in the estate should rightfully hold. The target itself, however, is an outcome standard, in that say, for example, 24 per cent of prisoners are in cells designed for less. Also, targets have tended to 'evolve' over time as outcomes exceed target levels. Furthermore, although crowding targets have been part of the formal performance-management regime, they have not usually been part of the formal assessment process for governors.

It is apparent therefore that this standards regime combines different types of standards simultaneously. Different actors may also relate differently to these standards, and this would seem to underline the need to look at the problem in a more holistic way. Standards will provide structural integrity in the system but will also adapt and evolve with governance arrangements and pressures on the system. To characterize this as a straightforward shift from one type of standard to another may be empirically observable in part, but it also oversimplifies complex and inherently dynamic relationships between the two. Let us first examine in more detail the two standards used in the prison system – Certified Normal Accommodation (CNA) and Operational Capacity (Op Cap).

4.2 Two capacity standards

In recent decades, two standards have defined and shaped capacity in the prison system – Certified Normal Accommodation (CNA) and Operational Capacity (Op Cap). Both have become part of the lexicon of prison policy and management, the former an input-oriented standard and the latter more outcome-oriented linked to operational performance of the prison.[2]

(i) Certified Normal Accommodation (CNA)

> It's a contradiction in terms. It's normal. It's a misnomer. Certified *normal*. It would be normal if we didn't have to overcrowd, but we always have to overcrowd. It's sort of legally dishonest. We trot it out. And we don't think about it. (Interviewee's emphasis in italics)

The term Certified Normal Accommodation (or 'CNA') is a modern articulation of a much older practice of certifying prison accommodation to ensure that it meets basic standards.[3] This practice has been in existence since around the late 1830s, a period that marked the beginning of attempts by government to standardize and centralize what had previously been a highly decentralized prison system. The 1839 Prison Act created legislative basis for the development of the 'separate system' of prisoner confinement, the principle being that prisoners should be held in single-cell accommodation as a means of punishment and encouraging reflection and reform. As part of this provision, legislation stipulated that no cell should be used for such purpose 'which was not certified to be of such a size, and ventilated, warmed, and fitted up in such a manner as might be required by a due regard to health [...]' (Ruggles-Brise, 1921, p. 64).

The struggle to impose greater uniformity on the physical environment of prisons continued throughout the 1840s and 1850s, and with the building of Pentonville prison in 1842, a blueprint for the single-cell 'separate system' was established (Fox, 1936, p. 64). The local and regional gaol system tended to resist standardization from the centre (Ruggles-Brise, 1921, p. 66), however, gradually more formalized Prison Rules began to emerge which set out basic input-oriented standards for prison cellular accommodation. The 1865 Prison Act pushed this along considerably, requiring all cells to be 'certified by an Inspector of Prisons that they satisfied all the requirements of the [Prison] Rules' (Ruggles-Brise, 1921, p. 68). Yet, there remained difficulties for central government in actually being able to enforce these Rules with any great consistency (Hobhouse and Brockway, 1922, p. 55).

The creation of Prisons Commission in 1877 helped to alleviate these implementation difficulties, as central government through the Home Secretary assumed control and administrative power over local prisons. Cell certification continued to be emphasized as an important part of the Prison Rules. Whereas previously Inspectors had been responsible for certifying cells, the responsibility shifted to the Prison Commission, and subsequently in 1963 at the abolition of the Commission, it transferred into the Home Office where it remained until 2007 (then transferring to the Ministry of Justice). From 1877, therefore, responsibility for evaluating and certifying the conditions of prison accommodation has been situated inside the government department responsible for running prisons.[4]

Although the Prison Rules stipulated that every cell should be certified for 'proper standard of size, construction, heating, lighting ventilation and equipment' (Fox, 1936, p. 64), there was no prescribed specification of what constituted a standard cell. (This was largely due to the diversity of physical accommodation in use.) The 1949 Prison Rules stated that cell certificates should 'specify the maximum number of prisoners to be accommodated at any one time in such a room or ward and the number so specified shall be not be exceeded without the authority of the Commissioners' (SI (Statutory Instrument) 1949, 11.1). The increase in the prison population from 1945 onwards, however, began to place pressure on prison estate, and this fed into a 'loosening' of the doctrines of the separate system and return to the practice of accommodating three prisoners in cells designed for one.[5] The 1949 Prison Rules incorporate this pragmatic flexibility by stating that 'provided that where it is necessary for special reasons the Commissioners may authorize the accommodating of not more than three prisoners in a cell' (SI 1949, 11.2).

Throughout the 1950s and 1960s, this practice of tripling prisoners in single cells became widespread in local prisons (Weiler, 1992; O'Friel, 1994). Prisoners were tripled (and not doubled) in single cells due to the fear that they would engage in homosexual activity, and this cultural fear would last well into the 1960s. Terry Weiler and former Strangeways governor Brendan O'Friel both highlight the commonplace characteristic of tripling of prisoners.[6] As O'Friel (1994) explains, 'the impression given by the reports is that the practice of "tripling up" was not seen as a policy change but as a temporary expedient. As such it was not to be publicized or questioned' (p. 20). Despite this, the prison system continued to certify cells and other units of accommodation in order to specify an 'uncrowded' capacity of the national estate. Indeed, at least since 1949, the Prison Commission and Prison Service have reported annually on 'accommodation available for ordinary prisoners' (SI, 1949) and these data have provided an assessment of uncrowded capacity.

CNA has not changed fundamentally since the early 1980s (PD (Prison Department), 1988; Her Majesty's Prison Service (HMPS), 1992a, 2001). As Table 4.2 sets out, it has been a measure of the 'uncrowded' capacity of a prison, 'the number of prisoners that the establishment will hold without overcrowding' (PD, 1988). It is input-oriented in the sense that it is a measure which has defined the number of prisoners which the prison *should* hold given the physical constraints of the accommodation available. The detail of the definition itself has been strengthened to incorporate more specific technical criteria (such as ISO standards), and it has evolved to incorporate more qualitative language such as a 'good, decent standard of accommodation' as defined by the Prison Service (HMPS, 2001). Governors and area managers are responsible for certifying uncrowded capacity of all cells and other units of accommodation, and the Prison Service has been responsible for monitoring certification and ensuring that it is up-to-date.

The 1952 Prisons Act is commonly cited as the legislative basis for CNA today, stipulating that 'no cell shall be used for the confinement of a prisoner unless it is certified by an inspector that its size, lighting, heating, ventilation, and fittings are adequate for health [...]' (Prisons Act 1952, Section 14). For many interviewed it has been a vital basis for regulating and controlling abuses of the system. One former top official summed this up:

> CNA comes from the Prisons Act in 1952. We were still coming out of the post-war. Presumably CNA was seen as a proper regulatory

Table 4.2 Certified Normal Accommodation and Operational Capacity

	Certified Normal Accommodation (CNA)	**Operational Capacity (Op Cap)**
Definition	Measure of uncrowded capacity in prison. Represents a 'good and decent standard of accommodation'.	Total number of prisoners that a prison can hold without serious risk to good order, security, and proper running of the planned regime.
Type of standard	Input-oriented, but the system has never specified objective input standards (e.g. m^2 per prisoner).	Output and outcome-oriented.
Primary focus of the standard	How many prisoners each individual or unit *should* hold.	How many prisoners the whole prison *can* hold without risk to health, security, or safety.
Threshold between	Uncrowded and crowded.	Acceptably crowded and unacceptably crowded.
Type of judgement involved	Applied to judgements about how many prisoners should live in each cell (lighting, ventilation, heating, equipment, etc.).	Applied more widely to the quality and capacity of infrastructure and facilities available in the whole prison.
Who makes the judgement?	Governors and area managers.	Governors and area managers.
Level of monitoring and enforcement	Department and Prison Service.	Department and Prison Service.
Role in resourcing the prison	No specific role.	Prison is resourced based on the Op Cap.
Legislative basis	The principle of cell certification but no reference to specific CNA.	No specific reference to Op Cap.
Used since	1980 specifically the term 'CNA', but cells have been certified and assigned uncrowded capacity since 1830s.	Early 1990s.

> framework against genuine acts of indecency. At the heart of that is a genuine intent to regulate what could be a completely corrupt environment. If CNA hadn't been invented, then would there be something like it now? Absolutely.

Although the Act provides legal basis for certification, it does not provide specific objective measures with which to quantify certification. As Weiler (1992) puts it, 'there has at no time been any statutory provision prescribing standard or minimum measurements for cells' (p. 31). Indeed, throughout the 1980s, critics have argued persistently for the introduction of objective metric standards, which could be used to evaluate whether prison accommodation was satisfactory and whether it was improving or deteriorating.[7] Intentions over the years have been expressed by politicians to develop codes of minimum standards but these have generally fallen by the wayside (King and McDermott, 1995, p. 11). Since the early 1970s, European Standard Minimum Rules for prisons have specified similar input requirements on space and access to facilities, but politicians and senior officials have paid scant attention to these unenforceable guidelines (King and McDermott, 1989). This has led to scathing commentaries by the EU and other international organizations over the years on physical standards in British prisons (Human Rights Watch, 1992).

Although 'capacity clauses' in legislation have been recommended over the years, they too have never been enacted. The most prominent example came after the 1990 Strangeways riots, as part of the recommendations made by the inquiry into these serious riots by Lord Justice Woolf (Home Office, 1991a). The only recommendation of twelve that was not accepted by the government was to introduce a limit on capacity of prisons at no more than 3 per cent above their CNA.[8] In instances where prisons went above CNA for a specific length of time, ministers would be required to appear in Parliament to provide reasons why, and give assurance as to when these overloaded prisons would be returned to uncrowded levels. Introducing legislative protection for an input measure of this kind was seen widely as a hostage to fortune for the government.

Based on publicly reported CNA data, it is possible to calculate levels of crowding above CNA. For each type of prison, Figures 4.1–4.3 show the number of prisoners held in prisons which are at different levels of crowding or under-population. Bars above the x-axis show the number of prisoners in prisons crowded above CNA, and bars below show the number of prisoners in prisons which have free capacity under CNA.

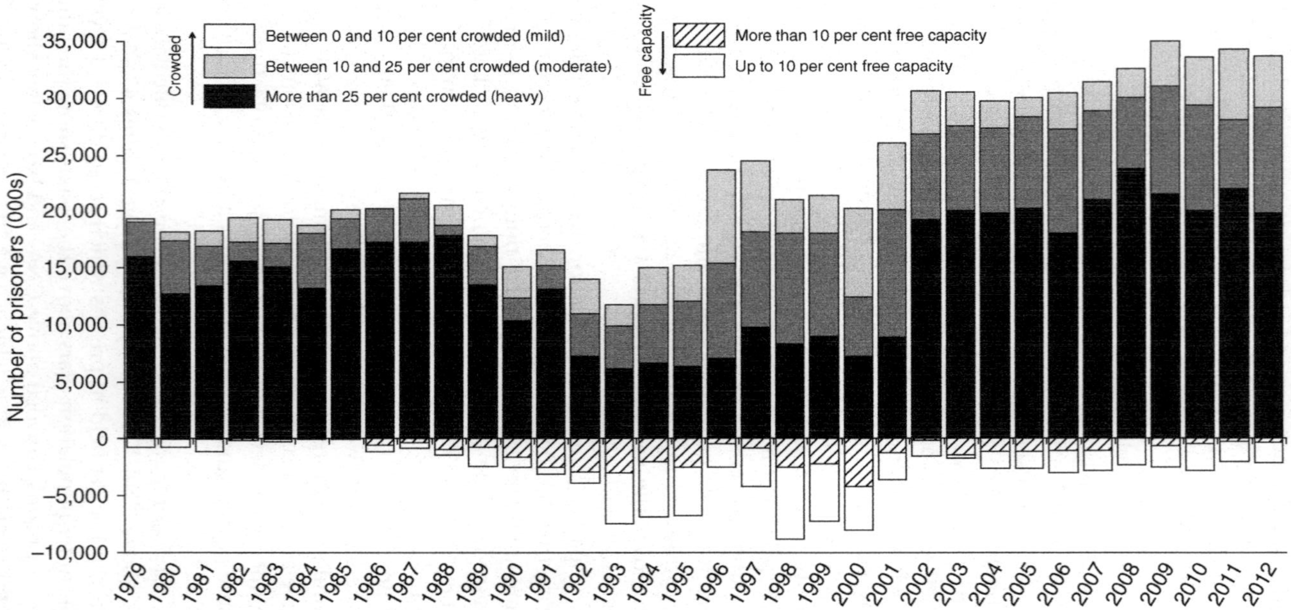

Figure 4.1 Crowding in local prisons and remand centres, measured against CNA

Source: Prison Department and Prison Service annual reports, 1979 to 2004. Ministry of Justice data publications, 2005 to 2012.

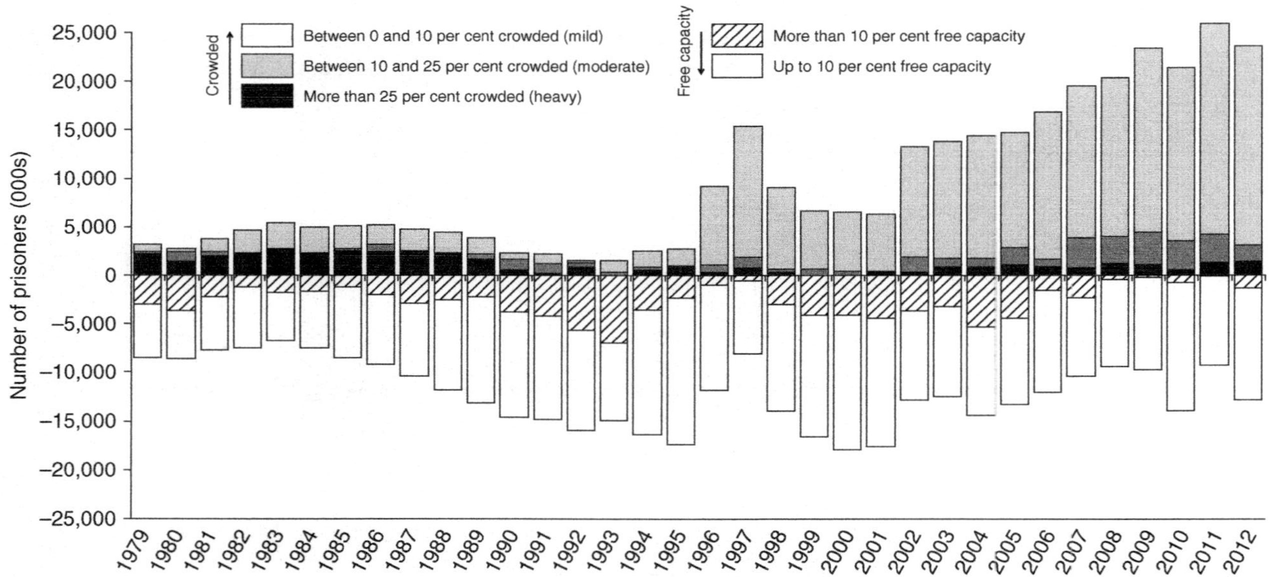

Figure 4.2 Crowding in adult closed training prisons, measured against CNA

Source: Prison Department and Prison Service annual reports, 1979 to 2004. Ministry of Justice data publications, 2005 to 2012.

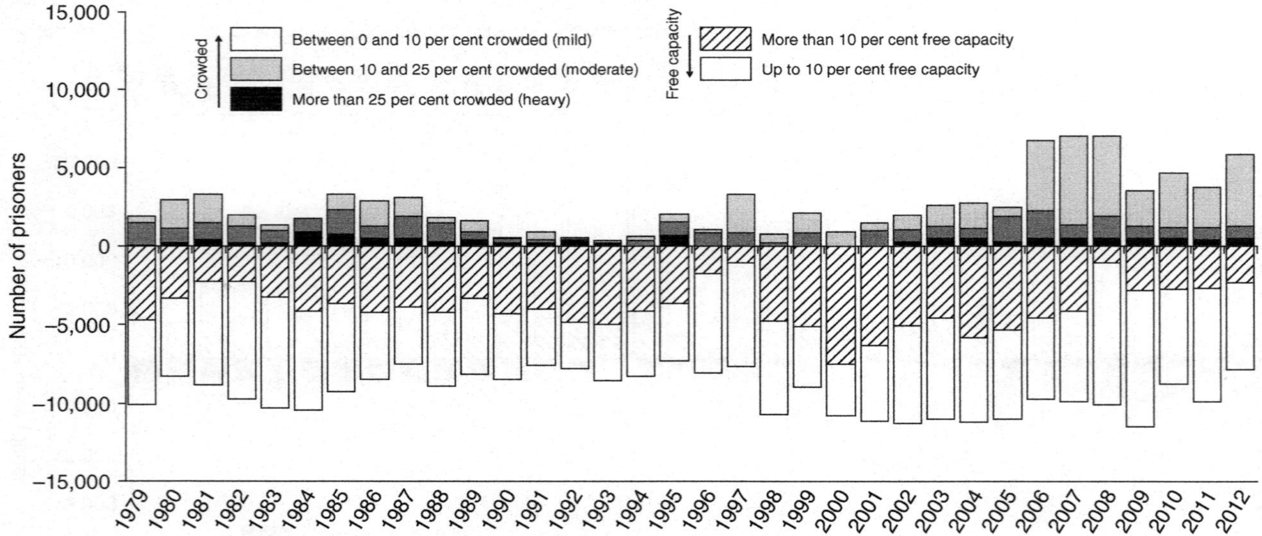

Figure 4.3 Crowding in all other types of prisons, measured against CNA

Source: Prison Department and Prison Service annual reports, 1979 to 2004. Ministry of Justice data publications, 2005 to 2012.

The different bands in each of the bars represent different thresholds of crowding or free capacity in individual prisons. Darker shaded bars congregate around the horizontal axis, and show more intense levels of crowding or free capacity.

Historically, local prisons and remand centres have carried the burden of crowding in the system. Figures 3.5 and 3.10 have already shown how the problem of crowding is still very much in the system in the 2000s, despite the fact that the worst excesses of crowding prisoners three or more to a single cell have all but disappeared. The practice of doubling prisoners in single cells has become commonplace across the local prison estate, and this accounts for a level of crowding in the late 2000s, which looks equivalent, quantitatively if not qualitatively, to crowding levels in the 1980s. Closed training prisons and other types of prisons have by design been protected from crowding, as these establishments have tended to accommodate longer-term prisoners. As the data shows, however, pressure on the system since the beginning of the 2000s has meant that training prisons have started to tip above CNA.

(ii) Operational Capacity (Op Cap)

In the months following the disturbances at Strangeways prison (Manchester) in April 1990, politicians and senior officials began to think more directly about the need for more rigorous standards governing capacity in the prison system. For many years prior, the system had coped with levels of crowding way above CNA and, as many interviewees have acknowledged, the Strangeways riots were a major and very public shock to the system, a turning point in the way the system thought about standards of decency and order. As one former official put it, 'it taught the system a lesson about how far you can push people'. Another reflected:

> [Strangeways] was the major catalyst. The Service was floating around being managed by civil servants without too much of a direct operational focus. The Strangeways riots followed by Bristol and Dartmoor, highlighted the paucity of our response. It exposed the paucity of our regimes in local prisons.

By Spring 1992, the Prison Service had developed a code of standards for all its activities, a large part of which addressed the problems of crowding and the need for some kind of ceiling limit on what local prisons could be expected to take (HMPS, 1992b). As Table 4.3 shows, the actual population of most large locals had been well above CNA for many decades, and CNA had not provided any kind of effective capacity ceiling for the system.

This breach of CNA was entirely normalized. As one former official explained, 'in the 1980s CNA wasn't something that we considered. You just knew that you were in a very overcrowded prison. You didn't see it in the light of being 65 per cent overcrowded, or breaching some guideline or whatever.' This governor described a period of reflection and more intensive thinking about conditions, justice and fairness in the prison, in the period between Strangeways, Woolf, and the publication of the White Paper *Custody, Care and Justice* (Home Office, 1991b). He continues:

> So we became principled in that we said we won't hold more prisoners that than which the cell was designed for. We'll get rid of tripling. And we got rid of that. And it became about certification of single and double cells. That period, 1989 through 1992, was a highly intense period of that.

During this period, the Prison Service introduced Operational Capacity (Op Cap) into its official guidance for governors (HMPS, 1992a). Op Cap was defined as 'the total number of prisoners that an

Table 4.3 Percentage crowding in major urban local prisons, 1979 to 2012[9]

	Average percentage crowding above normal accommodation *(Three-year averages from year listed)*										
	1979	**1982**	**1985**	**1988**	**1991**	**1994**	**1997**	**2000**	**2003**	**2006**	**2010**
Male adult locals											
Durham	42	40	52	51	61	51	36	15	19	59	52
Leeds	86	94	102	86	40	21	26	57	52	39	33
Manchester	60	53	60	8	–6	12	19	24	29	28	25
Liverpool	48	38	46	36	31	15	18	15	18	16	7
Birmingham	77	82	86	74	48	40	45	31	26	29	33
Pentonville	20	38	45	27	9	21	23	28	31	30	32
Wormwood Scrubs	24	19	29	10	32	14	–8	–15	5	7	8
Brixton	48	48	42	45	25	22	11	17	32	31	22
Wandsworth	16	11	20	19	7	4	8	19	30	41	55

Source: My analysis of data from Prison Service and NOMS annual reports. Positive figures denote percentage crowding above CNA and negative figures denote free capacity below CNA.

establishment *can* hold without serious risk to good order, security, and proper running of the planned regime' (HMPS, 2001; my italics). Its introduction was part of a plan to 'set out revised procedures for certification of inmate accommodation' (p. 1), and a measure of 'authorized capacity of the establishment'. It would legitimate an acceptable degree of crowding above CNA. Whereas CNA was a standard that distinguished between states of crowded and uncrowded, Op Cap became the measure that distinguished between 'acceptably' and 'unacceptably' crowded.

Op Cap hinged on a professional judgement, an agreement between the area manager and the governor about where the upper limit should be set based on a range of factors including infrastructure and facilities available, and what the prison could reasonably be expected to hold. In theory, the prison would be resourced to meet Op Cap. This standard therefore turned the input-oriented CNA on its head. Whereas CNA was a measure of what a prison *should* hold, based on an aggregated total of the certified space in each individual cell or unit, Op Cap was an outcome measure based on a judgement about what the prison *could* hold. Rather than starting with individual cells and working up to a capacity total for the whole prison, Op Cap involved a kind of retrospective rationalization of what individual cells could be expected to hold given a judgement about the available capacity in the prison as a whole.

Op Cap could not therefore be separated conceptually from the performance of the prison. The consequence of this is that it leaves large scope for interpretation about what is 'acceptable' performance and what level of capacity is required for that. Whereas CNA specifies this from the start, Op Cap is the capacity standard you get at the end of the process as a by-product of establishing a satisfactory operational equilibrium of the prison. As the next section below discusses, these decisions are subject to a wide range of managerial, political, financial, and cultural pressures. They also leave considerable scope for incremental re-adjustments in capacity – normalization of deviance – the marginal effects of which may be relatively easy to justify and absorb into the existing operations of the prison.

Table 4.4 confirms that Op Cap has stretched independently of CNA by anywhere up to nearly 1,000 places year-on-year since 2004 (the first year for which Op Cap data are publicly available). Most of this stretching has taken place in local prisons in which the pressure to accommodate increased receptions is most directly felt. Closed training prisons have traditionally been protected from population pressures

Table 4.4 Estimated stretch of Op Cap away from CNA, 2004 to 2011

	2004	2005	2006	2007	2008	2009	2010	2011
Total headroom *(prisoner places in 000s)*	3.3	3.2	3.2	2.5	2.5	3.6	4.9	4.2
Total capacity stretch	–90	700	420	360	930	–110	390	540

Note: Total headroom refers to the gap between Op Cap and the prison population. Total capacity stretch refers to the extent to which Op Cap increases independently of CNA in each year.

over the years, and therefore tend to show a closer relationship between CNA and Op Cap. All other prisons, semi-open and open, show a relatively close relationship between CNA and Op Cap, suggesting that population pressures in this part of the estate have never necessitated stretching of Op Cap. An extract from the 2006 Prison Service annual report corroborates the estimates in Table 4.4.

> Operational Capacity increased by 767 places during 2006–2007, partly as a result of 300 new CNA places being provided through newly constructed house blocks [...] but partly too as a result of agreed increases to overcrowding (i.e. increases in Operational Capacity) at specific establishments. (HMPS, 2006, p. 16)

So it is clear from the data that Op Cap can be shown to stretch when under pressure from increments in demand. As relatively small increments every so often, these may be easily rationalized and absorbed. Although Op Cap can be seen as a meaningful upper limit to prison capacity, many interviewees have been sceptical about integrity of the measure. More sceptical senior officials interviewed were inclined to see Op Cap as much a bureaucratic innovation to 'define away' the problem of crowding as a measure to set a limit on what the system could be expected to absorb. As one former senior official put it, 'this is all the product of highly imaginative and creative civil servants who have drafted the way out for ministers on some pretty tricky issues. It is a device.' As another pointed out, 'in the early nineties, with the increase in population, the problem was dealt with by a new term Operational Capacity...which means how many can you squeeze in without breaching health and safety?'

It is difficult to second-guess motives of officials in this respect. This is particularly so as it has not been possible to trace the exact origins of Op Cap during this period,[10] despite extensive interviewing with officials who would have been closely involved during that time. This suggests that the introduction of Op Cap took place relatively inconspicuously, most likely a product of a 'mid-level' managerial decision that did not get onto the radar of senior management and was adopted as a bureaucratic tool for rationalizing a manageable (if not ideal) level of crowding in the system. It is however worth pointing out that the level of crowding during 1992 was almost at its lowest point throughout the whole thirty-year period. Furthermore, the publication of the *Custody, Care and Justice* White Paper in 1991 had captured a sense of optimism in the prison system on the back of the Woolf agenda for change (Home Office, 1991b). These two factors suggest that there would not have been immediate pressure on ministers or senior officials to invent ways of redefining the crowding problem. Indeed, as many interviewees have reflected, crowding was beginning to be seen at that time as part of a bygone era.

By the late 1990s, however, the rapid and largely unpredicted increase in the prison population meant that much of this optimism about the system returning to CNA had dissipated. Senior officials had begun to work on the basis that CNA had become a largely redundant standard, at least for the local prison estate. One former senior prison official confirmed as much:

> At some point during the Labour period and Martin Narey's period, it became accepted that we were no longer going for the uncrowded estate. We accepted that overcrowding was permanent and endemic. I can't spot the point where that happened exactly, and I was very near to it all.

Both CNA and Op Cap continued to be used and reported as official standards of capacity and crowding. The Prison Service, and latterly the National Offender Management Service (NOMS), continued to publish CNA figures for individual prisons on a regular basis. Against this, Op Cap has been used as a pragmatic threshold of acceptable levels of crowding above CNA, an important device for legitimating flexibility in the system particularly during times of population increase. I now examine in more detail the varying perceptions of standards, their strengths and weaknesses.

4.3 Perceptions of how these two standards have performed

CNA has long been, and continues to be, the baseline convention for assessing the extent of crowding. Prison reform charities, press and media, and many officials and professionals working in the system, have long sustained CNA as this standard. Officials interviewed have often seen it as an unambiguous, even 'quasi-scientific' concept, based on a judgement about the number of prisoners a cell is designed to hold given specific technical and environmental guidelines. As one governor of a large local prison put it:

> [CNA] does not feel very ambiguous [...] as a governor. And crowding means the number of prisoners that are required to live in accommodation that is not designed for that number of prisoners. It's pretty simple really.

For many decades, leading campaigning groups such as the Prison Reform Trust (PRT) and the Howard League have used CNA as the sole benchmark for prison crowding, with little or no reference to Op Cap at all. And many governors and officials had sympathy with this approach in principle. As one suggested:

> CNA still needs to be there. That is the true capacity [...] the uncrowded capacity of the jail. Everything above CNA is overcrowded. I would get very anxious if the centre stopped reporting the fact that we are holding two prisoners in a cell designed for one. If the cell is designed for one, it should have one.

The question remains, however, how long a public-policy standard can fail to be adhered to before it is declared obsolete as a meaningful standard. As many senior officials and governors have pointed out, in policy and operational terms, CNA was commonly seen as something which had little or no direct bearing on the day-to-day resourcing and operations of the prison. As one experienced governor put it:

> I don't think there is anyone anywhere who is working on how to end overcrowding. It is not a real policy issue. None of those projections which get published in annual reports say anywhere how CNA is going to meet demand. It is working assumption that is never spoken of.

Rarely did governors not know what their CNA was when asked, but many confessed to having to go and look it up in preparation for our interview. A former senior official in population management explained that he 'never ever referred to CNA' during his time. In interviews with private-sector prison directors, the concept also seemed a distant concern. It was really only the fact that most private-sector directors had come from the public sector that a conversation about something called CNA was possible at all.

We might therefore ask how and why this standard has stood the test of time. If, as the quotations above suggest, civil servants have been so adept at the 'dark arts' of defining away problems, why have they not applied these skills to defining away crowding by formalizing this widely acknowledged view that CNA is an obsolete standard? After all, in most local prisons, the principle of 'doubling up' with a bunk-bed and a screened-off WC has become so commonplace that it would in theory be relatively easy to make a case that the new 'normal' in local prisons involved sharing a bunked cell with another inmate. Despite seeing the logic in this, many interviewees were sceptical that it would ever happen. As one governor put it:

> They dare not change it because of the row. All ministers will be advised that you can't change this without a god-almighty row. With the PRT, Ramsbotham,[11] questions in the Lords and in the House, the Home Secretary or Justice Secretary painted as a monster.

In fact, many interviewees have suggested that maintaining CNA as a measure of crowding allows ministers to point to overload of the prison system and implicate the judiciary in attempts to reduce the level of demand. As one former governor and senior member of the Inspectorate put it:

> Don't you think that that is the game being played? Actually most people want to reduce the number of people in prison. They can't come out and say it, because it looks as though they are treading on court territory. Which they have no right to do, and will be challenged in parliament by the opposition. So all the time, what they are saying is, look at the state of our prisons, we've still got massively more people in our prisons than we ought to have. Look at what the CNA is! That is about as far as people like Jack Straw are prepared to go in saying we have too many people in prison.

Many also agreed with the idea that CNA has in fact provided senior officials, governors, staff, and unions with a device to show how the system has operated successfully and valiantly under a perpetual demand-side pressure. One former Treasury official explained:

> It enables the NGOs to castigate government for not having a proper sentencing policy to keep the population at a sensible level. It enables the government to say 'oh gosh, we are trying to deal with all these prisoners'. It also enables ministers to say 'really, judges, will you please stop sending all these people to prison'. And it enables governors to say 'aren't I doing a tremendous job, packing in all these prisoners'. So that is absolutely true, everybody gains from it. There isn't anybody who would be arguing for getting rid of it, other than a mythical person who would be saying 'let's have a bit of honesty rather than this deception that goes on'.

There may be no less deception wrapped up in Op Cap. Discussions with senior prison officials have emphasized the importance of having sufficient flexibility in the system in order to be able to manage the population. As one former top official pointed out: 'When you are having to manage the whole system, your public-policy imperative is always going to be want to remain flexible. You constantly have to be looking at the options for what part of the system you can flex to be able to respond to new pressures.' One of these options is to be able to flex capacity standards. The invention of Op Cap has undoubtedly given this process of flexing a degree of legitimacy. The process, however, incorporates dynamics of recognizing the value of formal rules, yet also rationalizing increments of change to these rules over time. One former top senior official gave a candid account of this dynamic:

> Once you've made that rule and you know that you are going to break it, the next thing is to try to create that set of external rules, the next layer of the onion. What rule, which isn't quite so hard and fast, would we be able to adhere to? You wrap around these concentric circles of regulation.

Governors and senior officials confirmed that finding ways to stretch Op Cap had been a vital tool for coping throughout periods of population pressure. And as one former Prisons Minister put it: 'We don't work to CNA, we work to Op Cap. We stretch Op Cap. And the definitions change sometimes when you are under real severe pressure.' Senior officials interviewed described the kinds of incremental pressure which they would exert on governors to find extra capacity. This pressure would be channelled through the line management hierarchy of 'area managers'. One former experienced area manager described the incremental tactics:

> Systematically, as we ran that system, we went back to governors and said [...] 20? Is that your best offer? Why isn't it 22? Why isn't it 25? When you are talking about Op Cap, it is almost impossible to draw the line. You can always say, oh couldn't you have one more?

It is interesting, however, that governors expressed strong views about the integrity of Op Cap as a standard. Hardly any governors talked of having to transgress Op Cap, except possibly in cases of very short-term breaches in cases of 'lock-outs' from other prisons and late-night phone requests from area managers asking them to receive prisoners temporarily. Strong professional ethical standards were apparent here, as governors talked about their role in making sure that their prisons were safe and that they did not put their staff under undue pressure. There is much hanging on the ability of governors and their managers to predict a safe level of crowding, and stay on the right side of it. Many pointed out the fallacy in this; for example:

> A safe level of overcrowding? As if there is a safe level of overcrowding. At what level does it become unsafe? Nobody actually knows. We only know that it gets unsafe because something goes wrong. And then we go, oh dear. Didn't do that well, did we? That's where we are in the Service. We've not had disorder on a wide scale for years. So we think that we can edge it forward, keep pushing it up.

Governors were aware of the pressure from above to make capacity available. They were also aware of their responsibility as civil servants to do their best in terms of freeing up capacity during times of population spikes. An agreement between governors and area managers would be reached in the context of the situation, and this would depend to a large extent on the nature of the personalities involved and the urgency of the situation. Nevertheless, many governors have described instances during their careers when population pressures have led them to accept increments in population. As one put it:

> Anything can be justified. The new unit I opened was meant to be 180. And I was told by the area manager, can you find some overcrowding in there? I said no. He said, well let's have a look. And he

> said, well let's double this landing. So we went from 180 to 210. There was no assessment of the risk produced for me as a governor. It was just that we will have 30 extra prisoners in there. The question always comes. Could you find some more overcrowding?

Many governors talked frankly about the potential career-limiting effects of resisting pressures from their area managers. Older and more experienced governors tended to see themselves as more resistant, willing to say no to requests from the centre which they deemed unreasonable. One local prison governor explained the considerations involved in refusing to fill a bus with prisoners on overcrowding drafts: 'I declined to fill the ten. I do that more than my predecessor did. I'm a fairly senior governor. I've been governing jails since the late nineties. I know how to play the game. I've also got no career aspirations.' Often governors talked about putting in requests to decommission accommodation which was dilapidated or considered unusable. They talked of such requests being denied, particularly during times of population pressure, and in certain instances perceived resistance as damaging to their career prospects. As one governor put it:

> I closed a wing at a time of great capacity stress. I said it was unfit for human habitation. And I would not back down from that. There was a huge amount of pressure to say that the facilities, with a bit of extra work, would be habitable [...] I knew that the moment I left the prison, they would nobble a new governor, and it would go back into operation, and surprise, surprise, that is exactly what happened.

Despite this strong command-and-control dynamic, governors also suggested that over the years there have been clear incentives for them to find ways of stretching Op Cap. Receiving more prisoners was cited commonly as a strategy to secure extra financial resources for the prison, which could then be channelled elsewhere to make up shortfalls in the budget or boost provision of programmes and other services. Particularly in local prisons, taking another ten or twenty prisoners meant doubling up ten or twenty single cells, and often the marginal impacts of this kind of increase could be absorbed within the existing regime. Commonly, it would come with new 'per prisoner' payments, which might not necessarily require an increment in staff cover. As one governor said:

> Crowding for us was an advantage. There was a unit in HQ and if you went and said you could provide fifty extra places, they would say

how much money do you want? And with that money you paid for the same staff that you were cutting from the budget.

In the last few years, governors and senior officials suggest that these financial incentives to find extra crowding have not been as readily available, as the centre has become more knowledgeable about real unit costs involved and as financial resources have become more tightly allocated.

We have seen therefore that both CNA and Op Cap have incorporated strengths and weaknesses. Each standard has been originated for specific purposes and they are both quite different in the principles they embody and in the role they play. Independently, however, neither one nor the other can be said to be sufficient to provide structural integrity in the system and at the same time respond to changes in external environment, not least the rising prison population. It is in the relationship between the two standards, a form of control through counterbalance that the basis for structural integrity is found. I now turn to this relationship.

4.4 Control through counterbalance between standards

It is the relationship between CNA and Op Cap which has been the foundation for standards in prison capacity in recent decades. CNA still constitutes a significant moral capacity standard, and according to many it is still a relevant and desirable standard for the long-term planning of the estate. It is still, to use a term which has surfaced frequently in interviews, the 'gold standard', even if most local prisons have not been close to it for the best part of the last fifty years. Op Cap, on the other hand, regulates the elasticity of stretch away from this baseline, and is subject to a mix of different considerations, pragmatic and professional, about whether this stretching is safe or secure. As one former Prisons Minister put it, the relationship between the two 'tells me how much a prison is going to be focused on movement [of prisoners] and security, as opposed to the other functions that it should be discharging'.

Discussions with senior officials have shown how this counterbalance has become strongly conventionalized. For example, one senior NOMS official explained to me during an interview the semantic distinction between the terms 'crowding' and '*over*crowding'. 'There is no *over*-crowding. It is *crowd*ing. We don't have *over*crowding. We have crowding against our measure, which we have developed. It's our measure. It's not an external measure' (my italics to show emphasis of the interviewee). In clarifying this point further, we had the following exchange:

> *NOMS official:* Overcrowding would occur, for example, in an establishment when you had more prisoners than its evaluated Operational Capacity
>
> *Me:* So anything greater than Operational Capacity would imply overcrowding?
>
> *NOMS official:* Yes. But that materially does not happen. Except in exceptional cases where for example the Op Cap may be exceeded on a single night under extreme pressure.

As we have seen, however, Op Cap does and has stretched over the years, a fact which gives the lie to the argument that Op Cap is only very rarely transgressed. This may be the case, but if it can be shown that Op Cap stretches every so often, there is little need for it to be transgressed. This is a process which can appear invisible to the human eye, as any transgression is always assessed against moving thresholds. It is interesting how frequently the decision to stretch Op Cap is reported as having taken place during a previous governor's watch, and in this sense is pressure that governors' inherit rather than actually cause.

It seems therefore that the effectiveness of this counterbalance standard lies in its ability to offer different things to different groups at the same time. CNA has predominantly been a capacity figure for public consumption (indeed, it may be a reflection of the general level of interest of the public in prison conditions that an obsolete standard has sustained so long without challenge). Op Cap, on the other hand, has been a management figure for internal consumption for those responsible for running the system. By maintaining CNA, the moral ethical and principled dimension is retained. By deploying Op Cap, operators are able to maintain both the professional ethical and pragmatic dimension.

Looked at it in the round, the overall effect seems compelling. Indeed, a report by the UK National Audit Office in 2005 on the management of the increase in the prison population reported that 'our analysis of the data since 1993 shows that the increase in the average prison population since 1994 has led to the overall number of people in custody exceeding the certified accommodation available each year, although the estate has kept within its operating capacity' (NAO, 2005, p. 10). Even the NAO, it seems, are willing to accept that the prison system can sustain a state of being overcrowded, yet at the same time manageably uncrowded enough.

As Chapter 8 discusses, contracts with private-sector prison operators have perpetuated this relational standard albeit in a more legally specified manner. Private-sector contracts talk in terms of a contractually specified number of prisoner places to be made available, plus option to crowd in increments usually up to 30 per cent. Typically, these optional increments incur extra payments from government to the contractor. Over the years the public sector has experimented with Service Level Agreements (SLA) between prisons and the commissioning centre, designed to emulate commercial contractual approaches. SLAs, for example, have been used as a result of market testing. This approach gives governors some degree of predictability over a three-year budgetary period about the number of prisoner places that they are obliged to make available. Many argued that in reality these SLAs would be vulnerable to old-fashioned command-and-control requests from the centre however. One senior official explained the brutal facts of the matter:

> Be under no illusion that if I were told to put an extra 50 prisoners into Manchester tomorrow, they'd be going into Manchester tomorrow. No ifs and no buts. Unless you made it a crime. Legally, it's pretty straightforward. Can I do it? Yes. Is it decent? Well, yes. Bit more of a grey concept in the middle. But if I really need to put 50 prisoners in tomorrow, they would be going in tomorrow.

The combination of the demand-led environment of prison and the pragmatic command-and-control cultures that have existed in recent decades tends to work counter to attempts to establish hard-and-fast input standards for prison capacity, or indeed, attempts to emulate more legal-commercial approaches.

4.5 Conclusions

The account of the evolution of CNA and Op Cap in this chapter has shown a much more complex and nuanced picture than just a simple shift *ex ante* to *ex post*, or input-oriented to outcome-oriented modes of standard. We have seen how both standards have emerged in different ways and for different reasons. We have also seen how both standards incorporate weaknesses and strengths, which mean that independently they are inadequate to protect the system entirely from capacity stress. As a means of control through counterbalance, however, both measures have provided an acceptable and workable equilibrium between integrity and flexibility, and one which has something to offer different interests in different ways. This counterbalance seems key to understanding how the whole standards regime has maintained legitimacy and some degree of pragmatic effectiveness.

The counterbalance relationship echoes the discussion in the last chapter about countervailing dynamics of managerialism. Op Cap has emerged as a classic managerialist tool, one that has given licence to ministers, officials, and governors to be able to 'normalize deviance' and justify increments of capacity stress. In this sense, it has been the 'manager's measure', a wholly pragmatic device with which to cope with population pressure, while at the same time squeeze existing capacity in the system. But we have seen how Op Cap has been only half of the standards story. The counterbalance is maintained by another standard, CNA, which seems peculiarly 'pre-managerialist' in nature, i.e. a quasi-moral imperative. CNA has not shown any of the hallmarks of a meaningful standard; it has been cherished yet largely ignored in any actual sense. Yet, these two concepts have become inextricably linked, and have provided a standards ecosystem in which CCS has been able to sustain.

The relationship between Op Cap and CNA has also gone some way in helping to see why it necessary to look at the problem of crowding and capacity stress in a more holistic way. Thinking about the schema in Chapter 2, Op Cap has been the legitimating managerialist tool that has allowed the system to cope with a sudden increase in the prison population. Yet, at the same time it has allowed the system to hold onto the 'ideal world' standard of CNA, which by definition has become an artefact of obsolescence for those running the system. For those inside and outside the system, CNA has also provided a baseline against which the system can be assessed as inherently failing and unable to do much in terms of rehabilitation until the system is brought back to its 'normal' level of accommodation. This in turn feeds into direct and benign resistance on the grounds that the system (or actors within) is being asked to operate way above its normal capacity. The paradox is, of course, that it has been doing so in broadly acceptable ways for many decades.

The holistic approach is also necessary to highlight how different actors have tended to have different orientations towards these different standards, depending on their relationship to or their position in the system overall. Also, we have seen how actors at all levels must rationalize and reconcile internally the implicit tensions between the two. At times we must expect them to deploy these standards instrumentally vis-à-vis other actors for their own interests or protection. It is only by looking at these orientations, choices, and behaviours of actors across the system that we begin to understand the dynamics of how the standards ecosystem has worked over the years.

In the next four chapters, I develop in more detail this actor focus – looking at senior ministers (Chapter 5), top officials (Chapter 6), prison governors and staff (chapter 7), and private-sector prison operators (Chapter 8). There is a change in emphasis from managerialist themes relating to the system as a whole, to specific perspectives of these actors in the system. In order to understand their predicaments and behaviours, we need to see them as operating as part of the whole. The corollary to this is that in order to understand the whole, it is necessary to 'atomize' the parts and understand the system as the dynamic outcome of interactions between these constituent groups. The key theme running through each of these chapters is one of 'constrained autonomy'. On the one hand, actors have autonomy to affect or influence capacity stress from their position in the system. Yet, by dint of their position in the system, they are also constrained in how far they are able to do so.

5
Senior Ministers and the Limits of Their Influence to Resolve the Capacity Problem

> There are deeply entrenched cultural points. If you are going to reform this or any other part of public life, you have to have an absolute driving clarity at the centre of what you are going to do. You need the officials, the professional leaders of the service, the politicians, all involved [...] If there is not the coherence driving it forward, then it is terribly difficult to make the changes you need to make. (Former Labour Home Secretary)

Political science has often tended to explain the outcomes of public-policy systems in terms of the 'high politics' involved. Rikerian notions of political strategy and manipulation, for example, are based on the implicit assumption that the success or failure of policies depend upon the ability of political elites to engineer them from the top down. Governance concepts of 'steering' also imply similar 'dark arts' of design and manipulation. The implication is that it is the politicians who are ultimately responsible for the success and failure of policy systems, and that if we want to understand the causes and dynamics behind CCS, we should look for the answers at the top of the system. Policy success or failure, we are led to believe, is a question of political leadership or lack of it.

Although there may be merit in this perspective, we should also keep in mind that even senior ministers are but part of the system, and are likely constrained by the forces and dynamics that come to bear on them as a result. Let us assume that these ministers have all the political will in the world, and that they may possess dazzling skills of political heresthetics and manipulation. Such attributes, however, may be insufficient to bring about desired change or reform. As we have seen, the high political level is only one level, and policy outcomes must be seen as outcomes of all the levels working as a whole. Rather than seeing the problem as failure of the minister per se, the problem therefore may be more the failure of the minister in the context of the system in which she must operate.

Our holistic view so far reminds us that it is likely to be too simplistic to view the problem of chronic capacity stress (CCS) as simply the failure of political will on the part of ministers. Of course, in some cases, it may be exactly this problem that stops change from happening. But it will not always be the case. Even ministers must contend with the constraints of the system, and despite their best efforts and the nature of events, these constraints may contribute to limiting the extent to which change is possible. Ministers, like all other actors in the system, may therefore experience partial success and partial failure in their attempts to influence CCS. They must also find ways of managing their own position vis-à-vis other actors and pressures, and in doing so maintain some degree of manageable and acceptable equilibrium. This is the first of four chapters that narrow down the perspective to look at how constrained autonomy of actors plays out in different ways at all levels of the system. We start by looking at the nature of constrained autonomy and equilibrium for senior ministers over the years.

5.1 The view of crowding from the top of the system

Autobiographical accounts of former Home Secretaries betray the personal stresses involved in being the top political official in charge of the prison system. Accounting for a sizeable chunk of the Home Secretary's portfolio, prisons have in many ways been an 'elephant in the room' policy issue, something which can just about be coped with when lying quietly, but something which also has the power to cause huge disruption (and fear of disruption) if it is aggravated. Douglas Hurd (2003) reflects on sleepless nights in the mid-1980s worrying about prison capacity. 'News from prisons still very edgy,' he writes, 'Wandsworth obdurate... Wandsworth suspend industrial action,... but we are not through yet... Prisons filling ominously fast despite my sacrifice of July [extended remission]... Woken by the children at 3am and lie fretting about prison population' (p. 348). Kenneth Baker (1993) describes the uncertain existence of the Home Secretary, 'much more the victim of day-to-day events than any other minister. He is answerable for many decisions, some of them highly controversial, which are actually taken by other people – chief constables, prison governors, probation officers, and the parole board' (p. 425). Most Home Secretaries, Baker points out, 'cross their fingers and hope that things will not go wrong in prisons while they are in office' (p. 454).

Home Secretaries have been well aware of the problem of CCS in prisons, and have acknowledged its debilitating effects. In his memoirs, Willie Whitelaw wrote pessimistically of the late 1970s, 'the conditions quite frankly appalled me, and the extent of the modernization required depressed me deeply' (1989, p. 171). As another Conservative minister put it, 'it's bad in a moral and humane way. But it's also bad from a value for money point of view. It's a waste of money'. On doing things to engage prisoners, another former minister reflected, 'it's very difficult to do much in a prison which is overcrowded. You've got less time for leisure, less time for actual working, and that makes prison life incredibly difficult. It creates huge stress for officers, and prisoners. Prisoners get very bored, angry, fed up, sullen. It doesn't prevent them committing crimes to come back again'.

Ministerial reflections remind us too of the chronicity of certain aspects of the problem. Roy Jenkins wrote of his term in office (1974 to 1976) that

> I overreacted to this ephemeral public (or press) hysteria about escapes, and tilted the emphasis of prison regimes too much towards security and away from training and work. I ought to have been steadier under fire, but it is easier to say this in retrospect than it was to sustain it during the barrage of daily bombardment. (1991, p. 205)

Willie Whitelaw wrote in 1989 'if we persist sending to prison large numbers of petty offenders, and indeed of non-violent offenders, we risk using our prisons for the wrong purpose' (1989, p. 234). Both statements, it seems, ring just as true when read in the context of the situation at the end of the 2000s. As one former Home Secretary put it during an interview, 'the slightly depressing thing is that the sort of things that were being said, thought, felt, and done when I was Home Secretary are not very different from what is being said and done now. Except that the numbers are much greater.' Table 5.1 gives a broad overview across the last three decades.

At the heart of the predicament for ministers over the years has been keeping the prison system in some kind of acceptable capacity equilibrium. For the Home Secretary in particular, the predicament can be scoped more widely in the sense that they are responsible for the policies of the criminal justice system and, in coordination with the judiciary,

Table 5.1 Overview of thirty years of Secretaries of State and prison capacity

	Brief summary of policy and political focus on prison capacity during term of office	**Key events, landmarks, and crises**
May 1979 **Willie Whitelaw**	Government responds to severe criticisms of the prison system by the May Inquiry, i.e. crowding, under-investment, and failing industrial relations. New prison-building programme and attempts to reform parole follow. Also pragmatic measures to reduce stress, e.g. 1980 Act enables use of police and court cells.	May Committee inquiry Sept. 79 Prisons Inspectorate est. 1981. Early 1980s – industrial relations unrest and 'lockouts'.
June 1983 **Leon Brittan**	Continuation of prison-building programme and focus on taking forward recommendations from the May Inquiry, and early managerialist reform. Further reduction in minimum qualifying period for parole.	
Sept. 1985 **Douglas Hurd**	Crisis management of prisoner and industrial relations unrest. Reforms to remission period for good conduct in 1986. Criminal Justice Acts (CJAs) 1987 and 1988 increase remission of sentences for good behaviour. From 1987, more intensive focus on policies to reduce the size of the prison population. Supported by continued prison building. Managerialist reforms also gain momentum. Early plans to introduce private sector to curtail power of the POA.	1986 National strike action by prison officers and prisoner riots. May 1987 'Fresh Start' agreements abolished staff overtime. 1989 Further serious rioting and local industrial disputes.
Oct. 1989 **David Waddington**	Period of industrial relations disputes and series of major riots leading up to Strangeways – massive shock to the prison system and catalyst for change. Inquiry into these riots commissioned from Lord Chief Justice Woolf.	Widespread local POA disputes and prison unrest.

Continued

Table 5.1 Continued

	Brief summary of policy and political focus on prison capacity during term of office	Key events, landmarks, and crises
Nov. 1990 **Kenneth Baker**	Government responds to the expansive recommendations from Woolf. Capital investment to abolish practices of 'tripling' of prisoners in single cells, and 'slopping out'. Government policy sets out a new agenda for prisons, focusing on standards and conditions, expansion of the private sector, and non-custodial alternatives to reduce the size of the prison population. This is formalized in the CJA 1991. Further managerialist change 'post Lygo'.	April 1990 Major rioting at Strangeways prison, Manchester. April 1991 Woolf Inquiry published 'Custody, Care and Justice' White Paper published Sept. 1991. Brixton prison escapes July 1991. Dec. 1991 Lygo report on management in the prison system.
April 1992 **Kenneth Clarke**	CJA 1991 Act seen as too liberal and encroaching on judicial independence. Reversal of some of its more 'liberal' policies. CJA 1993 formalized this reversal. Prison Security Act 1992 intensifies efforts to reduce prison escapes. Managerialist reforms culminate in creation of the Prison Service agency April 1993. First chief executive, Derek Lewis, appointed from the private sector. More punitive discourse on crime in parliament.	First prison contracted to private sector (The Wolds) May 1991. Blair becomes Shadow Home Secretary July 1992. James Bulger murder Feb. 1993.
May 1993 **Michael Howard**	Continuation of punitive rhetoric, and shift of policy focus towards austerity of prison regimes and deterrence. Short-sentence prison population rises dramatically from 1993. Free capacity from the prison-building programme is filled up. Two high- security prison escapes from Whitemoor and Parkhurst dominate the middle of his term, and contribute to the controversial sacking of Derek Lewis. Increase the policy focus on reducing prison escapes. CJ and Public Order Act 1994 confirms that POA industrial action unlawful. Crime (Sentences) Act 1996 introduces mandatory sentences.	Howard states that 'prison works' in his 1993 conference speech. Sept 1994 – 6 IRA prisoners escape from Whitemoor prison. Jan 1995 – 3 prisoners escape from Parkhurst. Oct. 1995 Derek Lewis sacked as CEO of the Prison Service.
May 1997 **Jack Straw**	New Labour government emphasizes need for more joined-up criminal justice system, set out in the Crime and Disorder Act 1998. Continuation of Labour 'tough on crime' stance. Focus on zero high-security escapes, but also new spending on prison regimes and new prison capacity in the private sector. Pragmatic approach to reducing pressure on prisons through use of early release schemes. Renewed focus on performance management.	Oct. 1997 Prison Service Review strengthens ministerial oversight. Home Detention Curfew (HDC) introduced Jan. 1999. June 2000 'Laming' report on performance management.

June 2001 **David Blunkett**	First year of term marked by sudden rise in the prison population, and crisis-management response. Bouts of isolated but serious rioting. Early attempts by Blunkett to broker agreement with senior judiciary on sentencing changes to reduce pressure on the prison system. CJA 2003 creates the National Offender Management Service (NOMS), launched Feb. 2004. Also set up a Sentencing Guidelines Council to coordinate sentencing reform.	April 2002 Lincoln prison riot. First 'Carter' report on the penal system Dec. 2003. Nov. 2004 JIRPA agreement between POA and Prison Service on 'no strike action'.
Dec. 2004 **Charles Clarke**	Clarke gives a speech to the Prison Reform Trust in Sept. 2005 setting out long-term rehabilitative vision for change. Pressure on available prison capacity rises throughout his term. Scandal of unauthorized release of foreign national prisoners leads to Clarke's sacking.	April 2006 Foreign national prisoner release scandal.
May 2006 **John Reid**	Prison capacity stress and Reid secures funding from Treasury for an additional 8000 prison places. Emergency measures are also introduced in Oct. 2006 to get the prison system through a period of acute capacity shortage.	Emergency measures announced Oct. 2006.
June 2007 **Jack Straw** ***Minister for Justice***	Straw introduces End of Custody Licence (ECL) in order to deal with acute capacity pressure. National strike action in Aug. 2007 breaks the no-strike agreement. Straw commissions a second Carter report on prison system and NOMS reform, formalized in the Offender Management Act 2007. This envisages expansive of prison capacity to 96,000. Plus other measures to reduce prison population.	Acute prison-capacity crisis June 2007 – introduced June 2007. Aug. 2007 National POA strike. Second 'Carter' report Dec. 2007.
May 2010 **Kenneth Clarke** ***Minister for Justice*** *(replaced Sept. 2012 by Chris Grayling)*	New Conservative–Liberal Democrat coalition government from May 2010 announces 'rehabilitation revolution'. Clarke leads a range of reforms seeking to transform the rehabilitative effectiveness of prisons. These include introduction of rehabilitation performance standards, pilot schemes for 'payment by results' for rehabilitative outcomes, innovations for delivering rehabilitative services through 'social impact bonds, and further expansion of privately managed prisons. Continued pressure to run the system at close to 100% capacity.	Coalition White Paper sets out the path to 'rehabilitation revolution'. Pilots for 'payment by results' introduced in Peterborough and Doncaster prisons. Flash disturbances across UK cities in Aug. 2011 contribute to an increase in the prison population to 87,000.

for shaping the level of demand for prison. By introducing new laws on crime which incorporate provision for custody, or by revising existing laws to increase the scope for custody, ministers are by definition making decisions which impact on the level of demand for prison. Also, in shaping government-policy responses to major societal events such as rioting or high-profile cases of murder, ministerial decisions impact on the level of demand. The other side of the Home Secretary's responsibility has therefore been to make sure that the system is set up to deal with the demands made of it.

Table 5.2 gives an overview of ten groups of measures which ministers may employ in order to sustain some kind of acceptable alignment. These distinguish between 'wider legislative, judicial and sentencing' factors (on the left), and 'direct executive measures' (on the right). Each group of measures has associated trade-offs in terms of costs and benefits for ministers. Revising legislation to reduce the level of demand for prison may offer a long-term solution, but such strategies are likely to be costly politically in the context of a government, and indeed a society, which favours tough and more punitive approaches on crime. Similarly, attempting to influence the sentencing behaviour of the judiciary is likely to be less costly for ministers in terms of having to finance additional prison capacity, but they are also likely to be politically expensive in terms of being seen to encroach on judicial independence and being seen to be excessively soft on crime and punishment.

On the right-hand side of Table 5.2, there are other things that ministers can do to relieve capacity stress which, broadly speaking, bypass the need for judicial agreement. Building new capacity, for example, may be financially costly and require ministers to reduce investment in other potentially more beneficial areas of spending. Similarly, pushing the system to stretch and absorb higher demand through cost-efficiencies or acceptable quality shading may bring benefits, but the risk here is that it is impossible to know at what point the system will break. Also, the benefits of executive release may be quick and relatively low cost, but again they run the risk of aggravating the judiciary and providing political opponents with ammunition for attack.

The predicament for ministers is therefore one of combining these various options in order to manage potential imbalance and keep the system in some form of stable equilibrium. Ministers, as the top political officials in the system, have considerable scope and autonomy to shape the system over which they preside. It is clear that the top ministers have in one way or another been able to stamp their priorities and beliefs on the system, and certainly in many of the conversations I have had with them, they have been clear about what it was they were able to change

Table 5.2 The range of options available to ministers for balancing demand and supply in the prison system

	Wider legislative, judicial, or sentencing measures	**Executive measures available to actors in the prison system***
Front end *(i.e. what goes into the system)*	**Pass legislation which reduces the use of prison** – long-term cost-efficient, but does not provide immediate relief and may be interpreted as too liberal. **Influence the judiciary to send fewer people to prison** – low-cost measure with quick results, but very difficult to get judiciary agreement.	**Build new capacity into the system** – takes the pressure off, but need Treasury agreement and other causes lose out. **Squeeze existing capacity in the system** – avoid costs of new capacity and increase cost-efficiency, but at some point the system will break or become more disruptive.
Back end *(i.e. what comes out of the system)*	**Introduce suspended sentences or viable non-custodial alternatives** – maintain judicial independence, but these schemes may be ineffective and not provide quick solutions. **Bringing forward eligibility for parole or automatic remission** – low-cost measure which maintains judicial independence, but may be unpopular with judiciary, political party, and the public. **Introduce sentences with specific conditions for release** (e.g. indeterminate or IPP) – maintain judicial independence, but can be unpredictable in terms of how they work in reality.	**Introduce early release schemes or remission for good behaviour** (e.g. 'tagging' such as Home Detention Curfew HDC) – reduces pressure on the system, but higher costs of running schemes and political risk of failure. **Other executive release schemes without monitoring** (e.g. End of Custody Licence ECL) – quick mechanisms to release pressure quickly, but highly unpopular with judiciary and political parties. **Improve rehabilitative outcomes of prison in order to reduce demand** – desirable in the long term, but difficult to do and does not produce short-term fixes.

* Clearly, many of these executive measures require legislative approval.

by design. But at the same time, if we go too far in this direction, we risk underestimating the power of the constraints on ministers. In the next section I examine in more detail the extent to which senior ministers over the years have been able to shape the system and do things to reduce capacity stress.

5.2 Autonomy of ministers to shape and impact CCS

As a way of gauging the extent to which Home Secretaries and Ministers of Justice have prioritized the issue of prison crowding, I have compiled a picture of its salience in both British parliamentary chambers over thirty years.[1] Figure 5.1 shows the number of times ministers (and all parliamentary members) have mentioned the term 'crowding' or variations of it in relation to prisons. Four lines show the frequency with which members with different levels of responsibility for prisons have mentioned the term. Line 1 shows salience for the most senior politicians (Prime Ministers, Chancellors, and Home Secretaries/Minister for Justice). This may be a fairly crude proxy measure of issue salience, but I would argue it is one that provides a reasonably good indication of the extent to which the issue has been prioritized at the highest political level.

Amongst parliamentarians of all parties, there has been continual yet fluctuating 'white noise' mentions of crowding over three decades (line 4), and this is echoed by Prisons Ministers (Line 2) and their 'shadow' counterparts (Line 3). Focusing on Line 1 (solid bold), however, gives us an indication over time of how the issue has played at the very top of government. Clearly, the amplifications here are much smaller. Even small amplifications, however, can tell us something about the extent to which crowding has been prioritized. Between 1987 and 1991, mentions averaged consistently more than ten per year, reflecting a period of concerted political effort by Home Secretaries to eradicate prison crowding. The data suggests that this began under Hurd, and spanned the terms of Waddington and Baker. Indeed, throughout the 1980s, 'eliminating overcrowding by the end of the decade' was a specific policy objective for the Conservative government and a phrase much used by Conservative Home Secretaries (NAO, 1985, p. 6). As one former top official told me:

> Everyone knows about overcrowding. No one thinks very much about it. No Home Secretary comes in and gets fretful about it. I only worked for one Home Secretary who was brave enough to do something about it, which was Douglas Hurd.

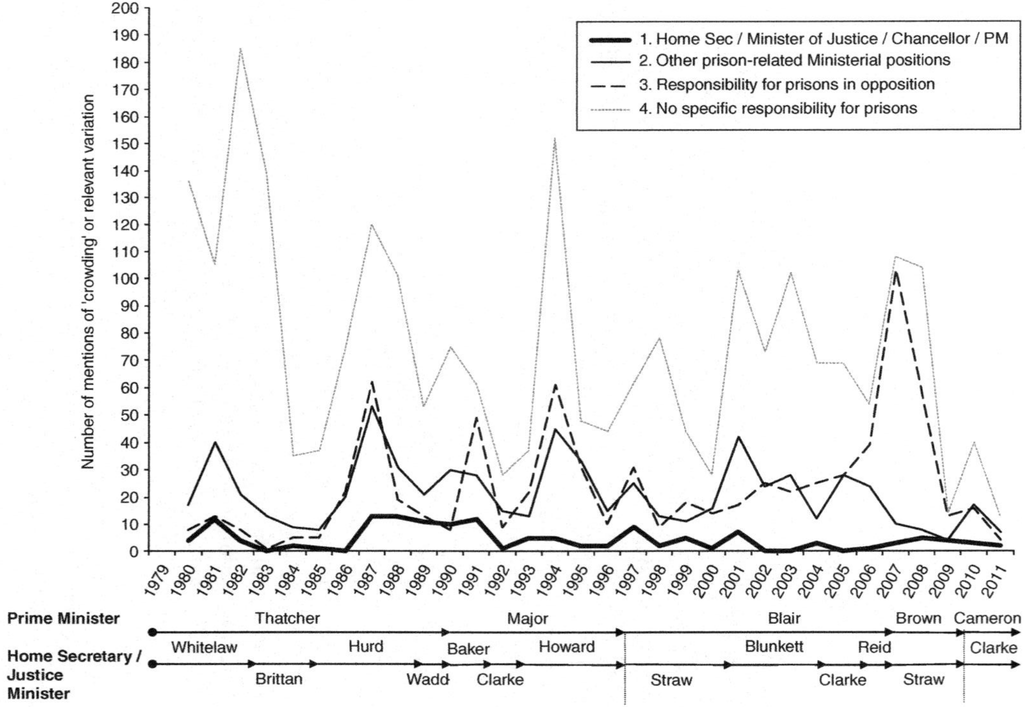

Figure 5.1 Number of spoken mentions of 'crowding' in parliament, by role of the person speaking

Source: Hansard and Millbank electronic search databases

In Chapter 3 we discussed what looks like a process of normalization of crowding during the 2000s. Indeed, the trend line from the mid-1990s onwards appears to support this idea. Despite the fact that crowding returns, salience of the issue never reaches these consistent heights again, apart from a short burst in 1997 with the change of government and 'new horizon' declarations by the new Labour Home Secretary Jack Straw. Even throughout 2010 and 2011, years in which the new Conservative–Liberal government was developing the early stages of its 'rehabilitation revolution' in the criminal justice system under Minister of Justice Kenneth Clarke, explicit references to crowding in Parliament remained conspicuously low.

Clearly, ministers have an important role in shaping policy agendas and priorities, in terms of what they say in public and in private about prisons. As one former Prisons Minister put it, 'politicians can come along and alter things immediately just by taking a different tone'. One way of profiling these variations is to look at what ministers have said about prisons in their annual platform speeches to party conference.[2] Coding these annual speeches allows us to look at the substantive balance in what ministers have said on prisons and sentencing over the years. Table 5.3 summarizes the findings of this extensive coding exercise. I coded all relevant prison and sentencing-related extracts from these speeches into six categories:

1. *custodial imperative and deterrent*: references associated with pushing the punitive and deterrent role of prison;
2. *reducing population pressure on the system*: references associated with encouraging non-custodial alternatives to prison and measures to reduce the size of the prison population;
3. *adding capacity to the prison system*: references associated with building new prisons, adding new resources, or extra capacity;
4. *rehabilitative goals and reducing reoffending*: references advocating measures to boost either of these two outcomes;
5. *increasing the powers of the judiciary*: references which advocate expansion or protection of the judicial powers;
6. *crowding, conditions, and coping in prisons*: references associated with the state or experiential environment of prisons.

Looking along the rows in Table 5.3, there are important variations in emphasis. Practically all ministers have emphasized the custodial imperative, i.e. the need to lock up certain offenders for certain types of crime. The relative variation in other factors, however, is interesting. The first four Conservative Home Secretaries (Whitelaw to Hurd) show

Table 5.3 How different ministers have emphasized different options for dealing with capacity stress, 1979 to 2012

	[1]	[2]	[3]	[4]	[5]	[6]
Average number of words across all years in office	**Custodial imperative and deterrent**	**Reducing population pressure on the system**	**Adding capacity to the prison system**	**Rehabilitative goals, and reducing reoffending**	**Given the judiciary more options for sentencing**	**Crowding, conditions, coping in prisons**
Conservative						
Willie Whitelaw	210	200	110	25	90	85
Leon Brittan	330	150	110	0	15	95
Douglas Hurd	205	240	125	15	65	120
David Waddington	215	145	135	0	70	40
Kenneth Baker	200	0	90	70	0	10
Kenneth Clarke	475	125	100	10	150	0
Michael Howard	485	50	25	0	70	5
Labour						
Jack Straw	65	50	25	0	20	0
David Blunkett	55	70	20	10	0	0
Charles Clarke	60	0	0	380	0	0
John Reid	60	30	0	0	0	0
Jack Straw	0	25	25	20	0	0
Conservative–Liberal						
Kenneth Clarke	160	220	0	720	50	0
Chris Grayling	250	210	0	920	0	0

Source: Conservative Party archives, Bodleian Library, Oxford. Labour Party speeches available online.

quite similar patterns. Each talks about the custodial imperative of prison (column 1), yet they also reference efforts to reduce the prison population in size (column 2) and add new capacity to the (column 3). These four ministers also reference 'crowding, conditions, and coping' in the prison system more than any other ministers subsequently (column 6), a reflection throughout the 1980s of the ministerial focus on eradicating crowding. Within this group of four, however, there are variations in the balance between more punitive emphasis (column 1) and more liberal or 'decarceral' emphasis (column 2). Brittan and Waddington tend more towards the more punitive side, whereas Hurd and possibly Whitelaw too tend towards the decarceral side. Of these four, only Hurd and Whitelaw reference rehabilitative goals of prison (column 4).

The last three Conservative Home Secretaries (Baker, Clarke, and Howard) encompass a transition in the system from 1991 onwards. The 1991 Criminal Justice Act was in many ways the culmination of this sustained emphasis throughout the late 1980s on decarceral policies. A more optimistic climate is reflected in the fact that Baker makes strong reference to rehabilitative goals in his 1991 conference speech. However, in the numbers for Clarke and Howard, we see signs of the strong shift towards a more punitive policies throughout the 1990s.[3] Clarke's speech to conference incorporates a much stronger line on the custodial imperative (column 1), and a commitment to reinstate many of the powers of the judiciary which were perceived to have been lost under the 1991 Act (column 5). Four subsequent years of Howard amplified and consolidated this transition. In his four speeches to conference, he hugely accentuates the custodial imperative, and severely cuts emphasis on decarceral policies (column 2) or adding new capacity to the system (column 3).

The most striking thing about Labour Home Secretary speeches from 1997 is that they mention prisons and sentencing much less than those of their Conservative predecessors. This is partly explained by the fact that their speeches have become shorter and pithier. But it is also explained by the fact that Labour ministers have said much less about prisons and sentencing, and have focused more abstractly on themes of crime and criminal justice. No Labour minister has referenced any themes relating to 'crowding, conditions, or coping' in prisons (column 6), despite the fact that crowding has risen continually since 1997. Despite the wider point that the numbers seem much smaller under Labour, we still, however, see the same kind of balance between custodial imperative and decarceral options. These patterns are not strong, however, and by the time that we reach Reid and Straw in the bottom two rows, these speeches barely contain any substantive references to prisons. The one striking anomaly in this general pattern is the very high emphasis of Charles Clarke on the need for rehabilitative reform.[4]

Since May 2010 and a new Conservative–Liberal coalition government, we have seen a radical shift back towards rehabilitative principles as part of the declaration of a 'rehabilitation revolution' (Conservative Party, 2008; Ministry of Justice, 2010). It is difficult to imagine a more forthright challenge to the idea of a collapse of a rehabilitative ideal at highest political levels, and this is illustrated in the numbers for Clarke and Grayling in Table 5.3. A major emphasis in this ambitious programme of change has been the piloting of 'payment by results' schemes and other mutualized initiatives designed to create direct incentives for actors to focus on rehabilitative outcomes and potentially be rewarded for it (Bolton and Savell, 2010; Nicholson, 2011). And interestingly, for the first time ever, government published statistics on reoffending rates for individual prisons, in an effort to begin to strengthen accountability (albeit indirectly) between individual prisons and their localities. This reflected a renewed commitment to the rehabilitative ideal at the highest levels of government.

Looking also at the data on parliamentary mentions of 'crowding' in greater depth, we can shed further light on these differences between Conservative and Labour ministers' attitudes to capacity stress. For each mention of 'crowding', I recorded whether the speaker was implying that crowding was a supply-side problem (i.e. a problem of not supplying enough capacity), a demand-side problem (i.e. a problem of excessively large prison population), or a combination of both.[5] Tables 5.4 and 5.5 show results for Conservative and Labour governments, distinguishing between members 'With ministerial responsibility', 'With responsibility in opposition', and 'No specific responsibility'. Table 5.4 covers all mentions during Conservative governments from 1979 to 1997. Looking at the top left field in the table, 27 per cent of mentions by Conservative members with ministerial responsibility suggest that crowding should be seen as a supply-side problem, i.e. one of not providing sufficient capacity to deal with demand. This compares with 23 per cent of mentions by Labour members with some kind of responsibility in opposition who implied specifically it was a demand-side problem, i.e. one of an excessively high prison population. For Conservative ministers, therefore, crowding was predominantly talked about in terms of 'under-supply' of capacity in the estate.

Table 5.4 Percentage of references implying supply- or demand-side interpretations of crowding: under Conservative governments, 1979 to 1997

Crowding implies...	**With ministerial responsibility**	**Responsibility in opposition**	**No specific responsibility**
Supply-side problem	27	1	9
Demand-side problem	3	23	11
Both	15	12	10
No specific reference either way	55	64	70
Total per cent	100	100	100
Total number	*509*	*356*	*1481*

Source: Analysis of Hansard and Millbank electronic search database.

Table 5.5 Percentage of references implying supply- or demand-side interpretations of crowding: under Labour governments, 1997 to 2010

Crowding implies...	With ministerial responsibility	Responsibility in opposition	No specific responsibility
Supply-side problem	9	7	6
Demand-side problem	5	19	17
Both	9	9	8
No specific reference either way	77	65	69
Total per cent	100	100	100
Total number	*256*	*379*	*865*

Source: Analysis of Hansard and Millbank electronic search database.

Focusing on the same trends during the Labour governments from 1997 onwards (Table 5.5), we see far greater ambivalence amongst Labour ministers on the root causes of crowding. Here only 5 per cent of mentions by Labour ministers imply that crowding is a demand-side problem (compared with 23 per cent in opposition). It is also interesting that 9 per cent of mentions by Labour ministers imply that crowding is a supply-side problem. This is nowhere near as high as 27 per cent under the Conservatives, but it is also higher than the 1 per cent recorded by Labour during their time in opposition.

All three data items in this section suggest interesting contrasts between Conservative and Labour. First, the issue of crowding appears to have been almost completely normalized by Labour ministers despite the fact that crowding itself has risen once again to aggregate levels almost on a par with the 1980s – even if it is a managerialist form of crowding. Second, the relationship with the judiciary is also marked in contrast. Conservative ministers have tended to view crowding less as a function of over-demand created through sentencing behaviour and more as a function of government's inability (specifically, the previous Labour government's inability!) to provide sufficient capacity. Labour ministers, generally speaking have been more ambivalent in their approach.

We have seen therefore how Home Secretaries over the years have been able to influence the tone and the priorities in terms of what is done to tackle CCS. We have seen continuity over time in some respects, but we have also seen important and nuanced variation in the way in which different individuals and different personalities have committed themselves to the problem. In some respects too, Conservative and Labour Home Secretaries have reflected the general orientations of their parties and the political climate of their time. Yet, at many levels, they have shown many similarities in their approach. One former Conservative minister said as much:

> Labour's instinct will always be to keep the liberal lobby happy, but if you look at what they've actually done, you will see that their record is pretty similar to ours. Expanded the prison programme, get a grip on regimes, issue guidance to courts. They are driven by practicality as were we. They haven't got the spaces.

In the final section of this chapter, I move on to look at some important constraints on ministers' autonomy to reform or impact on CCS, and how these have evolved as governments and ministers have changed.

5.3 Constraints on ministerial autonomy to reform the system

> It has to be forced. There has to be the political will to do it. To take on the civil service and the unions [...] you have got to believe in it. Is that the kind of thing that Ministers of Justice are interested in doing? In my experience, no.

The chapter so far has examined CCS as the outcome of the choices and actions of top ministers. Clearly, ministers do have an important influence, and have shaped the development of the system over the years in what they do and, often more importantly, what they do not do. As Newell (2003) writes, 'politicians could do so much to affect prison population and it is disingenuous to say otherwise' (p. 7). But, as I show in this section, ministers have their autonomy constrained by a range of factors, and hence any putative lack of political will must be seen in the context of these systemic constraints. As the quotation directly above suggests, political will or lack of it must be seen as contingent upon the range of constraints faced and the likelihood in the minds of ministers of being able to overcome them.

In this section, I examine six factors which can be said to have constrained ministers in their efforts over the years to do something about CCS in the prison system. These are relations with: the judiciary; managing the press and media; negotiations with Treasury; the Prime Minister and Number 10; the Prison Officers Association (POA); and their own top prison officials.

(i) Sentencing and relationships with the senior judiciary

Described by a former Conservative Home Secretary as 'extraordinarily tricky', the relationship with senior judiciary over the years has contained a fundamental paradox. In attempting to influence the level of demand for prison, ministers seek to influence sentencing behaviour of judges and magistrates. The more that ministers are seen to influence, however, the more the judiciary are inclined to resist and disengage, thus perpetuating the problem. During times of capacity surplus, ministers may feel only weak compulsion to interfere with sentencing. During times of capacity stress, particularly the acute kind, ministers must find avenues of influence – but without being seen to influence. And as a former Lord Chief Justice explained:

> There is no pressure [on us] from politicians because they get the Lord Chief Justice jumping down their throat if they start telling judges not to send people to prison. They do occasionally. They allow themselves to get pulled out by the Lord Chief Justice, probably privately, who says this is none of your business, don't start telling the judges not to send people to prison for so long simply because you haven't provided the prison spaces.

Traditionally, Conservative ministers have been more inclined to accept the principle of judicial independence in sentencing, and this is indicated by the data in Table 5.3. Ministers have commented on the strict separation between the executive and judiciary throughout the Conservative era, and a clear normative line on the obligations of the executive to provide sufficient places to accommodate demand, whatever that might be. As one Conservative minister put it:

> To try to get the courts to take responsibility for where we have fallen short is quite wrong. That corrupts justice and justice must be independent. It must work without reference, in an ideal world at least, to practicality, and it must never be governed by practicality. In other words, you should never say I would send this man to prison but I can't because there isn't enough space.

Despite this, Conservative (and Labour) ministers have found ways to modify remission and parole, and introduce other measures such as suspended sentences, all with a view to reducing the size of the prison population.

Labour ministers have also taken the view that the executive should not encroach on judicial independence. However, throughout the Labour era we have seen a more pragmatic approach, which implicates the sentencing behaviour of the judiciary as part of the problem, and has sought to reformulate the relationship between ministers and judiciary as one of 'partnership' towards decarceral outcomes. This has interesting countervailing dynamics. On the one hand, Labour rhetoric since the mid-2000s has accentuated partnership approaches with the judiciary (NOMS, 2006; Ministry of Justice, 2007; Jacobson et al., 2008). Yet at the same time, this pragmatic approach has aggravated senior judges and magistrates. The introduction of early release schemes has been an example of this kind of aggravating pragmatism. These schemes have played an important role in allowing the system to run at continually high levels of capacity. They have, however, done little to build trust between the judiciary and Labour ministers.

Ministers reflected on the difficulties of maintaining trust in this relationship, and the tendency for agreements to unravel and momentum to dissipate throughout their time in office. Labour ministers, in particular, described the problems of striking a balance between encouraging the judiciary towards decarceral policies, and the need to impress custodial imperatives on the public. One former Labour minister reflected on what he saw as the 'schizophrenic' nature of the messages coming from ministers and judiciary:

> All the elements of the system pull against you. When you are passing legislation like the Criminal Justice Act, and you get into parliament and you've people pushing one way and speaking the other. That's the battle. There was an effort. There was a coherent penal policy in the making, but not necessarily in the delivery. And it didn't come off.

Over the course of a term in office, ministers describe a process of general unravelling:

> You do begin to lose grip. And it accelerates away from you. If I had my time again, I would make a supreme effort to say to [senior judiciary], because we had split responsibilities, look can't the two of us just sit down? When I got round to doing that with the judiciary, the answer was no. We are prepared to sit down and talk about our pensions. But we won't sit down with you because you will want to interfere with what we are doing. That I might have been able to pull off early in my term, but by the end? No.

The inclination for ministers has been to lay the blame for a rising prison population on the judiciary and sentencing behaviour. The judiciary in response argue that they are merely following the legislative basis and associated guidelines laid down by Parliament and the executive. As one senior political insider put it: 'The judiciary won't take responsibility because they see it as government's role. And the government won't do it because it's perceived as shortening sentences and being weak. It's hopeless. It's actually a basket case.'

For ministers who are in office for relatively short periods of time, there is often insufficient opportunity to build trust and momentum. For those who are in office longer, as these quotes suggest, there is a danger that trust and momentum both dissipate and cannot be re-found. Again, there are frustrating countervailing effects here in that long periods of time are required for trust to build up, but change over long periods of time also increases the potential for other variables to intervene and undermine trust. Since 2007 and the creation of the Ministry of Justice, courts and prisons have been under the same ministerial portfolio, in theory reducing the tension between senior ministers and judiciary on prisons. Even this move however is unlikely to soften the fundamental reluctance of the judiciary to be influenced or seen to be influenced by ministers of any kind.

(ii) Politicians, the tabloids, and public opinion

The quote from Roy Jenkins earlier in the chapter gives a flavour of the anxiety ministers have felt towards the potential for 'hysteria' to break out in the tabloids on some aspect of prisons. Practically all ministers interviewed acknowledged this anxiety, and the distortions and knee-jerk reactions which ensue as a means of controlling the damage and being seen to deal with the crisis. Ministers frequently talked of the inherent unpredictability of the tabloid press, and constant potential to be 'blind-sided' by stories which come from somewhere deep in the prison system and are picked up by the press. As one former minister put it: 'The press really make it. They decide. On suicides, for example, you get it at the right time from the press point of view, and you'd think it was the only suicide for 50 years, and it's all down to the minister.'

It is interesting that ministers are frequently accused of 'meddling' in operational matters, but as ministers often pointed out, it is largely because it is they who ultimately must appear at the despatch box and account for what has happened. As one former Director General reflected, 'these things are, to a large extent, driven by the populist media. Tabloids have a big influence because they will pick up on these big cases. The politicians respond to that, as it is them who have to do something about it at the end.' Politicians reflected on the consequent need to think in terms of how tabloid newspapers would react to policy reforms, and to limit the prospects of tabloid storms. As one minister put it, 'you've got to sell it to the reader of the *Daily Mail*. You've always got that political balance between rehabilitation and protecting the public and punishment. It's a very delicate thing.' Often a media storm can upset the balance for ministers and cause them to renege on agreements already in place. One former Lord Chief Justice reflected on the destabilizing effects:

> It does happen. [Former Home Secretary] had a real go at it. When the tabloids started howling, he was the first to drop it. He would argue that I am wrong on that. But I felt very angry at the time as I had contributed to the judiciary being exposed, and when it went wrong it was explained away as a lack of resources.

Ministers have also reflected on the difficulties of presenting rehabilitative reforms to the media and public, and relatively low political pay-offs involved. As many have pointed out, ministers have rarely lost office (or even lost face) on the back of disappointingly low rehabilitation rates in prisons, or continual breach of CNA. If expectations are low in this respect, then ministers are unlikely to suffer politically from sub-optimal outcomes. Losing prisoners to escape, serious riots, or being seen to make life too comfortable for prisoners, however, has been perceived to have much more costly consequences for ministers. Numerous interviewees, for example, talked about the quid pro quo agreed between Home Secretary Jack Straw and Director General Martin Narey at the start of Labour's first term. Straw would support Narey's plans to push for investment and activity in rehabilitative programmes in prisons in return for Narey making sure that high-security escapes remained at zero level. Indeed, the data in Table 5.2 illustrates an ambivalence at the top of the political system over the years towards rehabilitative outcomes of prison. As one former prison professional put it, 'that sort of serious thinking about how to get the best out of the prison system is only fleetingly considered [...] at best [...] in the media, and in political terms, it plays very little role'.

(iii) Negotiations with the Treasury

Interviews with former Treasury officials have surfaced what we might see as a default sceptical attitude of the Treasury to prisons and funding prison capacity. As one former official put it, 'prison is low down the list. It is a waste of money. They don't make anybody better. They don't cut reoffending rates. They cannot be said to work in any sense, and the cost goes way past the profit from them.' The Treasury has therefore been an important influence on the ability of ministers to manage capacity and the prison population. Indeed, a former Labour prisons minister who subsequently became Chief Secretary to the Treasury, pointed out, only half-ironically, that 'the most influence he had had as prisons minister was when he became Chief Secretary' (to the Treasury).

To depict the Treasury however as a dogmatically stringent actor is too simplistic. As we have seen in Chapter 3, ministers have been able to secure considerable capital funding for prison building throughout the 1980s and early 1990s. Whitelaw writes of his gratitude to Geoffrey Howe, Chancellor of the Exchequer in 1979, for the considerable sums of money agreed for new prison building (Whitelaw, 1989, p. 170). A similar injection of funds came in 1991 on the back of the Woolf inquiry, in 1997 in order to fund rehabilitative programmes, and throughout the late 2000s for 'emergency' prison capacity. Officials also pointed out that by the late 1990s, arguments that you got the best out of public agencies by squeezing them to their absolute limit had come to be seen as 'unsophisticated' in the Treasury, as the approach became more progressively formulated to allow agencies budgetary leeway to 'invest to save'. As one Treasury official described it, 'we end up buying reform [...] using extra capacity to get something in return'. Indeed, officials argued that the Treasury had been keenly interested in the rehabilitative potential of prison during the early 2000s, and had been willing to release new money into the system to target reoffending, but had been disappointed by the lack of results. In more recent years under the Conservative–Liberal coalition, rehabilitation has become a much stronger policy priority, but the Ministry of Justice faces budget cuts of up to 25 per cent in the area of prisons, and therefore transformation must rely on alternative sources of funding such as 'social impact bonds'.

Generally, however, the Treasury have played a role in holding the prison system's 'feet to the fire' over the years. Often ministers would agree with the argument that Treasury follows an approach of constructive under-supply. As one minister explained:

> The Treasury will say, you seem to be coping with finding places for the prisoners we've got now. And we've no reason to believe the numbers will grow significantly. So I'm sorry, you know the situation

> we are in [...] we just can't find the extra funds. In fact, we expect a saving from you again over the next three years.

Ministers described 'heated' exchanges between themselves and Treasury officials over expenditure agreements in the normal spending review rounds, but also for supplementary funds, which become necessary during the spending cycle in order to accommodate increased demand. A former Labour minister reflected:

> The Treasury? Don't even go there. It was like taking teeth out. You'd think you'd got an agreement and then it slipped away when it came to the Spending Review. It would be the last thing on the agenda. You'd get some vague agreed promise that would slip away. Because you were always having to counterweight one thing against another.

The perspective from Treasury officials, however, was that often the requests for capital resources coming from the Home Office seemed excessive and based on insufficient justification. As one Treasury official reflected:

> We got a letter on asylum and prisons asking for a tonne of money. £1.4 billion over three years on the capital side. There was a tonne of resources that seemed to have been plucked out of thin air. And a warning that we would need more in future. That was from the Home Secretary.

Officials also talked about games of brinkmanship between ministers and the Chief Secretary, the outcomes of which would tend to feed into the perpetuation of pushing the system to ever higher levels of capacity, and then crisis response at key junctures. As one former top prison official explained:

> You always play dare, in which the Treasury says to the Home Sec or Justice Sec, it's your job to manage the population, we're not building for you. And it is for the Home Sec to decide whether they believe that, or whether they just hold their nerve and do nothing, until eventually it is going to be a public scandal, at which point money will arrive at very short notice and you will have to spend it quickly.

Treasury officials talked about how Home Secretary John Reid, for example, had approached the Treasury in late 2006 in order to stave off the impending capacity crisis of summer 2007. 'Reid asked for 15,000 new places, we gave him 7,500. It wasn't entirely new money, we just gave the Home Office flexibility to move funds around. If prisons are your priority, we said, then act accordingly.' Departmental officials interviewed suggested that these new places were not considered particularly good value for money, but they had been necessary as part response to the acute shortage. One official reflected on Reid's ability to use impending crisis as a lever for freeing up funds.

> I kind of admired his ingenuity. He had convinced himself that the Home Office was in crisis. Foreign national prisoners were at the top of his agenda. Prisons were connected in his mind with trouble, and he liked the idea of himself being the white knight and riding to the rescue with 8,000 places.

(iv) The Prime Minister and Number 10

As former ministers have pointed out, the Home Office has tended to be a portfolio which defines success in terms of 'lack of failure' rather than anything more positively couched. As one former minister put it, Prime Ministers have 'usually put a safe pair of hands inside the Home Office, and hoped for the best'. Indeed, Prime Ministers have generally taken a back seat on prisons policy, beyond a concern that costs are kept down and that there is sufficient capacity to accommodate demand. Conservative ministers agreed that Conservative Prime Ministers Thatcher and Major left their Home Secretaries to get on with managing the prison system.

On Thatcher's approach, one minister reflected:

> The Home Office generally had very little interference from Margaret Thatcher when she was Prime Minister. Partly because Willie reassured her. And also partly, and I know this to be true, her shrewd political judgement that there were no stars to be obtained on Home Office subjects.

On the cost and stability issue, Thatcher was interested in her Home Secretaries keeping control over the system and not letting situations or pressures get out of hand. This minister continued:

> She was interested in the cost. Therefore to some extent she would have accepted the Treasury attitude. She had a natural Treasury approach to this. But not a strong one. She was pleased, specifically.

> She said this to me. The Home Office is very quiet now. She liked that. She didn't want total eruption.

Under Major, Home Secretaries Clarke and Howard emphasized a more punitive penal rhetoric and policy (Balen, 1994; Crick, 2005), and this, by and large, found continuity under Blair. Blair and Number 10 played a more direct role in driving tough lines on crime and prison, and Labour Home Secretaries were aligned with this message, both in finding ways to deal with ever-inflating prison population and keeping the system secure and quiet. Indeed, the particular power relationship between Blair and Gordon Brown in the Treasury often constrained Home Secretary autonomy. Interviews with officials surfaced quite startling examples of the Home Secretary being sidelined on negotiations on prisons, and deals made bilaterally in private between Blair's office and Brown's aides. It was reported, for example, that in response to the request for £1.4 billion from the Home Office during the early 2000s, Number 10 and Treasury agreed to release somewhere in the region of £250 million, a decision which was taken bilaterally, reportedly without the Home Secretary even being invited to the meeting.

(v) De facto power of the Prison Officers Association

It is the prerogative and, in many ways, the right of the Prison Officers Association (POA) to do all it can to protect the interests of its members. However, ministers from both parties have commonly pointed to the threat of POA action as one of the major constraints on attempts at modernization and reform. About Labour Home Secretaries Jenkins and Rees in the late 1970s, Barnett writes that they 'preferred to defer expenditure on prisons rather than cut the size of prison staffs, much as they argued the desperate need for more prisons' (Barnett, 1982, p. 67). This in part reflects perhaps ideological inclination of Labour ministers of that era to keep one eye on the interests of the workers. It is also likely, perhaps crucially so, to reflect a more general reluctance on the part of ministers to do things to aggravate this powerful and potentially disruptive union.

Throughout the 1970s and 1980s, the POA commanded a powerful position, confrontational and militant in its style, and widely acknowledged to have a stranglehold over local prison cultures and practices, to the extent that many large local prisons were known as 'POA jails' (indeed, some still are). POA power was eroded somewhat as a result of the move to make national industrial action unlawful as part of 1994 legislation.[6] This Act was subsequently rescinded in 2005 to develop a more conciliatory and cooperative style of industrial relations. The removal of this section was followed by the establishment of a mutual no-strike agreement,[7] which critics describe as 'an important symbolic step, but one which has made little day-to-day difference' in the relationship between the Prison Service and the POA (Bennett et al., 2008, p. 128). National industrial action in August 2007 demonstrated the frailties of this agreement, and, once again in 2008, inciting industrial action by officers was made illegal. For many in the system, however, the POA retains its de facto power. One current governor summed up this widely held view:

> The POA ignored a high-court injunction and they decided to do nothing about it. If I was one of thousands of POA members, I would listen to them when they say, don't listen to your government, don't listen to your governor, we have proved that we are powerful to see this through. On a scale of 1 to 10, how influential are the POA in all of these things we are talking about? About 9, I would have thought.

At high political levels, many shared this view. A former Permanent Secretary of the Home Office suggested that 'the POA were just off the scale and would not be prepared to accept no-strike agreements and would threaten injunctions and all sort of things'. Despite some degree of modernization in the union, many believe that an unreformed and confrontational style is still the norm.

Officials reflected on the opportunistic tendencies of POA strategies during times of acute capacity stress. On numerous occasions, POA officials have offered ministers to take more prisoners into their jails in return for selective benefits. In March 2008, for example, during a visit by the prisons minister to Birmingham prison, a large local with a reputation for having strong POA influence, the POA offered to take more prisoners into the prison in return for increased numbers of staff. As officials acknowledged, this was a 'very seductive message to ministers at the time', one that put management on the back foot, and encouraged ministers themselves to return to managers and push them to look for opportunities to stretch the existing capacity of the system.

The combination of constraints here poses difficult predicaments for ministers. During times of capacity stress, they must to a great extent rely on the cooperation and efforts of prison staff. This puts the POA in a strong position, however, both because it is itself a vital part of the crisis response, and because the threat of industrial action can be used instrumentally at the highest political level. At the same time, however, ministers are aware of the threat of the union, and are inclined to want to introduce measures to curtail this power. The threat of private-sector competition and market testing has been an important aspect in this respect. Ministers have felt the pressure from the Treasury to push market testing and other competitive measures, yet at the same time, they have also had to have regard for the political consequences of aggravating or being seen to test the union. But these ministers are also under pressure from the Prime Minister to keep the prison system quiet and not risk widespread disruption.

(vi) Reliance on and resistance from senior officials

This interface between ministers and the top executive officials has been another potential source of constraint for ministers over the years.[8] The principal–agent dynamics are complex though. Ministers clearly rely on their top officials to deliver a quiet and cost-effective prison system, yet at the same time, they have also been inclined to be frustrated by the system and by those who wield considerable de facto power by being the ones who are able to 'deliver' it. Blunkett (2006), for example, writes scathingly six months into his first term as Home Secretary:

> Some of these Home Office officials are the worst, most obstructive, miserable, disengaged and disinterested group of people I have ever come across, which indicates a degree of demoralisation and complete lack of leadership. (p. 343)

Such ardent criticism must, it seems, be filtered to some extent, yet at the same time it also reflects the frustrations of a senior minister, and the limitations in being able to reform a large and complex bureaucratic system which is under continual pressure. In Blunkett's writing, this principal–agent conflict is continually visible. Set against the difficulties outlined above in maintaining trust with the judiciary, we see how the minister must find some kind of equilibrium between two competing pressures. Blunkett (2006) writes in March 2002:

> We've had three meetings during the course of the week on the rising prison population, but I've just got to hold my nerve and not allow myself to be pushed around by officials who always manage to get ministers to end up being the fall guys. Because managing the Prison Service in difficult circumstances falls to the managers, but executive release, which releases them from having to manage it in that way and lets the safety valve go, that's down to ministers. (p. 360)

Other ministers, Conservative and Labour, have had to deal with the constraints of senior officials. Extensive literature and interviews have highlighted the problems Michael Howard had with Derek Lewis (Lewis, 1997; Widdecombe, 1999). Numerous interviewees have talked about the tensions between Charles Clarke and Martin Narey, former Director General of NOMS. Clarke's vision for rehabilitative change was seen by officials at the time as completely unrealistic given the pressures of having to manage the prison population. And former officials reflected on the anxieties of John Reid towards what his departmental officials were telling him, and the political risks of acute capacity stress.

> You could tell John Reid didn't trust the Home Office, so he felt he needed to second guess everything. If they do trust you, by and large, they let you get on with it. He thought his job was on the line daily. He said, if I have to let people out of prison, I'll lose my job. When you are thinking that, you've got your eye on the numbers haven't you.

I examine this interface between ministers and top officials in more detail in the next chapter. In this section I have tried to illustrate, albeit briefly, how managing the relationship with top officials is just one aspect of a much wider nexus of constraints on ministers. As many experienced politicians have pointed out, it is possible to change the system from the top, but this requires a strong top minister, with sufficient time in office, and the right combination of external and internal factors pushing for the same kind of change. As one former minister pointed out, 'it takes a long time for a Home Secretary to change anything. It's a big boat and it takes a long time to turn. If you are only there for two years, you can't do very much.' As another pointed out, 'your Home Secretary may change, and because it is a long-term business, you need long-term consistency. If you don't and the person coming in has a radically different approach, then the whole thing gets messed up'. While ministers are in office, however, they must find a way of balancing all of these dynamics, as well as their own aspirations for changing the system.

5.4 Conclusions

I have tried to portray some of the most important aspects of what ministers must face in dealing with the issue of crowding and capacity stress in prisons. Clearly, it has not been a comprehensive historical account, but rather an attempt to show the main dynamics of constrained autonomy from their perspective at the top of the prison system. The analysis has shown a great deal of variation and complexity through time. Yet we can reasonably conclude that the notion that problems with policy systems should be put down exclusively to the failures of ministers seems inadequate at least when seen in the context of the system as a whole. Clearly, ministers have certain autonomy to shape policies and attitudes towards capacity stress in prisons. But we have seen how this can only be partly justified in a dynamic and finely balanced context which sees the minister having to act within a nexus of constraints and uncertainties. As one former Conservative Home Secretary pointed out, 'it is not a problem of an unseen conspiracy. It's just that the problems are so difficult'. On the perceived risks and sensitivities involved, another explained:

> If you force a confrontation in this way, you are always frightened as a politician that the whole thing goes tits up, and you are back to riots and escapes and all the rest of it. It's a very delicate thing you are carrying, the prison system. Because it is so near capacity, and because there are very difficult things like suicides and so on, I was frightened of doing anything which let the whole thing go.

If these constraints outlined in the second half of the chapter were to exist independently of each other, then it may be easier for a committed and skilful minister to overcome them. Seen in a more temporal and dynamic context, however, in which different constraints interact and have cumulative aggravating effects, the overall constraining influences are more debilitating. We have seen how one thing leads to another, and another, and windows for opportunity become narrower and narrower. For ministers, the degree of instrumental control and influence must be continually sufficient to keep all of these countervailing dynamics in some kind of manageable equilibrium, and keep the whole system moving at least in the direction of desired goals and outcomes. In some ways, this involves completely unrealistic expectations of ministers' abilities to bring about change by instrumental design. As one minister put it, 'in life as in politics, you've got to know what the second and third step after you make the first one. If you don't, the first one is as far as you will get'.

For ministers in office, it is perhaps excessively cynical to suggest that they would not try for prison reform on the grounds of knowing the odds on its likely success. Most top ministers over the years have placed more faith in their ability to bring about change despite the constraints, and some of those would admit to having a good go. Yet for experienced insiders, those who have seen Secretaries of State come and go, we find much more deeply seated scepticism about the expectations and outcomes of ministers and their visions. As one former Permanent Secretary to the Home Office explained:

> I don't think anyone in the Ministry and in the Home Office expects success. We are all conscious of what can go wrong, and if [the Home Secretary] emerges having handled one or two public order situations well and if he [*sic*] has some generally approved legislation, that's really it.

On this muted note, we move on to look at the problem from the next level down in the principal–agent chain, the perspective of top officials in the system, and their own predicaments of constrained autonomy, both upwards vis-à-vis ministers and political imperatives, and downwards in their role as managers and 'deliverers' of a quiet and cost-effective prison system.

6
Top Officials and the Interface between Political and Operational

> The pressure of numbers means that everybody in the organization has to focus on management of the population. Some of the most talented civil servants I have worked with have been in the Prison Service, but they were constantly being asked to spend their time thinking about how to manage the population rather than applying their talent to thinking about things like rehabilitation. (Former top Prison Service official)

Attention turns in this chapter to the implications of constrained autonomy for senior officials.[1] Public-policy and public-choice literature assigns considerable scope to the top officials in the executive to shape their world, behave strategically, or finesse their situations according to their own interests, and so on (Dunleavy, 1991; Page, 1992). Whether it be the traditional model of civil servant 'mandarins', or the managerialist model of CEO-style civil servants, the top bureaucratic officials in leadership roles in large public-policy systems are often attributed extensive powers of autonomy in one way or another. However, the constraints of the system are often as powerful, and this means that we should be careful about exactly how much autonomy we attribute to these top officials who work at the interface between political and operational aspects of the system.

How have these important actors perceived their own ability to affect capacity stress? Again, as we have seen in the previous chapters with ministers, constrained autonomy can be complex and involve a whole range of different strategic and cultural dynamics. The reliance of ministers on their top officials to deliver a quiet and stable prison system means that their influence cannot not be overlooked or downplayed as some critics have suggested.[2] Accounts which characterize senior officials as having little influence over ministers run the risk of underestimating the *de facto* influence which officials wield simply by dint of their role in managing this potentially complex and difficult system. Looking down the system too, top officials are likely to have autonomy to shape the way in which the rank-and-file managers and staff operate. On the other hand, senior officials are civil servants and are there to be responsive to ministers' wishes and priorities. Attributing too much influence to top officials will tend to underestimate the constraints of this political accountability. And, as is the risk for any principal over groups of agents, top officials will be likely to experience the risks of 'moral hazards' and different types of benign and direct resistance from the system, constraining in turn their ability to respond to pressures from above.

As with the previous chapter, the aim here is to examine the dynamics of constrained autonomy for these top officials operating at the interface between political and operational. They play a key role in reconciling and transitioning the very different cultures of high politics and frontline operations. Like politicians, the range of constraints on their autonomy is complex. The chapter therefore aims to capture this complexity, and understand how these officials manage their own situations of constrained autonomy. As each of these four chapters seeks to show, it is in doing so that they contribute to the overall outcome of chronic capacity stress (CCS).

In the first section, I clarify some of the key public-management changes that have determined the structure and context in which officials must operate. This highlights a strengthening of operational experience at senior levels. I then discuss two key aspects of managing capacity stress in the system – shaping the prison estate and managing the population. The final two sections examine various aspects of constrained autonomy as perceived by top officials.

6.1 The shift towards managerial and operational cultures

There is something about the public policy of prisons that it has tended to produce a tradition of strong personalities in the top administrative roles. Historical accounts have brought to life the impact of these senior officials in shaping values, design, structure, and cultures of the system (Hobhouse and Brockway, 1922; Fox 1936, 1952; McConville, 1981). Names such as Joshua Jebb (1850 to 1863), Edmund du Cane (1877 to 1895), and Evelyn Ruggles-Brise (1895 to 1921) are all in their own way associated with key periods of development of the modern prison system since the 1840s.[3] Indeed, the history of the system is often told in terms of the bureaucrats, autocrats, and reformers who have presided over it.

The influence and efforts of senior officials must be seen, however, in the context of the systems in which they were operating. In his paper on Du Cane (the first Director of the Prison Commission), for example, Tibber (1980) describes his 'autocratic and military manner', as well as the continuous tension which existed between him and Home Office civil servants over the autonomy and independence of his Commission.[4] Du Cane was much criticized for the manner in which he ran the system, yet Tibber seeks to redress the balance by 'illustrating how frequently Du Cane found himself at variance with, and frustrated by, the hierarchies within which he operated' (p. 15).

Du Cane's predicament provides insight into the kind of 'culture clashes' which have shaped constrained autonomy for senior officials throughout history. At the heart of the cultural equilibrium we find the hierarchical and rule-based civil-service culture of the Home Office (and also the Treasury). Against this, opposing cultures have operated in countervailing ways. Military cultures have cut across those of civil service. As a former military man, Du Cane's style was seen as a 'red flag to a bull' for civil servants (Tibber, 1980, p. 11). Indeed, after his resignation in 1985, he was replaced by an Eton- and Oxbridge-educated career civil servant, Evelyn Ruggles-Brise, no less a reformer but also a 'safer pair of hands' in terms of his civil-service credentials. We have also seen how managerialist cultures have cut across those of established civil service. Also, the operational street-level cultures of running prisons have posed challenges to the more rarefied cultures of Whitehall and Westminster.

By 1979 the administration of prisons had been through a process of consolidation and reintegration back into Whitehall civil-service culture, as the Prison Department of the Home Office.[5] Throughout the 1980s, the Prison Board was predominantly made up of career civil servants, led by the Director General Chris Train, described by interviewees as an 'old-fashioned Whitehall mandarin' yet 'the first modern manager of the prison system'. Senior officials from that era reflected on what seemed to be a much greater freedom to bring together experts and develop reformist penal policy. As one former top civil servant described:

> I had an extraordinary amount of leeway thirty years ago. I could do an awful lot. I did it with governors and other staff. We had ownership of it. We thought it out together. I looked after the bureaucratic side of that [...] making sure it was in the law and that ministers weren't going to be upset. There is very much less of that now than I was able to enjoy.

That said, former ministers and civil servants resisted excessively 'rose-tinted' accounts of that era. The late 1980s was a period of extreme crowding and unrest in the prison system. Train himself wrote on page one of the 1987 Prison Department annual report of a 'nightmare-like sense, felt more sharply than ever before at the top of the Service [...] of all running and never catching up'. Nevertheless, these officials reflected on the broader mix of civil-service and 'prisons people' on the Prisons Board under Train's chairmanship, and a sense of optimism about the collective approach to tackling the problems of excessive crowding.[6]

As we have seen, the early 1990s was a period of upheaval, disruption, and change in the system. The creation of the Prison Service as an executive agency of the Home Office, and the appointment of chief executive Derek Lewis from the private sector, challenged existing equilibrium between civil-service and operational cultures. Lewis (1997) provides a damning account of the general state of management performance in the system, itself a stark illustration of how modern managerialist expectations can run counter to entrenched civil-service attitudes. The tension between the role of modern chief executive and civil servant answerable to ministers led eventually to Lewis's resignation in the aftermath of the high-security escapes 'fiasco' in 1994 and 1995. One experienced official reflected on the implications of greater managerial focus at senior official level.

> There's a view around that Derek Lewis got the sack because every time Michael Howard said he wanted to do something, Lewis went back to him with the bill. This is how much your policy will cost, Home Secretary. Have you got the money?

This impact of the Lewis era, and managerialism more generally, illustrates interesting countervailing dynamics. The shock of the prisoner escapes from Whitemoor and Parkhurst, and Lewis's very public departure led to the Home Office opting to bring the management of the prison system 'back into the fold'. This appointment reflected a renewed belief at political level that officials running the system should have operational experience. As one former senior official put it:

> There was always a cultural tension between people with operational experience and civil servants. But after the prison escapes, and this thing with Derek Lewis, there was a huge swing towards giving more

Table 6.1 Summary of key senior officials in the prison system, 1979 to 2012

	Top level management arrangements	
Key periods of change	**Director General (DG) and Prisons Board level**	**Regional or area structures and relevant senior officials**
1979 to 1993 Prison Department of the Home Office	1979 **DG, Chris Train** (career civil servant). Prison Board predominantly career civil servants. 1991 **DG, Joe Pilling** (career civil servant). Integration of operational and civil-service officials at Board level.	Devolved network of regional managers reporting directly to the Prisons Board. Relatively high levels of autonomy for governors, while Board deals with high level policy.
1993 to 2004 Prison Service as Executive Agency of the Home Office	1993 **CEO, Derek Lewis**, recruited from the private sector. Sacked by Home Secretary Michael Howard after prison-escapes fiasco. 1995 **DG, Richard Tilt** (former governor). 1997 **DG, Martin Narey** (former civil servant with experience of the prison system). Deputy DG **Phil Wheatley** (former governor).	Area managers introduced in early 1990s, and much stronger hierarchical management from the DG and the Prisons Board down through the prison areas. Start of more intensive national management of the prison population through area managers during this period.
2004 to 2007 Prison Service as part of the National Offender Management Service (NOMS)	2004 DG, NOMS Martin Narey. DG Prison Service Phil Wheatley (former governor). NOMS civil servants commission prison capacity from the Prison Service. Narey resigns in 2005. 2005 **DG NOMS Helen Edwards** (career civil servant).	Top layer of NOMS civil servants commissioning prison services from the Prison Service. Senior management of the Prison Service, plus area managers.
2007 to 2012 Prisons as part of an integrated NOMS	2007 DG, NOMS Phil Wheatley. NOMS Board consists almost entirely of former Prison Service senior officials. 2009 **CEO, NOMS Michael Spurr**, formerly Deputy DG to Phil Wheatley.	NOMS senior management, Regional Custodial Managers, and subsequently Directors of Offender Management (DOM) commission custodial services for their regions.

Note: Permanent Secretaries to the Home Office were also included as 'senior officials' in this analysis. Traditionally, these officials have played relatively minor parts in prisons policy and management, except in their work to oversee and advise ministers on prisons matters.

> responsibility to people with operational experience. The Home Secretary said we need people who know how to run prisons. Tilt was the first. He was succeeded by Narey who was a prison person but had wider experience in the Home Office. Then there was Wheatley who had no experience in the Home Office. He was prisons born and bred.

From 2003 and the creation of the National Offender Management Service (NOMS), we see further tensions between this more intensive operational focus at the top of the prison system, and the wider changes towards a more integrated penal system. This comes in two stages. During the first four years of NOMS, the top layers of senior officials were predominantly civil servants responsible for commissioning and coordinating prisons in conjunction with probation and youth justice. Whereas previously senior prison officials had been responsible for delivering the prison system on behalf of ministers, now they were responsible for providing prison capacity to commissioning civil servants in NOMS. These prison officials therefore found themselves in the role of 'agents' answerable to this new layer of senior civil servants as 'principals'.

This first iteration of NOMS largely failed to integrate prisons and probation. With a further round of integration of NOMS from 2007, a new senior-management structure was established, which dissolved the administrative interface between NOMS and the Prison Service, and subsumed the prison system into NOMS under a more integrated structure of senior management. Interviewees describe the political and bureaucratic manoeuvring that went on between the various key actors in prisons and probation systems. The outcome was that the new senior-management structure of NOMS, a joined-up agency responsible for prisons, probation, and youth justice, consisted almost entirely of senior managers from the prison system. Senior probation officials interviewed describe this as a 'coup'. Senior prison officials were less inclined to see it in these terms.

6.2 The managerial challenge of making the system work

A key theme already has been the extent to which actors emphasize their role in finding ways to make the prison system work. For senior officials, their perception of their predicament is exactly that. They perceive the constraints on them and do their best to manage them. This presents a compelling if sometimes precarious managerial challenge. Numerous interviewees have said as much.

> Our instinct is to make it all work. If we are guilty of anything, we have been too successful at making it work. Perhaps things should have fallen over some time ago. But that's not the culture of the organization. Sometimes on a wing and a prayer. Sometimes closer than we should. But we make it work.

At the heart of this challenge, there are two broad options for senior officials in finding ways to keep the system in some kind of manageable equilibrium: either

- expanding or shaping the supply of capacity in the system (such as building prisons, 're-roling' them, opening 'makeshift' accommodation, stretching capacity, changing staffing or investment allocations); or
- reconfiguring the way in which prisoners are managed in and around, or out of the system (i.e. maximizing the use of existing capacity in the system).

The first of these relates to planning and shaping the prison estate to accommodate demand. This is not just a challenge of having enough places, but rather, given the differentiation between types of prisoners and their various needs, it is a challenge of having the right kind of places in the right place at the right time (or near enough). Historically, for male adult prisoners, local prisons have received all intake from the courts and have fed 'training' prisons. For the much smaller female prison population, female prisons have tended to receive and hold onto their intake. There is also the young offender population, which although has been largely separate, in more recent years has increasingly been mixed with adult population. Each of these broad groups will have different security, programme, and resettlement requirements, and these are generally balanced against commitments by the system to keep prisoners as close as possible to their families and local support networks while they are in custody. It is not possible to examine these challenges in great detail here. I simply argue that, for senior officials, the management challenge involves finding a 'best possible' configuration of the estate given the constraints.

We look first at new capacity built over three decades. We have seen already how the prison-building programme throughout the 1980s helped to get crowding down to its lowest levels by the start of the

1990s. The dark shaded blocks in Figure 6.1 show new prisons built. The expansion of the estate up until the early 1990s was done mainly through the provision of new prisons built in the public sector. In addition to new prisons, the Prison Service added new house-blocks in existing prisons and 'modularized' units which have provided short-term accommodation in ready-to-use form. From the mid-1990s to 2005, these units were used widely across the system as quick response to the rapid and largely un-projected increase in the short-term prison population. From 2003 to 2009, new house-blocks in existing prisons made up most of the new capacity in the system. Figure 6.2 shows the same data by type of prison.

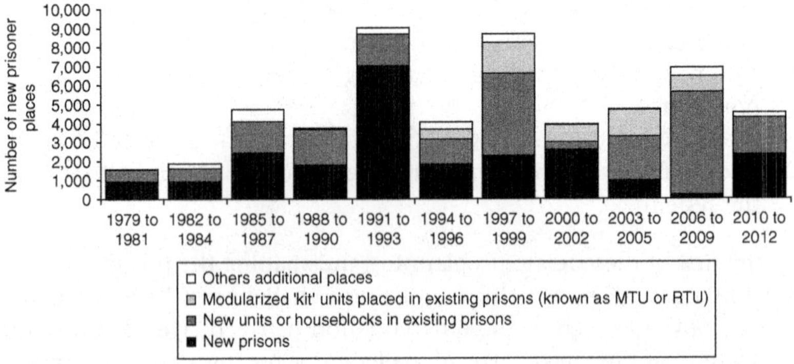

Figure 6.1 Number of new prisoner places, by type of accommodation

Source: My own analysis of data from Prison Department, Prison Service and NOMS annual reports.

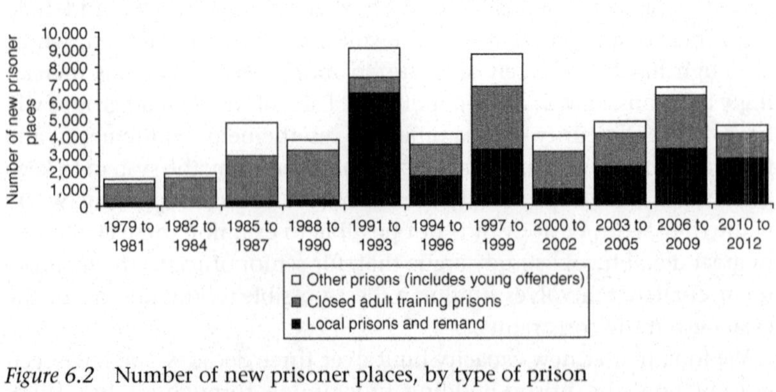

Figure 6.2 Number of new prisoner places, by type of prison

Source: My own analysis of data from Prison Department, Prison Service and NOMS annual reports.

The rapid rise in the size of the short-term prison population meant that senior officials found themselves having to source new capacity quickly as well as absorb the increase within existing accommodation. At Cleland House,[7] estates planning and emergency accommodation units were tasked with finding new ways to expand capacity at short notice during the second half of the 1990s. All officials interviewed from this period described the necessarily pragmatic, quick response, and often highly stressful nature of this work. This engendered often quite radical solutions, for example, the purchase of a prison ship *The Weare*,[8] as well as innovations with short-term modularized accommodation (NAO, 2005).

Although senior officials talked about the short-term value of these 'emergency' building solutions, particularly during times of acute capacity shortage, they also acknowledged the long-term obsolescence and costs which were built into the system as a result of this short-term expansion.

> *The Weare* is a good example. That was probably one of the best investments of the time. It cost £6 million and it produced 400 spaces in six months. To build a similar-sized prison, it would cost £93 million and take three years to build. So when it was built, it was a great use of public money for two years. But then four, five or six years down the line, when we kept giving it a lifespan, it started to be a misuse of public money.

Officials also characterized the command-and-control style of negotiations with governors: 'if I rang up the prison and said I'd like to come and look at the possibility of expanding accommodation, it meant I was coming to see them, if you know what I mean'. The practice of re-roling prisons or converting ex-military installations or hospitals, often at very short notice, has also been frequently used in responding to capacity shortages in super-quick time. Many governors and officials could tell 'horror stories', particularly from the 1980s and 1990s, about having to manage very quick conversions of municipal sites into establishments capable of holding prisoners.

The combination of the difficulty of building new prisons in the right place and the exigency of having to find new capacity at short notice has perpetuated the view that prison capacity has been sub-optimally distributed around the country. One former official summed up the overall effect of this, explaining that 'what you can't move away from is the fact the UK prison estate is possibly one of the most disparate almost randomly acquired set of buildings that you could possibly imagine'. Another official explained:

> We built in the wrong places. We continue to do so. I handed over to my successor a list of places in which there was no way in God's earth we should build any more accommodation. We came under pressure to deliver more. We built in all those places. And that is where you compound the strategic felony.

Inherent constraints curtail the ability of officials to shape the estate in optimal ways around geographical distribution of demand. Table 6.2 shows that London has historically generated by far the largest prison population, but has one of the smallest regional capacities and one of the smallest rates of increase in new capacity over thirty years. Officials described the constraints of finding suitable sites in the London, due mainly to the cost of land, difficulties in getting planning permission, and local political resistance.

> My team would come back and tell me this-or-that local authority have ten sites they've put into their strategic plans. Which do you

Table 6.2 New additional prison capacity built by region, 1979 to 2012

	1	2	3	4	5
	Average CNA in 1979	**Additional CNA places built, 1979 to 2012**	**Average CNA in 2012**	**Estimated CNA decomm.**	**Estimated population by home region**
North East	5,500	10,400	13,700	2,200	12,600
Eastern	2,000	7,400	8,800	600	5,500
South East	7,200	7,000	13,100	1,100	8,600
North West	6,700	6,000	11,000	1,700	13,000
East Midlands	4,400	5,000	9,500	0	5,800
West Midlands	3,300	4,800	8,100	0	8,700
London	5,100	3,300	7,400	1,000	18,600
South West	5,100	2,100	6,000	1,200	4,700
Wales	800	1,500	2,300	0	4,000
Region not known		6,200		(6,200)	
All regions	40,100	53,700	79,900	14,000	81,500

Note: All figures are rounded to nearest 100.

Sources: Data in columns 1, 2, 3 based on my analysis of data in Prison Service and NOMS annual reports 1979 to 2012. Data in column 4 calculated from columns 1 to 3. Data in column 5 is population by home region (as of March 2008) from the independent report on the England and Wales prison system by Lord Carter (Ministry of Justice, 2007).

want? I would say, find out which ones we are guaranteed to get planning permission for and I'll tell you which ones we want. The planning consent is a big issue [...] and the price of land.

Regions such as the Eastern and East Midlands have tended to be net importers of prisoners over the years. Whereas regions such as the North East, including Yorkshire and Humber, have tended to be relatively self-sustainable. In the period of thirty years from 1979 to 2010, only two new prisons had been built in London. This confirms what many officials have said about the inherent limitations on development in the London prisons, most of which are inner-city establishments, cramped for space inside and limited on the extent to which they can be developed outwards. Two additional prisons have been added in London since 2010, going some way to redress the balance (Table 6.3).

If capacity is perceived to be configured sub-optimally, it is the management of the population into, around, and out of the system which must, by definition, compensate. The more the capacity stress, the higher the rate of compensatory movement. Private-sector officials involved in running prisoner-escort contracts have pointed out this impact on movement in the system. As one contractor put it: 'We notice it in the prisoner transportation bit, because as the population increases, we find we are having to do longer journeys with prisoners. It works outwards from London.'

Table 6.3 Type of new additional prison capacity by region, 1979 to 2012

	1	2	3
	Number of new prisons built, 1979 to 2012	**Additional places in new prisons, 1979 to 2012**	**Other additional places in house-blocks or MTU/RTUs**
North East	9	5,400	5,000
Eastern	8	3,200	4,200
South East	6	3,300	3,600
North West	6	3,000	3,000
West Midlands	4	2,600	2,200
London	4	2,300	1,000
East Midlands	4	1,600	3,400
South West	3	900	1,200
Wales	1	800	700
Other not known			6,200

Note: All figures are rounded to nearest 100.

Source: Data in columns 1, 2, 3 based on my analysis of data in Prison Service and NOMS annual reports 1979 to 2012.

We have already seen in Chapter 3 how tighter centralized management of the national prison population has been an influential factor in coping with the rise in the short-sentence prison population. The shift to the area-manager structures in the early 1990s came with much stronger national population management function, which replaced the comparatively more devolved and independent regional structures. Top officials have recognized the benefit and necessity of keeping tight control over the movement of the population. One interviewee described the pragmatic outlook of former Director General Phil Wheatley in this respect: 'Phil always liked population management. He took the view that if you controlled the population, you could manage the Prison Service.' From the early 1990s, the Population Management Unit (PMU) began to tighten its grip on coordination and movement of prisoners through the estate in order to maximize capacity in different parts and to ensure that the system had space enough for new intakes from the courts. PMU has coordinated 'overcrowding drafts' from local prisons to other local prisons in order to maintain this balance.[9] Senior officials explained the importance of these continual movements to the system over the years in allowing it to function: 'We do overcrowding drafts into anywhere. They are an essential part of the business. You have to keep them going. You have to keep the programme going.'

Indeed, overcrowding drafts out of London local prisons have been a critical component of this 'life-support' mechanism, in particular being able to free enough space in London local prisons on a Friday night to absorb weekend traffic from the courts. A former head of the PMU explained that 'you would have to make sure you had beds in London for the following weekend. You would work the system two or three days beforehand.' Many senior officials acknowledged the logistical and human complexity of the population management process. As one former NOMS official explained, 'the algorithm of where you put [prisoners] around the country is something that is gobsmackingly complicated. The fact that it runs as well and as smoothly as it does is probably one of the working miracles by anyone's business.' I discuss this significance of the population-management influence and strongly centralized line management in the next section.

6.3 Autonomy of senior officials to influence capacity

Civil servants can be skilful operators in terms of finding ways to finesse versions of reality to their ministers. We have seen in Chapters 3 and 4 how entirely constructed targets for performance demarcate thresholds between 'success' and 'failure', and how these can be deployed by officials to reassure or pressure ministers. As one former minister explained:

> Senior officials would like their ministers to be comfortable. Yes minister, we are using the estate very efficiently, and yes minister, we are managing to keep up the number of constructive courses and so on. But they are not getting the educational activity and the constructive time spent they ought to be getting [...] Ministers will be fed rather cheerful statistics, such as we have managed to clock up about half an hour more constructive out-of-cell activity than last year. Whatever that means in reality is impossible to tell.

Top officials can therefore find room to shape from within the values and priorities of the system. Interviewees acknowledged, for example, the influence of Martin Narey during his time as Director General in establishing what has become widely known as the 'decency agenda'. This has done much to put the issue of decency at the centre of prison policy and life, and has linked to other important developments throughout the 2000s such as qualitative measures of 'moral performance' of prisons through tools such as MQPL (Measuring the Quality of Prison Life) (Liebling, 2004), and more systematic approaches to regime expectations encapsulated in concepts such as the 'core day'.[10] One current NOMS official characterized this widely held view:

> Martin Narey came along and took the view that security could be balanced with decency. Martin came with the agenda, which was then driven forward by Phil [Wheatley]. Those two were a strength. The development of MQPL, embracing pressure groups, bringing people in to do education. Bringing a more professional approach, it all helped stabilize morale.

Top officials have also not been afraid over the years to take a strong line with ministers and their permanent secretaries on population-management issues and make clear the limits of the system. As one put it, 'I would testify to the fact that Phil Wheatley held the line very clearly with ministers. And I would be surprised if you could find any examples of Martin [Narey] giving in on operational capacity.' Many others confirmed this view, particularly the strength of Wheatley over the years to resist pressure from above. As one put it, 'he accepts that ministers have to be kept reasonably happy, without lies being told.

But when ministers need to be confronted by an unpleasant truth, he will confront them.' Another NOMS official explained:

> The great thing that Phil Wheatley has done is to say that you can't go on doing that indefinitely. If you put me under more pressure, we will have to go into police cells. And that is something I can do and you can't stop me doing. And when I do, you will have the police on your back and you'll have to pay.

Another former top official reflected that

> Wheatley has taken a firm line on saying the prison system is full. He has turned shroud waving into a much more sophisticated and successful art. Because he has said any more than that is dangerous and I'm not going to preside over it.

Senior officials frequently acknowledged the strength of such advice up to ministers:

> It is quite compelling. It takes a very strong minister to go against that advice. If we do this minister, you are going to have riots in the prison. It's a very strong minister who says 'I don't buy that'.

Interviewees have also pointed out that experienced senior officials who know 'prison-craft', and can command respect simultaneously in the world of prisons, Whitehall, and Westminister, have been able to wield considerable power over politicians. As one put it:

> The Prison Service ultimately has government ministers by the throat. The great thing that Phil Wheatley has done is deliver a quiet Prison Service. When I was in the Prison Service, you had loads of escapes, riots, it was very traumatic.

The influence of Phil Wheatley in this respect has been mentioned time and time again as having been integral in ordering and quietening the system, and hence shaping the values and priorities along these lines. As one senior civil servant explained:

> The figure in the system is Phil Wheatley. When I was governor, I was extremely scathing about most bits of HQ because I worked there, but the one person I didn't ignore was Phil Wheatley. Unquestionable. It was good cop and bad cop with Martin Narey. The person who was directing you was Phil. He is hugely respected and feared by 90 per cent of governors. It has been a Wheatley decade.

This leaves the reader in no doubt about the ability of top officials to have an impact on the system. It is confirmed more widely. A former Prisons Board member reflected, 'there is a culture of autocracy. Everybody wants to see what Phil's view will be.' In recent years, particularly during the population crises from 2007 onwards, the impact of Wheatley's power was perceived as much by those above as those beneath working in the system. Numerous officials pointed out that the Permanent Secretary of the Ministry of Justice at the time, Suma Chakrabarti, had looked to bring back in a career civil servant at the top of NOMS to 'redress the balance', as one put it because 'Phil Wheatley is an incredibly powerful individual. Within the MoJ he is the most powerful DG, with nine tenths of all the resources.' For many, the decision to bring in Michael Spurr, Wheatley's Deputy Director General, on Wheatley's retirement in 2010, was a compromise between unquestioned operational experience and a move to bring control of the offender-management system back towards ministerial civil service.

Strong command-and-control cultures have played an integral part over the last fifteen years or so in allowing top officials to deliver the system. Senior officials and governors have frequently remarked on this prevalent command-and-control culture, and the subtle combination of quasi-autocratic and informal professional pressures that come with it. A former area manager reflected:

> Like all other area managers at that time, you'd feel pressure, and management would say, you've got to find me fifty places [...] I'd go to governors, I'd know their accommodation, and I'd say you've got to get ten doubled up on A Wing there, and on B Wing can you double up another ten [...].

As another official explained, 'when there's a crisis on, Michael [Spurr] sends a note saying please explore *every* option to overcrowd'.

As more experienced prison officials have observed, the rationale for command-and-control cultures of management reflects very real pressures to make the system work. Yet, this also reflects constructed norms, which can be used instrumentally by senior officials to finesse the impact of their decisions inside the prison system, and also to reaffirm dominant values and paradigms, which themselves are likely to be a source of power to these officials.

The function of population management provides a good illustration of how dominant values and paradigms can be reaffirmed and perpetuated by the behaviour and rhetoric of top officials. As Chapter 3 has outlined, the constant movement of prisoners around the system may be necessary to sustain the current national system at such high levels of capacity. Yet, the disruptive effect of this constant movement of short-sentence prisoners around the system makes it difficult to do the more ambitious rehabilitative work which the system itself professes to aim to do. The point here is that top officials can have the effect of reaffirming these priorities for the organization. Indeed, it is not unreasonable to suggest that top officials are likely to perpetuate perceptions of dependency on systems which themselves form the basis for their own ongoing authority. One current NOMS official reflected on the dominance of national population management:

> You create a national system, and we are able to respond to Ministers needs and pressures in real time. You create a kind of urgency and language and mythology around the whole enterprise that it takes an increasingly brave person to say, do you know what, come the 1st of November, PMU ceases to exist.

This is a complicated dynamic. I do not suggest here a crude picture of instrumental perpetuation of organizational elites through structural choice. Nevertheless, it is clear from the quotation above and many others like it that top officials do have autonomy and power to determine prevalent values and priorities of the system. If they are inclined to dismiss or reject the argument that the system should be geared more effectively to doing rehabilitative work, it is likely that this will filter into and shape prevailing culture in the system. When a current governor makes the point that 'there is an element of feeling comfortable and safe under this style of leadership', we have to accept this at face value to a great extent. But, at the same time, we should also view it as a cultural artefact reflecting the priorities and values which are shaped by those at the top of the organization. A former minister acknowledged the dominance of population issues throughout his time:

> I kept on saying that the key issue is that you must not start this from 'What is the size of the prison population?' You must start this from what are your social goals, i.e. reducing reoffending, or reducing crime. Or giving justice to the victim. Or other criteria. The capacity of the prison should not be the starting point. But that was the mind-set across the whole of the prison system.

For top officials, this kind of view may be seen as unrealistic or perhaps even naïve in the context of having to manage continual capacity stress. The conventional wisdom, often heard from senior officials, that rehabilitative goals are unobtainable as long as the system is run at prevailing levels of capacity may seem like a reasonable prognosis. However, many also acknowledge that crowding and capacity stress over the years have had considerable 'excuse factor' for the system not being able to achieve what it would like to in terms of rehabilitation. As one former top official put it:

> One of the realities about prisons for governors and staff is that overcrowding is somewhat of a comfort blanket. It's the excuse for not providing the sort of service which I always believed we could provide. I did work through a brief period where we started to see falls in the population, and started significantly to reduce the population in one or two establishments, because I wanted to see whether we could make a radical difference to rehabilitative activity. But it was too briefly lived. But it would have been a telling challenge if we had removed the excuse.

The reconfiguration of NOMS in recent years has done much to counteract the command-and-control culture in the prison system. The introduction of regional commissioning of offender-management services (under Directors of Offender Management, or DOMs) in 2007, provided leverage for a more regionally or locally based approach to offender management. Immediately, this created a direct incentive for regional managers to want to 'shape' the profile of their prison and probation populations, and consequently create impetus for holding on to offenders from their own region and displacing offenders from other regions. The power and status of old area managers (rebadged as Regional Custodial Managers) has also diminished as a result. The prison population continues to be managed centrally, along with monitoring and strategic expansion of prison capacity; however, regional commissioning has brought a countervailing dynamic to set against more excessive aspects of command-and-control management.

6.4 How senior officials are constrained by the system

As we have seen with ministers in the previous chapter, senior officials have developed a keen sense of the constraints on them in terms of their ability to influence capacity in the system. The fact that prisons are not in the right place means that prisoners have to be moved around to compensate. The fact that prisoners have to be moved around means that it is much harder to link them to local public agencies and charities. The fact that offenders experience disrupted services makes it likely that they will end up reoffending. All of these factors are examples of how sub-optimality is rationalized and coped with by those in the system.

Senior officials have frequently returned to the importance of the culture of coping, 'making things work', starting from situations which are 'not ideal', acknowledging that 'we are where we are', and so on. They have also emphasized the need to find a balance between managing the system and responding to the priorities of their ministers and governments. As one peer reflected:

> The successful civil servant has two characteristics. One is to run something or make policy that is effective. The second is to be good with ministers. Being good with ministers usually means finding a way to do what ministers want to do.

Indeed, the perception is widespread amongst top officials that it is their job to do what ministers want. As one current official explained:

> I was talking to my boss about some issue, and he said, 'The minister wants it'. And that I'm afraid is the show stopper in our business. If the minister wants it, and it's legal, the minister gets it. And rightly so. We are civil servants and we do what we are told.

More experienced officials have reflected on an increasingly politicized relationships with ministers over time. Officials in the Prison Department during the 1980s, for example, spoke of 'barely meeting a minister from one year to the next', and one former top official suggested that he 'did not meet ministers more often than 10 or 12 times a year'. This compares with accounts by top officials in more recent years which suggest a much more hands-on interest in the operational aspects of the system. Senior officials have frequently cited the tendency for what they have seen as 'excessive' intervention or 'meddling' by ministers in operational matters. The perception was that ministerial interest heightened dramatically during times of perceived crisis in the system. As one former official put it:

> The prison population, when it's fine, doesn't come near ministers. They will get nice, well-planned future strategy papers and it's a

> reasonably ordered situation [...] During a population crisis, it's very different. Ministers were involved in weekly crisis meetings. Daily, weekly, suddenly everyone wants to know the daily figures. The whole system cranks into white hot gear.

During these population crises in recent years, the issue has reportedly been closely monitored by Number 10. One official reflected that 'the level of political interference in the Prison Service got to a stage where the Prime Minister had an update with his porridge every morning'. Another former NOMS official described the process of keeping the Home Secretary up-to-date with the latest capacity situation:

> I used to get the numbers every morning. The Home Secretary wanted me in the next office to him. He didn't believe that we had it under control. And that we were really doing everything we could. So I thought how do we do this? We set up a huge roll of paper round the wall of the office. And wrote the numbers on it every morning with the increase. When he saw this, he said 'That's what I want to see'. I've still got a bit of it.

Senior officials responsible for managing the population during times of high pressure have described immensely stressful and close-run situations. In recent years, the system has operated with a planned capacity headroom or slack of 2,000 prisoner places. Figure 6.3 illustrates the problem of unexpected fluctuations in demand for capacity and the potential risk of running the system with inadequate levels of usable slack. During the capacity 'crisis' of 2007, the predicted 'Christmas dip' did not occur and the system was forced to operate at levels perilously close to full capacity. This explained the use of police cells in 2007 shown in Figure 3.7, and the introduction of the End of Custody Licence (ECL), a 'pressure valve' mechanism for releasing short-term and low-risk prisoners out of the system on eighteen-day early release in order to maintain the delicate capacity balance.

Senior officials described the intensive crisis-management approach to handling the population pressures during the introduction of ECL. It is clear from this analysis that ECL was a pragmatic demand-side response to a potentially unmanageable build-up of capacity stress. This illustrates also the potential misalignments between what Home Secretaries are saying in public about their own ambitious aspirations for the system, and the reality for senior officials of finding ways to cope with the pressures of day-to-day population. One top NOMS official

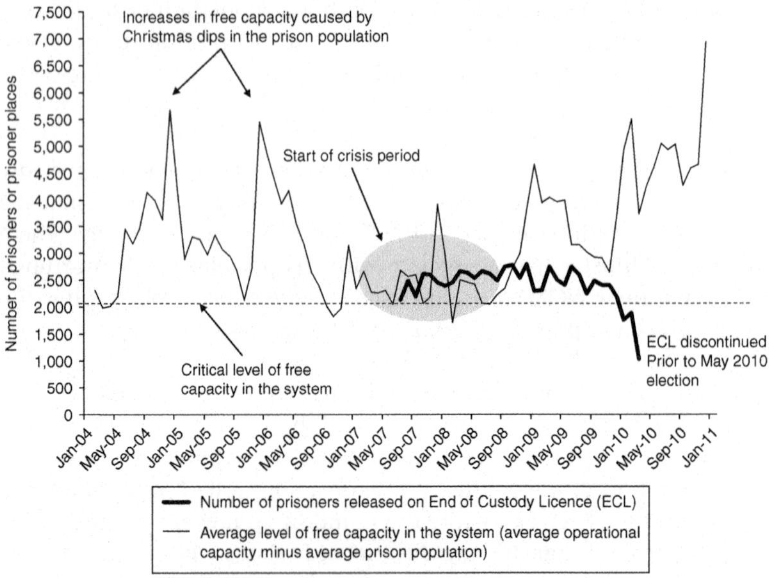

Figure 6.3 Estimated 'headroom' capacity in the prison system and rates of executive release under End of Custody Licence (ECL)

Source: My own analysis of Prison Service and Ministry of Justice data on prison population, CNA and numbers of prisoners released on ECL.

reflected on the speech by Home Secretary Charles Clarke in September 2005 which majored on putting rehabilitative goals at the centre of a strategic approach:

> When the Home Secretary stood up and made a speech saying that he was going to manage the prison population down, the point I remember was that it was never clear how he was actually going to do that [...] It didn't feel great because the projections were already starting to do adrift.

As shown in Figure 6.3, the missing Christmas dip marked the beginning of an acute capacity shortage in the system, brought about largely by the sudden increase of foreign national prisoners entering the system. This acute period was described by this official as 'like being in the eye of a perfect storm'. And as the graph shows, the use of executive release measures allowed the system to ride out this storm throughout 2007.

This period in the management of prison capacity illustrates the inherent challenges for senior officials in reacting to ministerial priorities. It also illustrates how changes in the nature of the pressures of the system can shape the range of options available. As outlined above, Charles Clarke had made his speech emphasizing the need for strategic focus on the rehabilitative goals of prison, and had also publicly voiced his reluctance to build new prison capacity in response to increasing population pressures. Officials describe a period for three or four weeks in the run-up to May 2006 when the prison population was rising by 600 a week, and the prospect of demand-side strategic action looked unworkable. During that same month, Charles Clarke was replaced as Home Secretary by John Reid, who brought to office an entirely different view towards rehabilitation and restricting the growth the prison capacity. As one official reflected:

> We were told in no uncertain terms. And to this day, it has been the minister's priority. John Reid sat there and said I don't give a stuff about rehabilitation. You find space to put them in. When push comes to shove, that's where any Home Secretary is. And you can see why.

As the system was moving towards this 'perfect storm', officials described a sense that it would be inevitable that they would have to build new capacity at some point in the near future. Reid managed to secure funding for a further 8,000 prison places as part of the next Treasury spending review.

The research has surfaced many other examples of this programmed need to finesse and work around ministerial priorities. Many officials have been able to identify occasions when they had put the case to a minister for a certain course of action, only to have the minister decide otherwise, often at the last minute or in a way which compromised these officials' own position. As one former official described:

> I remember going into a meeting with one minister having made the suggestion that we should close a particular prison. I had thought that he was in agreement. But half way through the meeting, he told the local politicians present that this prison wouldn't close. At the end, he shrugged his shoulders at me and said, 'I'm sorry, that's politics'. 'Fair enough', I said. 'I'll go away and make that one work.'

Another example involved a Labour minister, who having agreed with officials to market test clusters of prisons, at the eleventh hour and to the complete surprise of senior officials went back on this decision in the meeting with the POA. As one official closely involved suggested,

> Effectively [he] threw it up in the air and decided to look at it all again [...] You don't know what happened. Had the PM said you've got to do a deal with the POA? If he believed he could do a deal, he was sadly delusional. As an official, you don't always see what is going on behind the scenes. It came out of the blue for us.

Many senior officials interviewed have talked generally about the need to think strategically about the system over a much longer term. Indeed, in 2009 NOMS made public for the first time an 'estates strategy' which outlined some kind of long-term plan for prison capacity (Ministry of Justice, 2009). These same senior officials have, however, been sceptical about the viability of such strategizing in uncertain political environments. They have tended to regard development of a comprehensive medium to long-term estates strategy as something which is too difficult to do in a political environment, and therefore something for which responsibility is continually abrogated. One former Prisons Minister put this succinctly:

> If it was a well-run private company, it would have an important unit, there would be strategic planning, what is our market going to be like in five years time, how are we going to serve it, what are the developments and inventions. Lots of private-sector companies get it wrong and go out of business. But at least they know that they will go out of business. The Prison Service knows it will be in business so long as ministers want them to hold people sent by the courts. They feel powerless in that grip. How do you plan with any confidence and depth unless you have the responsibility? You don't do it. You might muse on the subject. And say it might be nice if such-and-such. But you don't do that hard thinking, and come to the conclusion of a policy you are going to stand by [...] if you don't have the responsibility.

Indeed, senior officials have been able to see the merits of trying to reshape and reform the prison system in such a way that it is more able to tackle rehabilitative goals. However, the imperative has also been to make sure that the system remains stable and politically quiet, and is able to absorb and cope with increases in demand. As one official reflected:

> The top management have been hidebound by these pressures. Keep it safe. Keep it stable. Let's not embarrass the ministers. Rather than 'is there a more effective way of doing this? Looking at what it costs the country. This is what I tell you with all my experience and so on'. It feels as though this kind of thing has been on the back burner for some considerable years.

For senior officials, the political constraints on their ability to manage and shape the system therefore appear very real. As the quotations and examples in this section have tried to show, there is a strong element of coping in their role, and in calibrating and adapting their own efforts to the inherent uncertainty and changeability of their predicament at the interface with the political domain. It is easy to see how top officials can feel powerless and unable to really shape their policy domain. It is, however, also easy to see how this can lead to incremental change or doing enough to get through acute crisis situations and see what things are like on the other side. In terms of their professional ethical world-view also, incremental change allows civil servants to rationalize things that they would rather not do into things which are acceptable given the situation.

6.5 Conclusions

We have seen in this chapter the complexities inherent in constrained autonomy of senior officials. In dealing with the pressures of crowding and capacity stress, senior officials have continually had to respond to the managerial challenge of making the system work. In planning and shaping the physical estate, we have seen how officials have found ways of optimizing existing and new capacity, while dealing with inherent political and practical constraints. Similarly, in managing the population, senior officials have sought to find ways of compensating for an 'imperfect estate' by moving prisoners around. Centralized population management has provided 'life support' to the system to allow it to mitigate problems of geographical and functional imbalance in demand and supply.

We have seen how senior officials are constrained by political choices and actions. Indeed, the managerial challenge of running the estate is carried out in an inherently political environment, and this perpetuates a sense of fatalism and a need to maintain as much reactive flexibility in the system as possible. Senior officials interviewed have consistently pointed out that crowding and capacity stress are determined by political choices which are taken above their level by ministers and governments. As one former top official put it:

> From the Treasury's point of view, if you spend in one area, you don't spend somewhere else. And essentially that is a political decision, so eventually they become political decisions; they are fixed between the people who have power. If you have a minister who has power, you do better than one who hasn't. So actually Michael Howard probably had quite a lot of power at one point. Jack Straw in the early days probably had power. Charles Clarke had very little power because he famously did not get on with Gordon Brown. He was never going to have any power with the Treasury. Neither did John Reid. The point is that you need to start analysing the politics, because the politics eventually decides what happens. Not the worthy work of officials.

Despite these political constraints, we have also seen how top officials have been able to have influence, indeed power, vis-à-vis departmental officials and ministers. In increasingly politicized environments, senior officials have benefited from being able to deliver a quiet and secure prison system, as well as one which can demonstrate improving value-for-money and progress against various performance targets. Within this they have been able to create and sustain influence, for example Narey's championing of decency and rehabilitative programmes in prisons, or Wheatley's 'prison-craft' management style at the top of the system which has been a major part in sorting the prison system out over the last fifteen years or so.

It is clear therefore that, over the years, the styles and priorities of top officials have shaped and reflected the particular dynamics of the prison system during that era. A looser and less politicized environment around prisons throughout the 1970s and 1980s may be seen as allowing greater scope for a mix of civil-service and operational cultures in the development of prison policy. As we have seen, however, these years cannot be seen in halcyon terms. The state of prisons and the prison system throughout left much to be desired. Indeed, it was managerialism and focus on operational aspects, which contributed greatly to improving conditions and performance in this respect. Yet, at the same time, the combination of politicization and managerialism has proved effective in winding the system tight during the last two decades, and finding the rationale to do so. This combination has arguably brought the system to a current point where it can sustain systemic crowding and capacity stress while at the same time perform satisfactorily against all or most of its targets.

7
Governors, Staff, and Strategies of Local Adaptation

> Mark Twain said that everybody complains about the weather but nobody does anything about it. Overcrowding is a fact of life. We have no control over it. We literally cannot influence it. Occasionally the DG has said things like 'it's dangerous' or 'we are not able to do our job properly'. We expect them to say those things because that's a way of getting resources. Our job on the shop floor is to get on and look after people we've got as best we can. (Former senior prison governor)

For most prison governors,[1] the idea that they and their staff can be implicated in sustaining crowding and chronic capacity stress (CCS) seems far-fetched. Conventional wisdom says that these are the concerns of 'high politics' and decisions way above their pay grade, and that the predicament of governors and staff is to cope with the stresses incurred and make the system work. Clearly, however, governors and staff form an important part of the prison system. Surprisingly, there are signs that they have been under-researched, despite the fact that their roles embody interesting and complex dilemmas of public management.[2] Governors face challenges of constrained autonomy in much the same way as ministers and senior officials, and their choices and actions are therefore vital components of keeping the prison system as a whole in some kind of manageable and acceptable equilibrium. As Bryans (2007) writes:

> There will always be a tension that exists between control from above in the form of rules, regulations, and directives, and the governor's autonomy, and the need for flexibility and personal influence in managing prisons, because of the very nature of penal institutions. (p. 181)

It would therefore seem necessary to at least entertain the idea that governors and staff would impact on the overall characteristic of CCS. If these conditions are, as I argue, symptoms of a whole-governance system, then we must at least attempt to understand how their choices and actions fit into this whole system.

This chapter therefore looks at constrained autonomy for governors. The first section discusses some of the wider perceptions of governors on crowding and CCS. In the second section, attention turns to the constraints from above on governors, in relation to increasingly managerialized and centralized coordination of the prison system. The third section examines the extent to which governors have had autonomy to shape their institutions, and barriers which they encounter in attempting to maximize existing capacity in their prisons.

7.1 Managing prisoners, cost savings, and renewing physical assets

It is not surprising that when prison governors, especially the more experienced kind, look at today's prisons they see a much improved system relative to the late 1970s and 1980s. Many governors reflected on the inadequacies in the system throughout these decades, what they saw as indecent and brutal conditions, dysfunctional regimes, lack of respect, and widespread rent-seeking behaviour by prison staff and management. As one governor reflected:

> What I would say to complaining governors is look me in the eye and say that the experience for a prisoner now is worse than it was in 1979. I can remember Manchester in 1983, the smell of excrement and urine at slop out, the abysmal food that we served, the relationship between staff and prisoners where every second word was 'fuck', prisoners weren't treated with respect, they weren't treated with decency, visitors were treated as if they were prisoners as well, the place was run for the benefit of staff earning massive amounts of overtime at fantastic cost, where racism and brutality was rife.

Another governor reflected on the morning regime (or lack of it) in a large urban local circa 1984.

> Each landing was called for breakfast. About 1,800 people going for breakfast. Everyone was locked up again. All that took place between 7 and 7.45. At 7.45 staff would go for breakfast and come back around

> 9. The 7.45 people would clear the yards, as people would throw pots full of shit out of the window. Often as a new person, you would get that job [...] the 'shit party'. Come 9, the rest of the staff would sit in tea rooms. Because there was no regime. Prisoners were gainfully employed making rolls or cups of tea for staff who used to sit in these areas playing cards or reading newspapers.

The qualitative shifts in how governors see crowding and capacity stress have been complex and, in some senses, paradoxical. For a start, the process of normalization of crowding has been strong over the years. Despite seeing the system as improved in many ways, governors also commonly reflected on this ever-present nature of the problem and an inherent tendency to normalize it and get on with things despite it. One governor reflected:

> We found the staff induction booklet from 1973 [...] I could have written it today [...] the governor back then talked about overcrowding being deeply unhelpful and the biggest problem he was facing. God knows how old you have to be to remember this prison as being not overcrowded. It's just the norm.

Governors, in fact, remarked that crowding appears so much the norm that it is not something a prison notices until it is not there or has been reduced. As one experienced governor pointed out, 'when it's *not* there [...] that's when you notice the difference. The last couple of months we've had spare capacity here, and it's been so much more relaxed'. Yet some governors also mentioned, perhaps ironically, that having slack in the prison also focused their mind on 'what the hell all these staff were actually doing every day anyway'.

Although governors have been inclined to see the benefits of being less crowded than usual, they have also pointed out that there are benefits to running at close to maximum levels (i.e. close to Op Cap). As a group of deputy governors in a focus group agreed, 'happiness is being full [...] because you know what you've got and what you have to do'. For governors in local prisons on the 'overcrowding draft' circuit, as it were, the worry was that in running with spare capacity, there was a danger that the prison would be destabilized by having to take overcrowding drafts at short notice. Paradoxically, therefore, governors saw the value of running at close to capacity, yet at the same time recognized the problem of crowding as a major constraint. This very much echoes themes discussed already in Chapter 4.

Starting with the issue of population management, we have seen that the national prison system relies heavily on continual movement of prisoners. Some local prisons tend to be more susceptible than others to this continual 'churn'. Figures 7.1 and 7.2 give an indication of the rate of movement through one of the largest local prisons, Birmingham. Figure 7.1 shows six main flows of prisoners in and out of a large local prison. Figure 7.2 shows the daily mean number of prisoner movements in and out of the prison in each of the processes outlined in Figure 7.1. For 2008, the average Op Cap of Birmingham prison was 1,450 prisoners. On a daily basis, reception staff at Birmingham processed on average around 35 prisoners out to court each morning, and around 28 prisoners back from court in the evening. (These are not necessarily the same prisoners given that some prisoners leaving Birmingham prison in the morning may return to another prison in the evening, or some prisoners from other local prisons or remand centres may be redirected back to Birmingham after court.) Generally speaking, around four-fifths of those who leave for court in the morning return to the prison in the evening.

The final bar in Figure 7.2 shows that Birmingham rarely went above its operational capacity during 2008, on exceptional occasions using its segregation unit and healthcare facilities to accommodate surplus demand for places. On average, the prison remained at around ten places less than its operational capacity – equivalent to running at 99.3 per cent of capacity! One current local prison governor explained

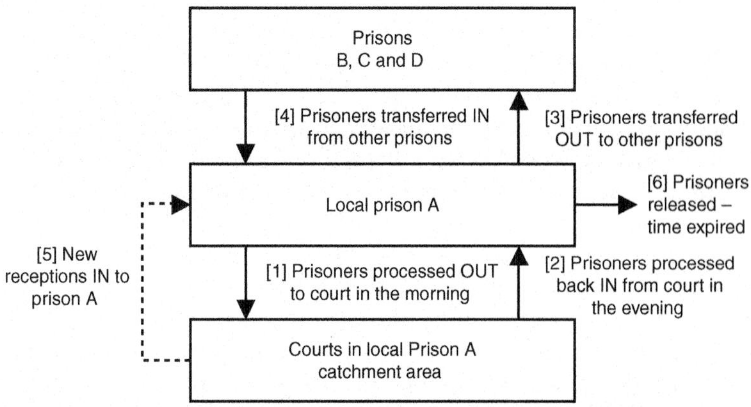

Figure 7.1 Flow of prisoners processed in and out of a local prison

Source: My own analysis of data provided by staff at Birmingham prison. Data covers weekdays only.

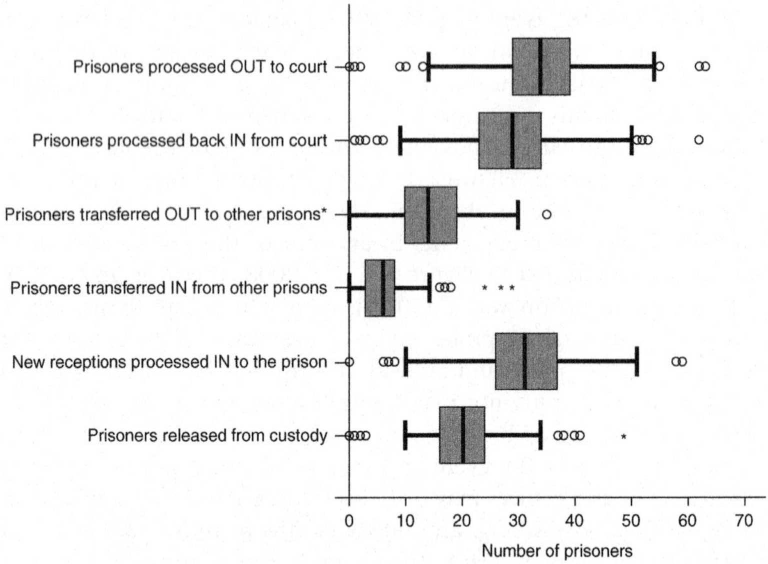

Figure 7.2 Box plots showing average daily movement of prisoners processed in and out of Birmingham prison, from January to December 2008

Source: My own analysis of data provided by staff at Birmingham prison. Data covers weekdays only.

the daily logistical challenges of having to operate at levels so close to tolerance.

> It does start to get more fraught when you are right at the top of the numbers. Because you are constantly trying to find spaces, put those people from similar religious, cultural backgrounds together. Smokers with smokers. Language with language. That's when it gets much trickier, when there's no space to manoeuvre. It's like one of those puzzles when you have to move the pieces around.

Many governors talked of the difficulties and stresses involved in identifying prisoners to go on drafts, and the soft (and at times less soft) skills required to get resistant prisoners to walk onto the bus under their own steam (a requirement of escort contractors). As one governor explained: 'It becomes part of life as a local prison. You develop mechanisms for coping with them, making them as comfortable as you can, and getting shot of them as quickly as possible.' As another reflected: 'One of the things we are depressingly good at is conditioning prisoners.

To say in the morning, you are going on a bus to the Isle of Wight [...] and nine times out of ten they do.' And as a former experienced official from the Inspectorate explained:

> That became part of being a governor. You don't want to do it. You don't like it. Other prisons would have it done to them. But you knew that you had to get shot of ten because you had ten coming in the door. The consequences of that for the way governors then thought about individual prisoners [...] they did become those pieces on the board that you had to move around just because that was what you had to do.

Looking for cost-efficiencies in the way prisons are run has long been an important part of governors' preoccupations – more so as managerialism has evolved. As one former governor and area manager in the mid-to-late 1990s put it: 'Three per cent was the mantra back then. You would be going round prisons saying, 'do I sniff waste here?' I was thinking like that. No doubt other governors were thinking like that too.' Current governors have talked about continued emphasis on this imperative for them to take costs out of their operations in the region of 4 to 5 per cent, and more recently 5 to 7 per cent. Governors generally manage to make savings of this kind, although often with some difficulty and systematic streamlining of staff working profiles. Nevertheless, governors were nervous about increasingly tough savings requirements from 2009 onwards as financial constraints tighten.

In most large local prisons, staff costs account for somewhere in the region of 80 per cent of the total budget. The potential for governors to find between 5 and 7 per cent savings year-on-year relies heavily on governors being able reduce staff numbers, and because of the difficulties in reducing head-count, governors have to rely on staff attrition or early retirement and not refilling these empty posts. As one current local prison governor put it: 'They are saying that you have to reduce the number of managers to show efficiency savings. They have told me that over the next five years, I need to make a saving of £330k. But we'll take it off you this year. How can I make a saving of £330k in one year? I can't do it unless I don't refill vacancies.' Another governor explained: 'In 2008, we got rid of seventeen staff from the books. Attrition, retirement, redundancy. I'm now running short of prison officers, knowing full well that I'll make efficiencies in the future when I don't refill them. The bit I'm running short on will help me reach that target.'

Another important dimension for governors concerns the physical condition of the prison estate, and the availability of capital funds to develop premises, or even do basic repairs to vital facilities. Most governors were realistic about financial pressures on capital investment, and could recognize a general problem of capital-thinning as one facing many other public-sector areas. Nevertheless, governors expressed worry about the difficulties in getting even most basic jobs cleared and funded. As one governor explained: 'There is a huge problem with the maintenance budget. I feel sorry for the works team. We are just not properly resourced, capital-wise, maintenance-wise, or staff-wise. It's a huge amount of work just to maintain the prison.' Some were sceptical about the risks of storing up obsolescence for the future. As one experienced governor of a Victorian local prison explained: 'We are banking up problems for tomorrow on the maintenance budget. If you don't maintain planned maintenance and replace assets at the correct time, if all you ever do is wait for things to break down, then you sow a recipe for disaster.'

Such pessimism may be exaggerated. In my visits to twenty-nine prisons, some governors were able to show me brand new modern facilities. Nevertheless, most governors were able to show me at least some fundamental issues with repairs pending such as severe damp, deteriorating plasterwork, roof leaks, and general obsolescence in basic facilities. A former area manager told me about these general repair problems:

> the message for years has been that there is no money to refurbish or repair. Unless it is absolutely crucial, to fix the roof or make somewhere safe from fire, the message has been 'don't commit the money'. I would get a chunk of money as area manager, and ask governors for their top five must-dos. The 'nice-to-dos' would never get a look in.

7.2 How governors are constrained by managers

Managerialist change has impacted on the role and functions of governors over the years. In his work on prison governors, Bryans (2007) distinguishes between broad four types: chief officers, general managers, liberal idealists, and conforming mavericks (p. 159). He identifies some 'clear trends' in the balance between these four types:

> General managers are increasingly replacing liberal idealists, as the work takes on an increasingly managerial flavour. Conforming

> mavericks are disappearing as diversity, variation and the governor's ability to shape the prison regime is being curtailed. The number of chief officers is growing as the Service comes to value people who will ensure compliance with orders and instructions. (p. 163)

He writes further that

> governors are now expected to be competent and professional managers who plan and deliver a public service within a set budget and to laid-down standards. They are expected not to be insubordinate, free-thinking, or openly challenge the current approach to prison management. (p. 169)

Greater standardization and oversight of governors grew out of findings from the 1979 May inquiry, and moves towards more systemic management throughout the 1980s. A 1984 Prison Department circular instruction (PD, 1984) set out a managerial framework for governors and their relationship to the centre, and from 1991, largely in response to the 1991 Lygo report (PD, 1991), an area-management structure was introduced for more integrated centralized line management. We have already seen in Chapter 3 how the intensification of performance targets also characterized the system throughout the 1990s and 2000s. In all of this, the role of governor was undoubtedly reined in, and made subject to much greater standardization and oversight. So much so that, by the end of the 2000s, governors commonly equated their roles to that of a store or franchise manager – supporting Bryans's general argument above. Whether this is seen as positive or negative development has usually depended on the world-view of the governor. Some governors interviewed have looked on this change positively, as part of an inevitable move towards creating a more consistent and cost-efficient prison system. Others have been more inclined to be pessimistic about the constraints on them as 'governing' governors.

Managerialist change, particularly from the late 1990s onwards, has also meant that large expenditure items have centralized as headquarters searches for economies of scale, and more consistent and effective services. Contracting for core services and facilities has been a major aspect of this change, from information technology and facilities management, through to prisoner-focused services. Hence governors have seen their capacity for direct control reduced as it has moved upwards to headquarters. This, by definition, has reduced the scope of governors to impact directly on the actual rehabilitative performance of their prisons. As a former Inspectorate official points out:

> If you think over the last ten years, governors are now responsible for things that they can't directly control. They are responsible for healthcare but they don't pay for it, and there is a separate system of governance and management by the Primary Care Trusts. They are responsible for education, but there is a separate system of funding and governance via colleges and what they are learning in skills councils. They are required to meet various accommodation targets and employment targets. They can't do that. They rely upon local authorities and the voluntary sector to deliver all of that. Increasingly they are sitting on top of a system but they don't have the levers in their office. The levers are in somebody else's office. And they have to work with that.

We have seen too how centralized control of the prison population can have disruptive effects on the governors' ability to target these rehabilitative services. Governors remarked on the power of population management, particularly in their ability to dictate transfer of short-sentence prisoners through drafts. Population Management's influence has been felt by governors during times of acute capacity shortage, and they have frequently referred to cases in which their own plans or initiatives had been scuppered as a result of 'Pop Man' interventions. Overcrowding drafts have been a disruptive factor which governors have confessed to be able to do very little about. One local governor described the impact on his establishment's own aspirations for dealing in the short term with prisoners' basic needs:

> What you lose are the softer outcomes, things that you would really like to deliver as a governor. We have a number of prisoners who we would be putting through courses, advanced thinking skills, drug rehab, and then we would be told that there is a bus scheduled with space for twenty prisoners who need to be moved out to make room for another twenty prisoners coming in from court. You get Pop Man on the phone and say hold on a minute... these people will benefit on a personal level. They are likely to be free from drugs by the time they get out. 'Don't care' [...] is the answer.

The most sceptical governors said that they 'could not remember the last time they won an argument with Pop Man', and that 'challenging the supremacy of Pop Man might be considered heresy'. Others would talk about how they tend to delegate these conversations to their allocations units, as one put it, 'because I just end up losing my temper'. Despite a healthy level of resignation to the dominance of Pop Man in times of capacity shortage, governors recognized that working constructively with Pop Man often led to mutually beneficial compromise. One former local prison governor talked about his own initiative to transform a wing of the prison into a training wing for prisoners from the region, on the grounds that this would help to keep prisoners 'close to home',[3] and allow the prison to work more constructively with local agencies to prepare these prisoners for release. Of Pop Man's initial scepticism to this plan, the governor said:

> Pop Man have their own agenda and their own life, and they didn't like me deciding what kind of population I was going to take in the new wing. My argument was that I'm not taking places away from the system as I'm freeing up training places that would have been filled in other prisons. Anyway, after a lot of argy-bargy, we managed to get that in.

Interviews surfaced a strong element of convention-following, particularly in the way in which governors 'finesse' the impact of population movement on their own prison and staff. Many governors could point to occasions in their careers when they had been faced with a van load of prisoners outside the gate after 'lock out', and a request from Pop Man to open reception and accommodate the prisoners. Governors would talk about a well-established routine of going through the motions of being seen to resist, and then agreeing to accommodate those prisoners.

> During Safeguard,[4] there was a pressure as duty governor to say I'm not going to accept these prisoners. So you'd go through the motions of saying to [the escort contractor], I'm refusing to accept these prisoners. They get in touch with the area manager, and then you get a call from him saying 'you will accept those prisoners'. So you go back to the staff, and say 'I did my best, but we've got to accept them'. You would do that to satisfy the staff. That would become the norm. It would be expected that you would stay on with those staff to process those prisoners. When it came to it, they would still go through the process as with every other.

Area managers have confirmed this almost standard expectation that prisoners would (and should) be ordered into prisons in order to avoid having to use police cells or other options. As we have seen in Chapter 4, governors and area managers are frequently insistent that they would not sanction crowding above the Op Cap (at least for any longer than one night). As one former area manager put it:

> When things got very difficult in the last few years, I would get calls from Pop Man asking me to agree to take prisoners into segregations units in London prisons. I remember pushing back on that because it was not right. It was a moral imperative.

The inclination amongst governors to be seen to be coping has been an important part of this relationship for many decades. Governors talked about this professional ethos to 'get on with the job', 'make things work', 'realize that we are not in an ideal world', and 'take a pragmatic approach'. By their own admission, at times there is a fine line between resistant and coping responses, and this can be seen as a professional weakness as much as it is a professional strength. One former female governor explained the predicament (with characteristic Prison Service humour) that many governors would face in dealing with excessive numbers:

> I would be thinking what can I do to mitigate this? I would never think, what can I do to get fifty prisoners out? I would be thinking, where can I put them? If rang up HQ saying things were a bit tense and I wanted to move say twenty prisoners on somewhere else, they would say [...] Where love? In your spare room? So you would never ask for help in that way.

There are contributing factors which feed into this widely held perception that governors take a large risk in resisting instructions from above. One important factor is the culture which has underpinned the way in which governors have been promoted over the years. Typically they serve on average somewhere between eighteen and twenty months in any one institution, before they are moved on to other establishments. Turnover of governors is therefore seen as relatively high, and appointment of governors is decided at the discretion of area managers and top officials. In this sense, the system is susceptible to the vagaries of personal relationships between officials and governors. As one highly experienced observer put it:

> It is very personal, the Prison Service. It's small enough to be personal. There's only 139 governing governors. So-and-so is a good person.

> So-and-so is struggling. It's a small cadre of people. It used to be distinguished by your ability to hold your drink at the Prison Service conference without falling over and ideally without hitting anybody. It's a bit like police. They work shifts. They spend a lot time with each other. They work in a closed environment. Not a popular job. It has all those characteristics of support, and knowing a bit too much about each other.

The structure of promotion tends to mean that good governors get moved around frequently, and many governors suggest that a 'prison-hopping' approach (i.e. taking opportunities when they arise) has tended to be the standard way to move on upwards. A general rule of thumb for most governors involves dealing with the effects of an 'eighteen-month syndrome', whereby the first six months are usually spent learning the establishment and dealing with the legacy of the previous governor, the next six months are spent trying to articulate a new vision for the prison, and the final six months are spent dealing with a staff group who begin to anticipate the governor leaving for another prison. Many governors acknowledged this syndrome. One suggested: 'You probably need to keep governors in post either to gain the benefits or feel the pain of their decisions. It's been a bit too easy to hit and run over the years.' Others pointed out that resistance amongst the staff group would also often be based on the expectation that the governor would be gone within eighteen months, and would be replaced with another most likely with different approaches and priorities. As one governor put it: 'The staff can play a waiting game, and they know that they have a good chance of winning.'

Governors talked about the culture of expectation that they are able to take new postings often with very short periods of notice. This has linked closely to the practice of moving governors for crisis-management purposes, where tried-and-trusted governors, who have developed reputations for turning round 'failing prisons', are brought in under emergency measures. This reflects again a commonly recognized culture of coping and crisis management over the years. Reaffirmation of certain governors as 'fire-fighters', 'fixers', or 'consolidators', for example, feeds into the continuation of this culture, and sustains a perception that this kind of crisis-management culture is part of the fabric which holds the system together. But as highlighted in the previous chapter, such 'bossist' culture is as much constructed by the managers and willing governors, as it is inherent in the system. One current local governor reflected on the difficulties of saying no to short-notice requests from senior officials:

> My first move from [Cat A prison] to [YOI *X*] was two days notice. I was rung at home on a Friday, and asked what I was doing next week? I thought he was planning to cancel my leave. He said I want you to turn up at [YO institution *X*]. You take it as a pat on the back that you are being asked to go into a dodgy jail to fix it. When I was at [YOI *Y*], to be asked to go to [local prison *Z*] was quite a compliment. I'm not sure what would have happened if the answer had been 'no'. I'm just not sure. I hadn't tested the waters. That is the culture we live in.

Many governors, however, recognize their ultimate position as civil servants, and part of the line of responsibility, or chain of command, up to ministers. As the system is organized, this is seen as the responsibility and obligation of their position. As one put it, 'we are civil servants; we are here to do what the government wants'. Other governors have been less inclined to see this as an important factor, and argue that contentious issues will actually be hammered out in discussion between governors and their senior officials, and that in reality the culture is less fatalistic than the analysis above suggests. As one current senior NOMS official and former governor put it: 'I don't accept this idea that governors are pawns who are terrified to say no. Governors tend to be quite strong characters on the whole, and they can be quite vociferous when it suits them.'

This leads to an important point over the years about the collective professional status of governors, and the extent to which they have been able to influence up the line for increased resources and constrain the negative impact of capacity stress. Governors interviewed have tended to agree that, as a collective professional group, they had been somewhat beleaguered over the years. Some suggested that the professional cadre struggled collectively to articulate pressures of crowding and resource stress up the line, and as stress has reached acute levels during recent years, there is a perception that 'the centre is less keen to listen to us than they were. There seems to be a feeling in the centre that we are negative, obstructive, and difficult'.

Anecdotal accounts from governors interviewed reflect a collective reluctance to question the judgement of senior management. Numerous recollections of Prison Service conferences depict a muted collective voice of governors from the floor, an observation picked up by many governors and chief probation officers during NOMS conferences in recent years. As one current prison governor reflected: 'I remember on a number of occasions at conference, governors being slapped down for being critical in public. Anyone else offering criticism looked at the floor. We sit there and say nothing now. That's the way it is.' This is reflected in the stringent restrictions on prison governors speaking to the press on 'national issues' relating to the prison system:

> The reality is that if you are going to trust us to run prisons, million-pound organizations, then you need to trust to talk to the press. Fleet St media will tell you that prisons always make the best stories. So it is politically very sensitive. We understand that. But a way of dealing with that is not tell us all we can't speak to them.

Over the years there has also been a level of distrust amongst governors about the extent to which senior management will support them in making potentially risky decisions. For example, many governors talked about the risks involved in deciding whether to release borderline case prisoners on Home Detention Curfew (HDC).[5] One governor conveyed the sense of uncertainty about likely support from politicians and top officials:

> When they introduced HDC, the prediction was that it would take 3,000 off the population. After it had been going a few months, it was realised that it was only taking 1,000 off the prison population, and they were concerned. David Blunkett held a reception for governors at Lancaster House. For free reception and warm talk. He said he understood the reticence towards using HDC, but he could assure people that they would be 100 per cent backed if day release led to an incident, as long as they had gone through all the process, qualifications, and judgements. There was an audible laugh in the room.

Signs of organized presence and political lobbying by governors have been visible since the late 1970s (SCPS, 1978; BAPG, 1979). Governors began to organize through the Prison and Borstal Governors Branch of the Society of Civil and Public Servants, and this developed through the 1980s into the formation of the Prison Governors Association (PGA) in 1987. Interviews surfaced a strong degree of scepticism about the effectiveness of the PGA, particularly in more recent years, to organize and articulate the collective professional views of governors. The development of the PGA as a visible and professionally accepted body has, in

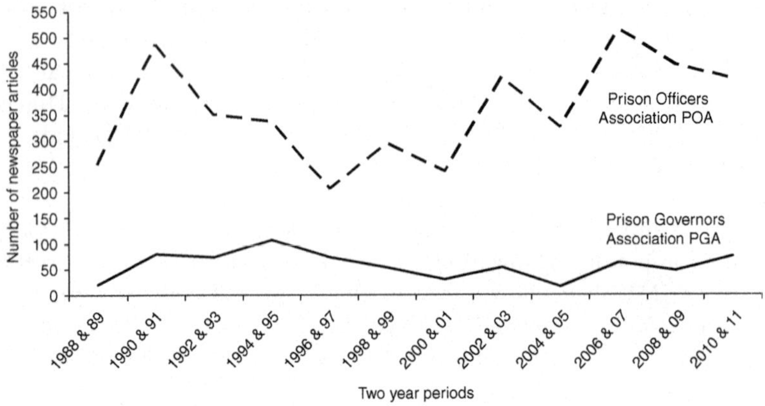

Figure 7.3 Numbers of mentions of Prisoner Officers Association (POA) and Prison Governors Association (PGA) in national newspapers

Note: References to 'Prison Governors Association' and 'Prison Officers Association' were searched in the following national newspapers and where applicable their Sunday versions: *The Business, Daily Mail, Daily Star, Daily Telegraph, Express, Guardian, Independent, Mirror, Morning Star, News of the World, People, Sun* and *The Times*.

Source: My own analysis of data from Nexis UK national newspaper database.

the minds of the great majority of governors interviewed, been weak. Governors generally agreed that it has suffered from little or no visibility, and press searches over the years confirm that the PGA has a consistently lower media profile than the Prison Officers' Association (POA) (Figure 7.3).

For many governors, the PGA has increasingly fulfilled the role of a union organization rather than something more akin to a professional association or Royal College. This had led to high degree of opt-out amongst senior governors, and many confessed to not attending PGA conferences and if possible 'sending a more junior governor'. As one experienced governor explained:

> The PGA, when it was first formed, it was run by senior people of some reputation who spoke with authority on professional matters [...] over time the PGA drifted much more to being more trade union and professional issues, and the calibre of people representing governors began to decline.

As one former top prison official put it, 'if governors were able to produce a professional association that was on a par with ACPO [Association of Chief Police Officers] for example, that would be a good thing. As a founder member of the PGA, I don't think it has ever realised its potential'.

7.3 Autonomy of governors to influence capacity in their prisons

For many governors, managerialism is associated with excessive constraint on their professional autonomy and discretion. The discussion in the previous section has helped to shed light on why this might be so. Linked to this is also a tendency amongst some governors to imply a bygone era of free-thinking and independent governors who had autonomy to run their prisons by their own design. It is peculiar that some look back upon this unchecked era throughout the 1960s and 1970s as something approaching 'halcyon days' for governing. Many others, however, perceive no such thing. As one put it:

> What may be seen as halcyon days of the governor would have been more related to the fact that there was no central superstructure. Some of the 'legendary' governors were quite dreadful in fact. There were questions about whether their behaviour would have been acceptable by today's standards.

Another former top official said as much:

> The days when idiosyncratic governors produced failing prisons were inexcusable. It isn't something most people want to go back to. I've seen the quality of governing improve during that period because governors have been freer to manage. There's been a lot more freedom for governors than I ever had. You see some really class governors and not much weak governing.

Managerialism, it seems, far from constraining governors, has also gone a long way to giving governors new kinds of autonomy. Indeed, New Public Management (NPM) principles should in theory have allowed governors more scope to shape and develop their prisons. As one former senior governor reflected:

> When I joined the Prison Service in the mid-70s, governors didn't have a budget. You sort of just ran your prison. You did what you could with overtime, you tried to stop escapes, but accepted the fact that prisoners might escape. It was the sort of ethos based on the public school system.

Managerialism allowed governors to become managers of their own budgets, shape the corporate and operational practices of their organizations, create structure and culture in which their staff can improve and develop, and so on.

> There can be very few jobs in the public sector where you still have so much freedom effectively to determine the character of what you are managing. There are reams of performance standards and targets, and everything else, but in practice there's a lot of scope to impose your personality and will on what is a multi-million pound organization.

Practically all governors interviewed articulated plans or visions about how they would like to see their prison develop during their term. As one governor reflected: 'You've got desires about how you want your own organization to grow, against the practicalities of maximizing available operational capacity. These are natural organization tensions, and I'm sure you'd get them in any commercial organization.' A strong tendency amongst governors, for example, has been to shape the type of prison population held in their establishments. Governors generally acknowledged a tendency to want to use population shaping in strategic ways in their prisons. They would commonly seek to stabilize the culture and attract funding by developing specialist or 'niche' functions. As one put it:

> I'm a Cat C prison which doesn't do many things very well. Being a Foreign National Prisoner centre would be useful. Doing something with X and Y wing with my sex offenders would also be useful. I need a niche in the market.

Another local governor however provided a more pessimistic interpretation of this shaping activity:

> There are very few public-sector organizations where I could have the sort of creativity that I have here now. But governors have to accept that we are part of a new changing financial landscape. And it's their own fault because they have just spent money willy-nilly on their own 'pet projects', which haven't made any sense to anybody [...] ever. For example, I've got this unit for elderly lifers. Why have I got that? I'm a local prison serving the courts. Because some governor has said, 'Oh I'll have that money, I'll do that for you'. But it's a pointless waste of resource.

New capacity put into existing prisons have come with new facilities which can be made available across the whole prison and, as many governors have argued, have considerably improved the overall quality of life and access for prisoners (and staff). As one governor explained, the caveat for providing new accommodation was that

> a lot more should be done in terms of broader service provision for the prison. A new multi-activity centre was built, reception was extended, a new kitchen. It had to be a package, it couldn't just be an accommodation unit on its own. That was successfully bid for and provided as part of the project.

In the final few pages, I turn attention to governors' ability to maximize latent capacity within their prisons. We have already seen in the previous two chapters how ministers and senior officials have by necessity focused on operational aspects of the system perhaps to the detriment of more strategic leadership and planning. We see similar characteristics in the role of governor. In many governors, for example, a chief executive leadership style is visible, and these governors seem less inclined to get directly involved in the operational minutiae of their establishments. For many governors, however, a major barrier to maximizing capacity in their prisons has been the inherent difficulties in being able to behave like chief executives. This has various aspects to it. For decades, prison cultures have exhibited paternalistic relations between staff and governors. These have tended to perpetuate excessive expectation that the top official in the organization is visible, accessible, and is the final arbiter on issues of contention. As one put it:

> We have had a very paternalistic culture over the decades, particularly with officers living on site and so on. The governor has always been seen as lord of the manor, a powerful and important individual, and some governors, myself included, say 'my door is open, come whenever you want'.

Although conventions of 'regularly walking the landings' and 'having an open office door' are widely seen as important aspects of being a good governor, those less inured in the world of prison culture, particularly those who had come from other professional backgrounds and had been exposed to other professional cultures, tended to view this kind of paternalism as something peculiar to the prison system, and for that matter, not a particularly effective way to run a large modern organization, even if it is a prison. One female governor with experience of public-sector leadership outside the world of the prison system summed this up most eloquently:

> My preferred style of management is more the leadership stuff. That I should not be involved in the day-to-day. That I should be strategically placed. Culturally it's very difficult, because there is still very much an expectation for me to be 'mother', almost. It only happened today. People come up with incredible minutiae. I do find it quite difficult. Staff do feel it is their right. It is like me saying to Phil Wheatley, 'Phil, can I have a minute?' For most people, it's like 'I haven't seen the governor in a month'. Well, so what? If I see Phil Wheatley once a year, I think, there's a result. In most organizations, you wouldn't expect to see the Chief Exec once or twice a month.

The development of the 'chief executive' governor role also partly depends on the extent to which the working structures and practices allow delegation of tasks and problem-solving to take place. Paternalistic cultures have tended to push problems and the search for their solutions back upwards, perpetuating the involvement of senior managers in these apparent minutiae of prison business. Many governors spoke glowingly of their management teams. However, many recognized this syndrome of 'problems coming back up' as staff tend to look up the hierarchy for assurance, accountability, and triggers for action. The quotation below from an experienced local governor illustrates one of the more extreme characterizations of this generally recognizable syndrome:

> Delegation really has to be shoved down their throats. It means holding them by the lapels, saying look at me, open your eyes, I'm talking. It's not that delegation comes back up, it's that you never delegated it in the first place. Often people have got to really senior levels with transactional attributes rather than leadership attributes. They have been on the same journey after all. You can get on quite satisfactorily providing you don't want to make cultural change.

Many governors also talked of the challenges they faced in attempting to improve staff cultures and working practices. Prison staff will tend to work in the same prison for many years, and the tendency for entrenched mind-sets and practices is considerable. Small yet intractable groups of dominant staff were often cited by governors as having what was commonly described as 'corrosive' and 'undermining' influence on the staff group as a whole. As one governor described it, 'they were taking advantage, so you never quite knew who was off sick, who was doing what, and managers were not controlling that'. For many governors, there were aspects of the staff culture in the mid-2000s in large urban local prisons that were reminiscent of bygone decades.

> [Large London local prison] in 2006 was equivalent to the British car industry in the 1970s. If individual employees are allowed to get away with not working hard, and are allowed to operate under poor working practices and are not well managed, they will take advantage. When that is systematically withdrawn from them, it is genuinely quite difficult.

Governors frequently talked about breaking down these dominant cliques as an important part of getting staff motivation on a positive upward cycle. They emphasized the importance of being seen to do this collectively as a whole-staff group, commonly describing the process in terms of 'a journey for us all' and recognizing that in many cases, 'you have go backwards to go forwards, but once we started going forward, we leapt forward quite significantly'. This linked to another common observation by governors that dominant corrosive cultures tended to normalize a kind of de-motivated and unquestioning culture amongst potentially talented and engaged staff. Governors pointed out that once the corrosive influences are neutralized, culture and working practices can be transformed onto a positive footing, and latent capacity can be released. As one governor reflected:

> What was interesting for me as a manager was the classic situation of people thinking they were happy but not realizing quite how unhappy they were. They thought that the position they were in was great, because they could get away with all sorts. The truth of that is that you slightly scratch the surface and what you found was high levels of stress and genuine absence. When you fix the corrosive stuff, people admit to being much happier.

In these observations from governors, we see a similar kind of syndrome to the one described in the Brixton reception vignette in the opening pages of this book. On the one hand, prisons appear to be working at close-to-tolerance capacity and having to find cost savings, yet at the same time, governors frequently acknowledge considerable obsolescence or dysfunction in the way capacity is currently deployed. In this sense, capacity stress can be seen as much a problem of dysfunction in the system as it is one of overload. In this sense, it seems characteristic of the prison system that it is able to conceal considerable amounts of latent capacity, which from time to time, can be activated and unleashed. As the next chapter discusses, this may explain partly why public-sector prisons have been able to respond so apparently effectively to market testing and performance-improvement measures.

As the next chapter will also show, for more ardent managerialist governors, particularly those who have been subject to private-sector commercial cultures, crowding and capacity stress become issues which can be neutralized or fully mitigated through improvements in management and governance in the prison. One current public-sector governor characterized this general view:

> Better organization allows you to be able to cope with and manage better serious operational problems [...] If you have that as the basis of systems, you are more able to cope with the personal issues that come out of things like crowding. You can give people confidence. If we can make that systematic you can have as much overcrowding as you want actually, and cope with it even better.

Such optimism about the ability of better management to neutralize the detrimental effects of CCS may be all very well, but the picture provided by governors in this chapter is more complex and nuanced. In a managerialist world, governors clearly have had autonomy to shape and influence their prisons, and many of those I have spoken to for this research have illustrated exactly this. The influence of a governor to change a prison cannot be underestimated and, in this sense, a lot of the myth-making around governors as 'fixers' or 'consolidators' must be taken at face value.

7.4 Conclusions

It is in the role of prison governor that we have seen perhaps the most interesting and paradoxical dynamics of constrained autonomy so far. In their position as top boss of their prison, as it were, they appear to embody considerable influence and status in relation to their staff and prisoners. Even the term 'governing governor' implies a kind of accentuated position of power, but also one that seems eccentric and anachronistic in a modern managerialist era. The fact that the governor must be seen as a 'governing' governor indeed implies a sense of redundant terminology – after all what else would a governor do but govern? This is perhaps just another example of a deeply entrenched cultural artefact of the system, much like CNA, something that embodies complex and countervailing dynamics. It is paradoxical, for example, that the position of governing governor of the prison should carry so much reverence amongst staff working in the prison, yet we have seen how the collective status of governing governors as a professional group is beleaguered to say the least.

It is clearly the case that governors have considerable autonomy to come in and change the tone and the culture of their prisons, much like in fact ministers have the scope to enter office and set the tone and the priorities of policy. Yet we have also seen in many different ways how these same governors are also constrained by the forces and realities of the system in which and with which they must work. Facing upwards, they have been beholden to ever-increasing line-management discipline and pressure to act as good civil servants and toe the line. It is remarkable, for example, that these top managers of multi-million pound institutions are not permitted to speak publicly to the press on issues deemed of national importance. Pragmatically, also, governors have had to play their part in a national prison system that has run consistently at levels of capacity close to 100 per cent, and the continual churn that this has caused particularly through large local prisons has fed into perceptions of coping and limitations about what can be done. Facing downwards, governors are also constrained by the cultures and technologies available to them in their prisons. Once again, they can only do so much to affect their situation in this respect – before that is, they are asked or minded to leave for another prison.

Just as it may be tempting to blame politicians for the problems of the prison system, it may also be tempting to subscribe to the pure fatalistic interpretation that governors are so far removed from the levers of decision-making that they cannot be implicated in any explanation for capacity stress and crowding in prisons. As I have argued, however, politicians may have autonomy to change things but they also are constrained by a great many forces beyond their control. In exactly the same way, but conversely, governors and indeed senior officials face undoubted constraints, yet they also have considerable autonomy collectively to influence the system. They are after all a vital and important part of it.

In some ways, this is just the same argument we used for ministers, but in reverse. The point is in both cases that these groups of actors must find ways of keeping their bit of the system stable and in some kind of manageable equilibrium. Governors may for very good reasons see themselves as powerless to affect characteristics of the system. But at the same time, they are by nature an important part in affecting and sustaining its equilibrium. We return to this systemic view of individual actors in the final chapter. Before I do this, however, I focus attention on one final actor and their own constrained autonomy – the private firms that run prisons on behalf of the state.

8
Privately Contracted Prisons: New Setting, Same Condition

> People in the public sector want to do good things, but the system does not allow them to do it. Whereas people in the private sector want to do good things, and the system supports them and enables them to do it. Everything about the public sector is just lack of trust all the time. If we didn't browbeat you all the time, if I didn't keep telling you all the time, you'd be out doing this and that. You mustn't do this and you mustn't do that. It's a very different way of looking at things in the private sector. (Former public-sector and now private-sector senior official)

The growth of the market for privately managed prisons and prison services is an important part of the story of chronic capacity stress (CCS). Accounting for around 15 per cent of total capacity in 2012, private-sector firms have established themselves as designers, builders, operators, and financiers of new prisons, as well as running other key services such as prisoner escorts and electronic-tagging schemes. The sector has done much to impact capacity. It has been a near-exclusive provider of new prisons since the early 1990s. And it has been used, in theory at least, as a source of leverage and innovation for improving the existing public-sector system. As the concept of constrained autonomy by now would have us suspect, it has partly been allowed to do this, and partly not.

As I will show in this chapter, constrained autonomy applies equally to the private sector. Private firms have a particular type of autonomy. They operate in a different environment, under different rules and cultures, and are able to do things differently, freed from many of the constraints that impact the public prison system. But they have also been part of the national prison system, and have been constrained by it. In the first section, I review briefly the growth and maturation of the private market, and highlight reasons why private-sector firms are constrained as part of a national prison system. Then I examine specifically the central role of the commercial contract in defining and managing the relationship between private operators and the commissioning authority.[1] Finally, I examine how the contract creates room for autonomy in managing capacity issues, and difficulties of replicating this in a public-sector context.

8.1 Constraints on the autonomy of the private sector

Public–private partnerships have been an important part of managerialist change across UK government since the mid-1980s. The prison system has been no exception. From the early 1990s onwards, it has grown what can now be described as a matured and well-established minority market share of privately managed prisons.

Early academic literature on private prisons[2] in the UK reflected intense scepticism (as well as ideological distaste) about the idea of extracting private profit from incarceration (Ryan and Ward, 1989; Matthews, 1989; Stern, 1993). In more recent years, accounts have become more circumspect, less inclined to question the underlying legitimacy of private prisons, and more focused on questions about efficiency, effectiveness, and accountability (James et al., 1997; Harding, 2001; Sachdev, 2008; Shefer and Liebling, 2008). Critics have also argued that the introduction of private prisons and the need for their regulation has also helped to focus regulatory standards across the wider public systems in which the private ones operate (Braithwaite, 2008). Furthermore, critics have examined the potential for therapeutic innovations in private prisons to refocus the values and goals of the system on rehabilitative outcomes (Genders, 2002, 2003). Despite these signs of an ever-stabilizing and legitimated private-sector market, other critics have continued to cast doubt on the moral and economic value of private prisons (Nathan, 2003). Indeed, the efforts of these committed individuals have been valuable in collating and publishing data on private prison markets.[3] This has helped to counteract the frustrating constraints of commercial confidentiality on the ability of the public to scrutinize value for money of these public–private partnerships.

The percentage growth in private-sector market share over the years has been broadly equivalent to the number of private prisons (Figure 8.1 and Table 8.1). 'Three firms, Serco, G4S, and Kalyx, have become established incumbent operators, with the GEO Group relatively newly established

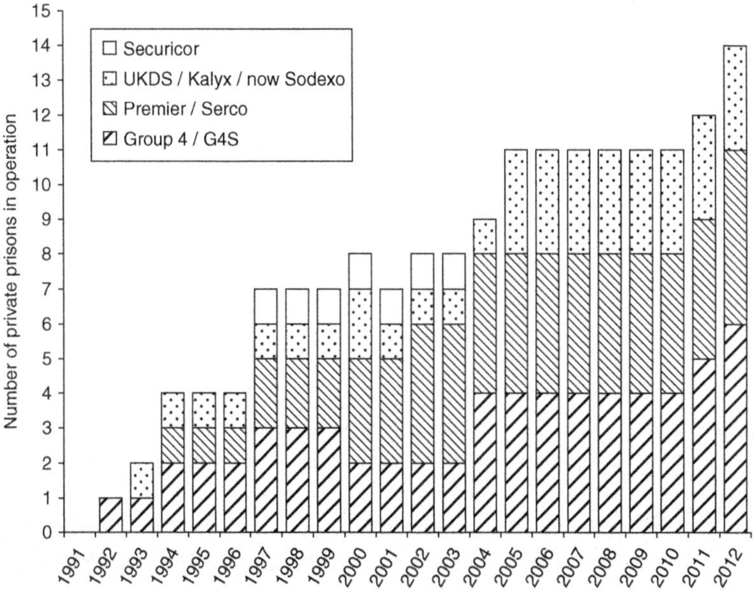

Figure 8.1 Growth in market share for privately contracted prisons

Source: Prison Service annual reports 1993 to 2004, and Ministry of Justice data 2005 to 2012.

as a competitor although currently not operating any prisons in the England and Wales system. Since the mid-1990s, government increased its total expenditure on private prison capacity from around £40 million to more than £350 million, at least a nine-fold increase expressed in terms of 2012 prices, and broadly equivalent to 9 per cent of total net operating costs of the prison system less capital expenditure.

Private prisons are fully integrated into the national prison system. They do not form their own separate system for particular types of prisoners. Any prisoner entering the system could in theory end up in a private prison subject to location and functional requirements of the prisoner. As part of this national system, therefore, private prisons do not have pure autonomy to follow their own interests or strategies. Indeed, as we have seen with other key actors, they are inherently constrained. It is worth outlining some important areas of constraint, which cast doubt upon arguments that the private sector can behave as an unchecked actor, able to extract excessive rents from the system over the years.

The first constraint relates to the basic *commercial and reputational* pressures on the contractors to deliver what government requires.

Table 8.1 Privately contracted prisons, since 1992

Year	Name *(city or county)*	Opened by *(now)*	Type	CNA at open *(Op Cap 2012)*
1992	The Wolds *(E. Yorks)*	Group 4 *(G4S until 2013 –then back to PS)*	Remand	320 *(360)*
1993	Blakenhurst *(Worcs)*	UKDS *(back to PS in 2001)*	Local	650
1994	Buckley Hall *(Lancs)*	Group 4 *(back to PS in 2000)*	Train (C)	350
	Doncaster *(S. Yorks)*	Premier *(now Serco)*	Local	770 *(1150)*
1997	Altcourse *(Liverpool)*	Group 4 *(now G4S)*	Local	600 *(1200)*
	Lowdham Grange *(Notts)*	Premier *(now Serco)*	Train (B)	500 *(920)*
	Parc *(S. Wales)*	Securicor *(now G4S)*	Local	820 *(1480)*
2000	Ashfield *(Bristol)*	Premier *(now Serco)*	YOI	410
	Forest Bank *(Salford)*	UKDS *(now Sodexo)*	Local	800 *(1370)*
2001	Rye Hill *(Warks)*	G4S	Train (B)	600 *(630)*
2002	Dovegate *(Staffs)*	Premier *(now Serco)*	Train (B)	800 *(1140)*
2004	Bronzefield *(Middx)*	Kalyx *(previously UKDS, now Sodexo)*	Local (f)	450 *(530)*
2005	Peterborough *(Cambs)*	Kalyx *(previously UKDS, now Sodexo)*	Local	820 *(1010)*
2011	Birmingham	G4S *(transferred from PS)*	Local	1110 *(1450)*
2012	Thameside	Serco	Local	600 *(900)*
	Oakwood	G4S	Train (C)	680 *(680)*

Notes: *Year* refers to year opened. *Type* refers to the predominant function of the prison at opening. CNA is reported as the full amount although it may have taken more than one year for the prison to reach its full CNA capacity. The consortium UK Detention Services is abbreviated to UKDS. HM Prison Service is abbreviated to PS. Figures for Op Cap at July 2012. Training prisons are abbreviated to 'Train' with security levels B or C in brackets. Bronzefield is a female prison (f).

Critics of the private sector have focused particularly on the risk that private prisons will seek rents and profits, squeeze costs, and cut corners in order to maximize financial returns.[4] Concerns around adequacy of staffing levels in new private prisons over the years, as well as high-profile failure of regimes and order, have tended to add support to such critical accounts.[5] Private-sector officials, however, have acknowledged that although problems of inadequate staffing and control have been exposed over the years, the sector has learnt from this and adapted by adjusting staffing levels upwards. As one official put it:

> After Dovegate and Rye Hill, Bronzefield and Peterborough were much more realistically priced. I don't think anybody again would

> go at the level of pricing that was present at Dovegate and Rye Hill. You also get worried about company reputation.

Indeed, in a commercial environment, reputational factors are seen as important constraints on rent-seeking. Directors[6] emphasized the commercial importance of running good prisons, and furthermore the fact that running good-quality prisons over the long term was commercially more advantageous than attempting to do things to maximize short-term profits. Contracts for private prisons, after all, tend to be long term over twenty-five to thirty years, and this requires a relatively long-term view from contractors. In fact, these officials argued that rent-seeking made little or no commercial sense:

> This is one of the common arguments you hear about the private sector. Everybody sees the private sector as being short-termist, cutting corners to make a profit, and wanting the prison population to go up and up. When actually the opposite is true. You can't do short termism because the minimum contract is twenty-five years. So you've got to win the contract when it comes up for renewal. You can't cut corners because, for a start, you are under about three times the level of scrutiny compared to public-sector governors. And what they don't realise is that if you cut corners you are not going to be operationally successful. And if you are not operationally successful you are not going to be commercially successful. You get penalized to hell on the contract so all your profit will go on fines. Your reputation will be crap and you'll never get another contract. So to be commercially successful as a company, you've actually got to be one of the best performing prisons.

A second important constraint on the private sector is the *professional-ethical* one, in the sense that a great many of their senior personnel have transferred across from the public-sector prison system. These officials have tended to be governors who have been recruited directly. Many, although not all, talked about reaching a point at which they felt frustrated or disillusioned about the public sector. Many directors pointed out that for those who argue that public sector is good and private sector is bad, it was important to keep in mind that private-sector prisons have largely been managed by governors-now-directors who had found severe shortcomings in the public sector. One senior official expressed this commonly held view:

> There is a perception that in the public sector there are only good moral altruistic people, and in the private sector, we are all capitalists.

> It couldn't be further from the truth. I've seen many more things that I find morally difficult in the public sector.

The third area of constraint is *logistical* in that private prisons must operate as part of the national prison system. One common criticism heard over the years has been that private prisons have been able to cream-skim the type of prisoners they receive (Ryan and Ward, 1989, p. 72). In the context of the England and Wales system, however, it is difficult to see how such cream-skimming can take place. All local prisons, including private prisons, must take prisoners from the courts in their catchment areas, and must operate in the wider national system. Both points mean that they have little or no influence over which prisoners come to them.[7] As one official explained:

> There is no system I know in which the private contractor has any control over the input which comes to them. They are either sent to them by the state or they have a catchment area. Under the most elaborate of conspiracies it is difficult to see how they control the numbers they get. They may be happy to see the numbers rise or fall, but you can't argue that they control it.

In fact, private prisons may end up receiving more difficult prisoners, simply because public-sector prison staff may view the private-sector prison as an opportune 'dumping ground' for their difficult prisoners. It is interesting, for example, that private training prisons have ended up in recent years with high numbers of indeterminate-sentence prisoners (known as IPP – Indeterminate sentences for Public Protection), effectively trapped in custody as a result of insufficient access to the programmes upon which their release is dependent.[8]

A fourth constraint results from public-sector *standardization and proceduralization* of private-sector operations. Public-sector officials have pointed out the importance of maintaining parity across the system as a whole. Private prisons are subject to the guidelines and regulations published by the Prison Service to control and regulate activities in prisons. Directors frequently complained about the administrative burden of complying with Prison Service Orders and Instructions, and often admitted to just ignoring many or phoning headquarters and saying that they would not do whatever was being asked of them. This tendency to resist requirements which are not specified in the contract is, however, usually balanced with reputational considerations about being seen to be a cooperative partner. Indeed, most directors acknowledged that they would do their best to accommodate requests where possible.

In recent years, as financial pressures have tightened, senior managers have sought to pare down prison services to a 'lowest common denominator' standard, which constitutes a standardized level of acceptable service quality across the system – a process euphemistically known as 'disinvestment'. For directors, disinvestment has often meant that they have had to scale back their own service provision in order to align themselves with national levels of performance. Private prisons may therefore effectively be required to under-perform in order to maintain parity with the wider public sector. One director explained the difficulties of integrating the NOMS requirement to shut down workshops and other commercial activities on Friday afternoons:

> The Prison Service closes down on a Friday afternoon. NOMS say they don't want a two-tier prison service. So they force me to replicate their close date. Again, contractually I don't have to do that. But as a good customer I look into doing that. But I can't close down on a Friday afternoon because I have to shut my workshops. Now the contract for the workshops here states that they must be commercially viable and generate revenues enough to pay for all education and teachers inside the contract. That's why I'm millions of pounds cheaper than equivalent public-sector jails. They don't pay for any education or city in guilds. So, at any one time, all the men in this contract on education and all those spaces is paid for by those workshops. So I say to NOMS, I can't close that down, unless you offset the lost revenue.

The final type of constraint relates move widely to *direct or benign resistance* within the system to the growth of private-sector market share over the years. There have been signs that private-sector firms had envisaged a quicker growth in market share. James et al. (1997), for example, report the announcement by the Home Secretary in 1994 that management of a further nine prisons would be offered to the private sector, bringing the total by 1997 to about 10 per cent of the prison estate (p. 157). Private-sector officials also suggested at a Home Affairs Select Committee in 1996 that they envisaged an optimal private-sector market share at somewhere near to 25 per cent (p. 169). As Figure 8.1 shows, neither of these aspirations has materialized. The market share has grown steadily, but not as expansively as many had envisaged.

This under-expansion might be explained by direct or benign resistance. In order for the market share to grow, it would have been necessary for the government to transfer existing public-sector prisons into private management, and we have not seen this programme of transfer throughout the Labour government years. Indeed, it was not until December 2010, seven months into the Conservative–Liberal coalition government, that the decision was taken to transfer an existing public-sector prison, Birmingham, into the private sector, thus making a strong statement about intentions to follow through on the threat of market testing failing public-sector prisons. This was followed by a decision to market test and subsequently transfer four more existing public-sector prisons – Northumberland, Moorland, Hatfield, and Lindholme – into the private sector. This has signified clear intention to grow the market share of the private sector up to more than 15 per cent of the total prison population.

Throughout the Labour government years, however, there was apparently more reluctance to push the private-sector market. In 2001, Brixton prison was formally submitted to a market test due to unacceptably low standards of performance. Views among top officials from that period were that had the private sector shown interest in taking on Brixton, then it probably would have been handed over in 2001. However, not one private sector firm submitted a credible bid to run Brixton. As one former senior NOMS official put it:

> Why would the private sector want to run failing prisons? They want to run good prisons, not really bad ones. It's all very well for the Prison Service to threaten these prisons with transfer, but they don't seem to realise that the private sector doesn't want them in the state they are in and the conditions they come with.

Officials also pointed to the political resistance to transferring existing public prisons into private management. In late 2009, before the decision to transfer Birmingham prison, a former senior NOMS official reflected on the likelihood that it would be transferred:

> Whether they'll actually go through with it, who knows? This is all about realpolitik. It's got nothing to do with management or whatever. It is about power struggles, I think. Until they grasp the nettle, contract out an existing big prison, I don't think they'll ever reach that 25 per cent market share. All they'll be able to give the private sector is the new builds.

Between 2001 and 2004, a period of intensive comparative benchmarking activity by NOMS, eight prisons underwent performance benchmarking, including Wandsworth, Liverpool, and Dartmoor, on the understanding that if these prisons failed to show that they were capable of improving their performance, they would be put up for market testing. The result of this exercise was that precisely none of these prisons were earmarked for market testing, with senior officials in NOMS stating that all of these prisons had risen to the challenge of implementing 'performance improvement plans'.

The dynamics involved in evaluating public-sector prisons are double-edged of course. Top officials have suggested that they had been willing to give prisons away to the private sector, but that these prisons had shown an ability to put together a 'competitive' proposal for performance improvement. As we have seen from earlier chapters, reluctance of ministers, particularly Labour ministers, to take on the POA has constrained the growth of the private sector. Senior prison officials and Treasury officials also described the practical difficulties of being in a position to judge one way or the other whether a prison's performance improvement plan is any good or not. Treasury officials admitted to not being able to help feeling uncomfortable about the extent to which they themselves could (or should) be expected to judge prison performance on the strength of what they saw. One senior Treasury official characterized this scepticism:

> This benchmarking, we didn't really believe in it. We weren't really sure in our judgements. It wasn't really our job to assess the quality of prisons. We felt slightly off our ground. In fact, we felt slightly stitched up by being on the panel in the first place. We felt that the people who should be doing this were the people who run private-sector jails, the people who can do a proper analysis of this. Not us.

The same officials also remarked on the general pressures they felt to give benefit of the doubt to the prison management and staff under review. The fact that these judgements were being made by senior prison officials raises questions about motivations for allowing public-sector prisons to fail performance tests. For senior officials in the public-sector system, the private sector has been the competition, and it should not be surprising that these officials would favour an outcome towards public-sector bids. One former top official also explained why it should not be so surprising that public prisons have consistently managed to evade being transferred.

> The public sector should always have an advantage if terms and conditions for staff are the same. There's no need to break off 10 per cent to give to shareholders. If it's sharply managed, the public sector would normally win if the terms and conditions of staff remain constant. Once the staff stop pratting about and the managers are decent, it's difficult for the private sector to win. Because they have got to make a profit as well.

One important constraint for the private sector in taking over existing public-sector prisons has been the cost of replicating public-sector pensions for staff transferred. One private-sector official summed up the problem as one of a difficulty in establishing a level playing field between public and private because of the duty to cover the cost of public-sector pensions:

> I know that we can't provide a public-sector pension for much less than 30 per cent. At the minute the MoJ pay 19 per cent. That's a big issue for us. If we've got a 10 per cent difference on staff costs, which is 70 per cent of the price of the prison, we are 7 per cent more expensive from the outset. The pensions bit is probably the final stumbling block because nobody wants to admit that public-sector pensions cost 30 per cent.

These five areas of constraint show how the complexities of the wider system impinge upon autonomy of the private sector, and cast doubt over arguments that firms have been able to engage in excessive rent-seeking. As the market has developed, the commercial and competitive pressures on these firms have increased, as have the bureaucratic and logistical constraints on the way they operate. With these constraints in mind, the next section moves on to look at the role of the contract in shaping the way in which private-sector firms and directors manage CCS.

8.2 The 'contractualization' of crowding and capacity stress

The contract is the crucial mechanism determining the way in which private-sector operators manage crowding and capacity stress.

It specifies the broad range of services which the contractor will provide, including required standards of output for those services, and the schedules of payments received and penalties due. It specifies an agreed number of managed prisoner spaces that should be made available. Operators are penalized for dropping below that number, and NOMS aims to ensure that all available spaces in private prisons which are being paid for are being utilized. Contracts also typically specify type and volume of programmes and treatments that will be provided, as well as key outputs such as 'hours of purposeful activity' and 'time out of cell' for prisoners. Performance against contracts is closely monitored by public-sector officials on-site in the prison and in NOMS headquarters.

For private-sector directors, the contract is at the heart of what they do and what they prioritize. As one current director put it: 'I do more than govern prisons. I run a contract. I manage stakeholders. Numerous interested parties.' The emphasis is on the need to manage and operate their prisons in such a way that they deliver against the terms of the contract. One top private-sector manager reflected on the objectivity and predictability it brings.

> The contract means that you begin to get away from 'personalities'. You've got a legally binding contract between an organization that wants a service and an organization that wants to make money and survive by delivering that service. I think that is the real secret to it. The contract makes things relatively simple.

There is indeed apparent simplicity to what directors are expected to achieve. They are charged with fulfilling all the service requirements set out in the contract, as well as complying, broadly speaking, with prison-system rules and regulations. In terms of their relationship with their own bosses, they are charged with delivering the contract within the pre-specified cost parameters. As one official put it:

> Here's a financial package with the banks that says that we will get an 8 per cent return. We don't want 7.8 per cent and we also don't want 8.5 per cent. We want 8 per cent. So if you go off line and you incur penalties, that comes out of the profit margin, and the bosses say 'we want our money'.

Although the concept may appear simple, the realities of delivering this for many directors have been demanding, particularly as in the early days of the market, contract terms agreed were often excessively tight. As one former director explained:

> Some of them were horrible. The problem is that the price can be absolutely too low. At that price, bad stuff happens and it gets frightening. The job of the director is to keep the cost line at a point below. That gap is profit. That's really important. But you are under such pressure. Because the price is too low. You've got staff turnover at 40 per cent. That's improved now. So if you let costs go, and say sure, we'll take more, we'll do more for you, and it's not in the contract, we'll try and help you, cost increases. And we all go home.

Contracts can also provide structural integrity and limit the extent to which capacity can flex and stretch. As one private prison director pointed out, the contract is a 'real legal document. It's got teeth and penalties. And it is both a sword and a shield.' It provides a basis for both parties to hold the other to account. It also provides both parties with a protective device, some kind of effective 'bottom line' with which to counter unreasonable requests. Directors also referred to the more subtle opportunities for benign resistance that the contract brings. They emphasized the importance of not being seen to be directly resisting requests from the Authority. However, more indirect methods of prevaricating could be employed in order to stall or deflect requests. One current director outlined an example which reflected many other similar techniques of using the contract to resist capacity stressing:

> They approached me last week and asked how quickly can you bring in another sixty in the new accommodation. I said I don't want to. They said please please please. I said that the contract says I don't have to for another five months because there is a six-month stabilization period. Now part of being a good customer is to be receptive to customer need, but by being receptive to the customer, I run the risk of destabilizing the prison and getting a whole range of fines and reputation damage. And it is written into the contract that there is a six- month stabilization period.

Over the years, contracts have become more sophisticated in the way they have specified crowding. Early contracts tended to specify a number of prisoners which the prison would be expected to accommodate, and any additional numbers over this maximum would involve expensive contract renegotiation. In more recent contracts, thresholds or 'escalators' of acceptable crowding have been built in from the outset, meaning that extra increments (typically a maximum of 30 per cent in 10 per cent stages) can be activated from the existing contract at prices which are pre-specified and part of the original bid evaluation.[9] As one former official explained:

> They've learnt to allow for change up front [...] contracts which build in more flexibility. At the time of the original tender, it is a highly competitive business. You have to think about what your competitors are going to do. If you are asked for CNA plus 20 or 40 per cent. You've got to be quite tight on that otherwise you may do yourself out of a job.

The challenge therefore for private operators has been to find a balance in the contract, allowing enough flexibility to accommodate crowding without undermining performance against the contract, while at the same time presenting as competitive a bid as possible. Private-sector managers and prison architects have described the detailed analysis and modelling that is done to find optimal cost-effective physical design specifications, which maximize flexibility of usage, and balance design quality, decency, and cost. One bid director reflected on how private firms build flexibility into their bids. This example relates to cell design:

> There are NOMS standards for cell sizes – single, larger, double. We had to make a call based on what we thought was the best configuration. If you only have single cells, you have to do a lot more building because there are a lot more walls. But if you have double cells, there are fewer cells which reduces your flexibility should some cells go out. It was more about costs and flexibility rather than being able to put two prisoners in every cell. The cells are 'larger' cells. They are not double cells. But they could take two people.

Private-sector officials also explained the importance of maximizing the usage of communal space and facilities. There is an incentive built in at the design and construction phase for physical space and facilities to be multi-purpose, so that capacity can be optimized in the operation of the prison. For these managers, this flexibility in use of facilities of the prison was seen as an important factor in allowing the capacity of the prison to absorb increments of crowding.

> It's easy for us because we are the ones delivering all the services. We say we need this much space for the programmes, this and that,

> you don't need to provide them all with separate spaces. What we do is provide them with nice rooms that can be used for a number of things. We will then have a booking system to make sure that the rooms are being used intensively, and we run it like a Regus business centre [...] well, actually the prisoners run it.

The development of the market has involved adaptation and learning in terms of building in flexibility to accommodate increases in crowding. Officials acknowledged that many of the earlier contracts, particularly those signed between 1997 and 2002, failed to build in sufficient capacity in order to deal with surges in the prison population. As one director explained:

> The effect has been huge. As a company, we made a mistake. We knew that the contract required to overcrowd to 30 per cent max, but we didn't build the purposeful activity centre big enough, and we won't make that mistake again. We built [our next prison] with a purposeful activity centre large enough to manage. That problem has caused me huge operational, management, and reputational difficulties in terms of achieving our purposeful activity targets.

Private-sector officials also reflected on the importance of modelling the staff-cost implications of crowding. If the increment is small enough, private-sector prisons may be able to absorb additional prisoners into the existing regime without increasing staffing levels. However, at some point, staffing levels will have to be increased to accommodate increased number of prisoners and to ensure that the prison can fulfil basic contractual obligations and sustain safe environments.

> Some steps for us would be more attractive than others. I think it was twenty-five. Say, taking the first twenty-five would be very attractive because we could absorb all the marginal costs, and probably not even staff up. That would be pure margin. Then you go to fifty, and you have to start recruiting staff, then that wasn't so attractive because your margin drops, and so on. We did a lot of modelling on that. We got to propose the steps. There's a lot of thinking that goes on behind that.

The risk for the private sector is that during times of population pressure, government may be likely to commission extra capacity, and then when pressure recedes, decommission them and leave the prison with costs of extra staff. As officials have explained, this accentuates the need to maintain flexibility in all aspects of physical and human resources. It also creates incentives for private prisons to move quickly and in large steps towards the maximal levels of crowding within contractually specified limits.

Table 8.2 shows how private prisons have been crowded above their original contract capacity. The first observation is that the profile of crowding mirrors closely the profile of crowding across the system as a whole. Local prisons are heavily crowded, closed trainings are crowded but to a much lesser extent, and youth and female prisons tend to be shielded from crowding completely. Broadly speaking, private local prisons during the last decade have been marginally more crowded than large public-sector locals. It is interesting that the 2011 NOMS annual report stated an intention to reduce crowding in private prisons by 460 places (p. 12) – still a relatively small gesture that will have seemingly little impact on the extent of crowding across the private sector.

These observations therefore cast some doubt over the extent to which the contract gives directors a basis on which to resist 'excessive' crowding. Clearly, the contract provides for financial payments for increments in crowding. However, even with this commitment to reduce crowding in private prisons, crowding levels in private prisons have been consistently above the 30 per cent threshold. Officials have argued that these excessive increments have come with new purposeful activity facilities. Also, directors have talked about the pressure to find ways of accommodating requests from NOMS to take more prisoners. One senior executive reflected on the similar kind of de facto pressure that we have seen in the previous chapter on public-sector governors. The reasons may be different in the private commercial context, but the general dynamic of rationalizing stretch seems broadly familiar.

> Sometimes we feel that if we don't look more than willing, and look to overcrowd and be accommodating, then we won't win new business. So you might say that it is fixed in the private sector, it is, that's our number, and they can't go over that. But in discussion, we always say yes because we don't want to be seen as being unhelpful.

This echoes too the discussion in Chapter 4 about the relationship between CNA and Op Cap. Contractualization of crowding has created a sense of legitimacy, and perpetuated the idea that it is possible to establish and maintain meaningful normative thresholds between what is acceptable and what is not acceptable. Discussions with directors have

Table 8.2 Percentage crowding in private prisons, 1992 to 2012

	Average percentage crowding above normal accommodation (two-year averages from year listed)									
	1992–93	1994–95	1996–97	1998–99	2000–01	2002–03	2004–05	2006–07	2008–09	2010–12
Male adult locals										
Wolds	*–21*	0	9	11	10	9	3	11	19	15
Blakenhurst	*–43*	*–2*	17	29	27					
Doncaster		1	29	39	38	46	42	39	47	52
Altcourse			6	21	33	60	57	57	63	48
Parc			*–13*	*–4*	5	20	21	26	40	30
Forest Bank					*4*	26	28	28	41	26
Peterborough							*–7*	6	15	13
Birmingham										34
Thameside										*–17*
Closed training										
Buckley Hall		*–9*	2	9	4					
Lowdham Grange			0	*–2*	*–1*	3	2	6	6	0
Rye Hill					*–2*	9	4	2	6	4
Dovegate						*–6*	0	4	6	5
Oakwood										*–42*
Young offender										
Ashfield					*–12*	*–27*	*–8*	*–5*	*–13*	*–32*
Female adult										
Bronzefield							*–11*	*–4*	*–3*	*–4*

Source: My analysis of data from Prison Service and NOMS annual reports. Positive figures denote percentage crowding above CNA and negative figures denote free capacity below CNA.

reflected exactly that same kind of rationalization and legitimation of 'acceptable' crowding.

> CNA represents a bygone era. But we do treasure it. I have to have a cell certificate which is signed off by the area manager. It's preserved in private prisons where there's a definition of what a prisoner place is. You've got to have light that works, a desk, and so on. There are about seventeen things which have to be added up. That's really important. If you've 800 cells, that is times 7 per week, times 365, and that is the amount of money you are going to get for the contract. So that gets repeated in the private sector contract.

In the private sector, the belief that crowding and capacity stress are issues which can be effectively mitigated and 'managed away' appears just as strong if not stronger. For many directors, as with many of the more 'chief executive' style governors in the public sector, the question of crowding appears as a 'false problem', partly an 'alibi' or excuse for sub-optimal performance and partly something which may be seen as an issue of secondary concern which should not in reality hinder high performance in a well-managed prison. These views reflect a purest form of the argument that crowding and capacity stress are 'constructed' figments of the system itself. One private prison director captured this prevalent view:

> It's a myth. I don't want to think about it. I don't want to create the pressure in mind that it is a difficult job. They will say, but your prison is only built for such and such [...] and you've got more than twice that number. But we don't focus on overcrowding. Or whatever. I don't want to get bogged down in it. The day I use it as an excuse, I'll use it until the day I die.

We have seen therefore a similar paradox to that discussed in Chapter 4. Public-sector governors argue that they rarely exceed operational capacity in their prisons, but acknowledge the fact that operational capacity of the system has stretched over the years as population pressures have increased. In the same way, private-sector directors emphasize the protective value of the contract, yet must also acknowledge at the same time that crowding has stretched quickly and, in most cases, way above the 30 per cent threshold. As I aim to show in the final section of this chapter, the output and outcome focus of the contract does, however, offer directors considerable scope for doing things to mitigate crowding and manage it away.

8.3 Operational autonomy and comparisons with the public sector

In this contract model, constraints act on directors from two different directions. First, they must deliver outputs and outcomes pre-specified in the contract. Second, they must be able do this within the confines of financial model agreed with their own bosses and financiers. Both constraints can be tight and can put considerable pressure on directors. These hard-edged commercial realities appear difficult to re-create in a public-sector setting. One of these officials contrasted the pressures and incentives for private-sector directors with those of public-sector governors:

> If I overspend in the public sector, my area manager sits there and moans, but I'm not going to lose my job, and it is not going to affect my bonus. If you are on a ten grand bonus in the private sector. It's fab. But you have to work hard to get it. The maximum bonus I can earn is £800 before tax. I do not get out of bed thinking I must work harder. It just does not motivate me.

Service Level Agreements (SLA) have been tried in the public sector to replicate this contract-style discipline. There was, however, widespread scepticism about the effectiveness of these mechanisms. Another local prison governor reflected on the difficulties of replicating this commercial discipline through SLAs in public-sector settings:

> This SLA requires me to do some stuff. I had my first SLA meeting. Who comes? Me. My performance person. My finance person. The DOM? No. Too busy. The RCM? No, too busy.[10] He sent someone on his behalf, who sat there and told me I'm missing my targets on drugs, electricity, and so on. He sent me eight 'improvement notices'. In a proper contract, that would be the end of the world. There's no budget for that and it's straight off the bottom line. Leave a gate open here [a public local prison] and it gets reported as an 'incident'. Leave a gate open in [a private-sector prison], and it's a thousand pounds. That soon changes behaviour.

The difficulty of transposing contractual-style accountability lies also in the conflict with command-and-control hierarchical structures of discipline throughout the public-sector system. This governor quoted above reflected also on the institutional and cultural limitations involved.

> How can you come to the table as independent parties, mediated by a document which we call an SLA, when the person across the table from you is your boss? It's not real accountability. You can't negotiate with someone who has a direct influence over your career. You ask 'Is the SLA the most important piece of paper around?' Answer [...] no it is not. The most importance piece of paper is your appraisal form.

Comparative autonomy of operation has meant that the private sector has been able to run prisons more cheaply over the years. Comparative estimates have varied because it is not an exact science. Critics have argued that the cost differential between public and private has gradually decreased as the public sector has taken costs out of the system, and as the private sector has been burnt from excessive under-supply of resources and absorbed the costs of operating in a wider bureaucratic system (Harding, 2001). Research and interviews tend to converge on a bare-bones cost differential throughout the 2000s at somewhere between 10 and 15 per cent (Harding, 2001, p. 285).[11] This ballpark estimate corresponds relatively closely to reported pre-tax operating profits for the private sector shareholders – in the broad range of 10 to 17 per cent annually.

A major part of these marginal cost savings comes from lower staffing levels in private prisons, and the ability of directors to deploy staff more cost-effectively. It is difficult to say in any absolute sense what the correct ratio of staff to prisoners should be in a prison, and it is possible to construct arguments each way for higher or lower ratios. As one senior public-sector official put it, 'you would probably never know what proportion of the staffing in a prison is preventative and what proportion is wasteful'. Nevertheless, private-sector prisons have managed to normalize considerably lower staffing ratios than public-sector prisons. Directors commonly talked about the comparative freedom to manage staff time creatively, as well as explore imaginative and more cost-effective approaches:

> In the public-sector world that I was in, a unit of eighty prisoners would probably have a manager and half a dozen staff on a daily basis. We run it with three staff. We are expected to deliver, and we do, the same standards as the public sector. Clearly we can do it, because we do.

Interviews have revealed large discrepancies in the numbers of core specialist staff in public and private prisons. One director talked about receiving a visit from a governor of a closely comparable public sector prison.

> He came round to visit. He was saying things like, 'How many nurses have you got?' I'd say I've twenty-two nurses. He said I've got eighty-five. It was an extraordinary number. It may be that prisoners there were getting a much better healthcare service, but it certainly was not eighty-five nurses better.

Directors talked about the benefits of more normal (as opposed to normal-abnormal) working environments for private-sector staff. For example, they emphasized the importance of a more balanced gender mix, and the much greater prevalence of female staff was strikingly obvious during my own visits to these prisons. Directors also talked about their own autonomy to invest in staff training and development. The corollary to this is the more credible threat in the private sector in which staff are clear that if they abuse excessively their working privileges, they are likely to lose their job. As many public-sector governors have pointed out, the private-sector approach to staff disputes tends to be 'dismiss and settle later' rather than the public-sector approach of letting grievance procedures drag on over long periods. As one official observed, private-sector arrangements tend to be less susceptible to escalation and gaming by staff and management:

> Within the public sector there are well-held game plans that everybody plays to. The game plans are not so clear in the private sector. You know, you play the game that way, the management plays the game that way, the POA play the game that way. Everybody knows what the rules are, we all go through the escalation procedures. It's been done for years.

Private officials have often talked about inherent obsolescence in the way many aspects of the system are designed. The Brixton-reception vignette at the very start of this book provided regular topic for conversation during interviews with private-sector officials. From a staffing perspective, directors pointed out that this was a good example of how it would make sense to use different types of staff in reception to carry out the repetitive work and redeploying more experienced staff in other more challenging roles. As one put it:

> We are a lot leaner in process and staffing than they are, given the numbers we put out every day. We'll use a mix of prison officers, clerk grades, and support grades, whereas if you go into a public-sector reception, you are predominantly dealing with prison officers.

One director talked of his own attempts to integrate reception procedures with prisoner escort roles:

> The model that I was working towards was that I'm the escort contractor and I'm coming into your prison to collect a prisoner. All you need to do is bung them into a holding cell. I'll get hold of him, do his searching, get his property, and I'll take him. And vice versa at the other end. If I don't do that, all my staff are doing is sitting round drinking tea. Offer it to the Prison Service. It wouldn't cost my staff any time because my staff are there anyway. I used to have conversations at Pentonville, saying I'll do it for you, and the governor used to say, 'No, the POA won't have it'. I wasn't asking for money. They would have made a saving.

Another private-sector executive reflected on cultural barriers inherent in the system which stop basic modernization of these logistical processes:

> If they could get into the twentieth century even and barcode the boxes where the kit is. It's not difficult stuff. We are bidding for PECS now,[12] and I was talking to them about making sure that everybody's property was such that we could use some form of detecting where it was. If you go to any Excel warehouse, stuff goes flying out, and it's not difficult anymore. But it's, 'Oh I don't know about that'. They would say what's the failure rate of that, about 3 per cent. Ooh, 3 per cent. Not sure we could tolerate 3 per cent. They are probably running a 20 per cent failure rate now.

Directors have also frequently talked about their autonomy to experiment with new technology. Most pointed out cases in which the private sector had led the way on integrating basic technology, for example, PIN numbers for phones, kiosks, in-cell telephony, and

IT education. One former director reflected on the apparent can-do approach to technology solutions in the private sector:

> I got some people from one of our partners to talk to me about this new in-cell technology. I said what I'd like to do is have this cell as a study bedroom, with a computer in it, and restrictions on access. These guys looked at each other and said [...] looks pretty straightforward. But it just doesn't happen here. It'll be years and years before that would happen at a public sector prison like this.

Electronic kiosks, in particular, have been used in certain private-sector prisons, but they are not used in the public sector. As one former official put it:

> I couldn't think of a single reason why you couldn't put kiosks in the public sector. Not a single reason. It depends what you are getting the kiosk to do. If it is stuff like booking a visit, contacting a drugs officer, it strikes me that that is quite useful. And it tends to reflect what is happening in the modern world.

Private prisons have begun to put telephones in cells in recent years, making the case that calls can be more easily controlled and reducing the likelihood of mobile phones coming into prisons. The installation of telephones in cells in public-sector prisons has been continually opposed by ministers, yet they are constrained from intervening when phones are installed in private-sector jails. One former private director characterized the kind of dialogue which takes place:

> We'd say can we have [phones] in the public sector? The DG would say we'd love to give it to you, but ministers won't accept it. Why's that then? Public perception [...] holiday-camp prisons. Ministers hate the fact it's in the private sector. They wanted us to take it out until we said to them we'd have to increase staffing again. And that would increase the price of the contracts. So they said OK, let them have it [...] but no more.

Governors often expressed scepticism about the motives for installation of new technologies in private prisons, arguing that it had much to do with 'looking good and ticking boxes' for the next retender stage. Most acknowledged, however, that they would welcome similar types of technological investment in their own public-sector prisons. And many were generally resigned to the combined constraints of political sensitivity towards use of prisoner-facing technology in prisons, and perceived lack of willingness to secure capital investment for prisoner IT systems.

Directors and their managers are under hard-edged commercial pressures to deliver on the requirements of the contract and to do so in budget. As long as they are able to do so, however, they can be shown to have autonomy to shape and manage capacity in their prisons. It is interesting here that directors have tended to stay in post for longer periods of time (an average closer to three to four years) than governors in the public sector. And private officials have suggested, if directors can successfully manage the basics of delivering the contract to budget, then the managerial freedoms create a much stronger incentive to stay in one place for longer. Of course, the relatively much smaller number of other prisons to move to helps to explain longer incumbency of directors.

8.4 Conclusions

When the first privately managed prisons were introduced in the UK in the early 1990s, much of the political rhetoric justifying their introduction emphasized how these new actors in the market would help to alleviate the excessive crowding prevalent in the system. As we have seen, the story of private-sector markets and their impact on capacity stress has been nothing of the sort. New markets may have brought with them a new setting, hard-edged contractual mechanisms for limiting excessive stretch in the system, and new cultures and ways of doing things that help to mitigate the negative effects of crowding. Yet we have seen exactly the same trends and pathologies at the heart of CCS, normalized to an even greater degree, and still, as much as ever, an overriding characteristic of the system.

The commercial contract has provided the framework for, by now, familiar countervailing dynamics. Its strength is that it provides some basis to resist what might be seen as excessive stretch in capacity stress. However, the distribution and scale of crowding in the private sector has moved quickly to mirror the public sector, and in many cases surpass it. Paradoxically, the contract offers structural integrity to directors to be able to resist, yet it has also offered a mechanism through which crowding and acceptable forms of capacity stress can be legitimated. By writing into the contract thresholds for 'acceptable' levels of crowding in these prisons, CCS is effectively normalized to an even greater degree.

An important part of this normalization process has been the argument that private prisons have greater autonomy to be able to mitigate and manage the pressures of crowding. In many ways, this is a compelling argument. In terms of their overall design, staff cultures, technologies, and general feel, private prisons have seemed on the face of it more 'normal' institutions in terms of what one would expect from modern-day public services. Fatalist cultures amongst directors and staff do not appear to be so prevalent. Many of these directors have come from jobs in the public sector and almost unanimously point to the much greater scope for autonomy and influence in their new private sector roles. It is perhaps no surprise that the experiments in 2010 with 'payment by results' schemes for rehabilitation in prisons were piloted first in private-sector prisons – Peterborough and Doncaster.

It is, however, in the nature of constrained autonomy that it warns against attributing excessive instrumentality to individual parts of the system. The ability of one part to bring reform or change to the greater whole is by definition constrained. As I have tried to show, there are important commercial, financial, political, and logistical constraints on the ability of the private sector to influence the system. They are both constrained from excessive rent-seeking, as well as constrained in the extent to which they are able to influence the rest of the system in radically transformative ways, particularly on rehabilitative outcomes. In this sense, they have reflected the prevailing norms across the system. We have also seen the limits to how far the undoubted autonomies and cultures of the private sector can be transferred into the system as a whole.

For government and the top public-sector officials involved, therefore, the predicament here embodies a tricky balance. On the one hand, autonomy of the private sector may be able to offer a catalyst, experimenting ground, or a means to driving improvement in the prison system as a whole. And to some extent it has. Yet, by dint of the very fact that it is a part of the system and is constrained by it, the potential for the private sector to change the system must also be seen as inherently limited. The countervailing dynamics are just as visible in the private sector as they are in the public sector. And this, although there may be gradual or incremental impacts on the system, is hardly the stuff of radical transformative change.

9
Chronic Capacity Stress: A Complex Condition

> An endless series of natural equilibria which are constantly shifting as pressures change slightly. It's like trying to design a bit of geology. The forces are far greater than you can influence. (Former governor and senior official in the Prison Service)

When the experienced governor of a large local prison tells you that you have to go back to 1877 to get to the roots of the problem of prison crowding, it is a pretty clear indication that the issues that you are dealing with have something chronic about them. In that year, the Prison Commission was established, marking what is widely seen as the beginning of the modern-era prison system in England and Wales. The implication is that as the system has grown into a large and centralized modern bureaucracy, it has also become somehow less able to do the things necessary to impact positively and effectively on the lives of prisoners. Blaming the best part of 150 years of public administrative change for sub-optimality in today's prison system is perhaps one of the more outlandish examples in this book of fatalistic response. Nevertheless, it illustrates nicely the kind of potentially paradoxical dynamics that can be found at the heart of a large and complex public-policy system.

Through the concept of 'chronic capacity stress' (CCS) we have sought to understand more clearly how a prison system has been able to sustain crowding over a long period of time, while continuing to function in broadly manageable and acceptable ways. We have seen how the system has not merely coped or scraped by, but rather has been positively successful in improving many important aspects of its performance. We have seen how the system has become more ordered, disciplined, and decent. And we have seen also a system that has focused more of its efforts and resources on trying to make a positive difference in the complex and chaotic lives of offenders in custody. Yet, at the same time, we have seen how the system has worked despite or against itself, in the sense that aggravating and compensating dynamics within have fed into sustaining aspects of failure, fatalism, and obsolescence.

We have found that the concept of stress in a human-dominated system can be potentially complex. It is a feature of the condition that its causes are as much related to the external pressures and demands laid on the system as they are related to the aggravating and compensating dynamics generated within. The case of prisons and prison crowding has shown us that a system can be under stress from all sorts of exogenous factors that are beyond its control. But it is also apparent that there is much in the system, its aggravating and compensating dynamics, that feeds into sustaining the actual and perceived stress. CCS has provided a heuristic for understanding the key strands in this potentially complex condition. It helps us to see how it is possible for a policy system to incorporate aspects of success and failure simultaneously as part of its essential equilibria. It also helps us to understand why it is necessary to look at the way in which policy systems work as a whole in order to understand their defining characteristics or features. As I have tried to show in the preceding four chapters, the basis for this kind of whole system understanding must be found in the way in which its constituent actors think and behave. Furthermore, in order to understand the thoughts and behaviours of these actors, we must look at the context of the institutions and cultures in which they operate. It is key therefore to CCS and the whole theoretical argument in this book that each of these three approaches – system, culture, and actor – are necessarily constituent of each other.

In this final chapter I bring together the four main aspects of CCS as discussed in Chapter 2, and the concept of constrained autonomy as seen from the perspectives of the four main groups of actors in the previous four chapters. I discuss the implications of constrained autonomy of actors for the each of the four parts of the CCS heuristic, and show how this integrated approach can help us to understand the extent to which the condition is chronic. My analysis of the theoretical approaches in the opening chapter of the book has allowed us a lens through which to see the problem of crowding and CCS in these terms. In following through empirically from this basis, we have also seen ways in which these individual theoretical approaches have revealed blind spots. I have shown that in order to understand the problem of CCS, we must look at it in this much more integrated way. As the chapter develops, I discuss the theoretical implications of CCS, and the prospects for alleviating or indeed escaping from it completely.

9.1 Individual actors, constrained autonomy, and adaptation

In the previous four chapters we have had an insight into the predicaments and trade-offs that key groups of actors face in trying to manage constrained autonomy. These actors play simultaneous 'principal' and 'agent' roles within interlinked principal–agent chains that run from high politics down through the management and operation of the system. They must contend with their own predicaments of constrained autonomy, and find ways of dealing with them so as to maintain some kind of manageable equilibrium in their own position. And in each chapter we have seen how the choices and decisions that different actors take can be rationalized as entirely understandable in the context of the constraints on them.

At any point in the system, we can pull on seemingly innocuous threads and reveal interlinked dynamics and constraints relating to CCS. Take, for example, this simple description by a deputy governor of the dynamics involved in agreeing to receive prisoners into the prison after the reception has closed for the night:

> There is some theatre in it. The duty governor is seen to stand up and say no, the bus is late, and we are not going to take these prisoners. Pop Man then either rings the governor or me. Are you prepared to order them in? I will always say yes. The alternative is that these hungry prisoners have nowhere else to go. The duty governor and the staff know that I will do that. It is everybody retaining their own position. And they are happy to do it with a bit of grumbling if they feel the area manager has ordered it.

In even this small and innocuous example, we see how system constraints and adaptation come into play. The duty governor, by agreeing to allow the prisoners in, is responding to the need to manage the interests of her own staff as well as those of the prisoners involved. She will also presumably be managing her own equilibrium, by responding to the pressures coming down from the area manager or 'population management' (Pop Man). Meanwhile, the area manager is having to respond to pressures coming down from headquarters to resolve this specific dilemma. And headquarters, as we have seen, are under pressure from politicians and from senior management to make sure that prisoners are accommodated without disruption, and so on. The outcome of this situation is presumably a marginal increase in capacity stress in that particular prison. The marginal increase in capacity stress is not by design, but rather by default in a system in which all actors are seeking to manage their own equilibrium as best they can.

Let us return now to the four aspects of the CCS schema discussed in Chapter 2, and look at each from the perspective of these different groups of actors. For in each of these four aspects we see exactly the same kinds of nuances and constraints as those in the example above. Moreover, we see how the decisions and behaviours of these groups feed into sustaining the overall condition of CCS. The schema must after all be seen as a general abstract concept, but in order to understand the actual dynamics, we must look at them through the eyes of the real-life actors involved. I summarize this in Table 9.1 and discuss each of the four aspects in turn.

At the heart of the CCS schema we identified a link between a putative *collapse of the rehabilitative ideal* and perception of a serially failing prison system (Loop 1 in Figure 2.8). At all levels of the system, actors have shown varying degrees of fatalism about their ability to impact on rehabilitative outcomes, both in terms of *a priori* normative orientation and practical constraints on what is logistically or feasibly possible (even with the best will in the world). For a start, many interviewees have reaffirmed a recurring and indeed quite dominant conventional wisdom that any discussion about improving the effectiveness of prison involves a fallacious assumption that prison should be the focus for improvement in the first place. One governor summed up this conventional wisdom by questioning the underlying premise of my research:

> You are asking the wrong question. Instead of saying how can we make prisons more effective, the question should be how can we reduce crime and harm in society. There are actually far more ways of doing that than prison. Constructing the argument around prisons works on an assumption that prisons are effective and ought to be used.

Thinking about how to reduce crime and harm, and about how to deal with offenders without using prison, are clearly both entirely worthwhile and good research questions. Yet there is clearly a troublesome paradox in using such argumentation as a reason not think about how to improve the impacts of prison. The paradox was illustrated by the public declaration of the Prison Governors Association (PGA) during 2009 which argued that prison sentences of less than one year do not work and could not be expected to have any rehabilitative effect (BBC, 2009). The peculiarity of such a statement lies in a wholesale negation by a professional group of its own instrumental impact. Admittedly, not all governors held this view, but many did and it reflected a deep-seated tension in the system about legitimate expectations of prison per se.

Clearly, any rehabilitative goals must be articulated and supported from the highest political levels of the system (top left field in Table 9.1). We have seen how ministers have varied in terms of their views and efforts on rehabilitative reform over the years. For those who have talked about having a go at reforming the system, most have found themselves stymied in their attempts. Ministers have reflected on seeing their best efforts unravel or dissipate as momentum is lost. Once momentum is lost, it is difficult to get it back, and invariably the reality of politics means that other priorities and issues deflect attention. Generally, ministers have been well aware of the difficulties of making the case for rehabilitative reform, and this has underpinned what we might describe as 'default low' expectations (despite ministerial vanity) at the highest political level about what can be realistically achieved during their time in office. Ministers have also reflected the sheer difficulties of changing cultures in the system and so on. And ultimately, there is an awareness that failure to rehabilitate prisoners is unlikely to undermine their political credibility, especially if they have not publicly declared an intention to pursue this policy outcome.

Senior officials, as civil servants, not surprisingly emphasize their role as one of responding to ministerial priorities. If ministerial priorities are not prioritizing rehabilitative goals, then they perceive that it should not be their role to redefine priorities on their minister's behalf. That said, however, the rehabilitative aspirations of the system have been explicit throughout the 2000s as part of the NOMS policy goals. And as Chapter 3 has shown, rates of reconviction after custody appear to have fallen by at least 7 per cent since 2000, if we are to take Ministry of Justice statistical modelling at face value (see Figure 3.12). We should interpret this figure cautiously as it is based on a notional improvement in rehabilitation, but at the same time it is indeed evidence that the system is moving in the right direction in terms of rehabilitation. It is interesting here that this particular piece of analysis is buried in a technical report by the Ministry of Justice on reoffending rates. When asked why this potential success had not been championed more publicly by

Table 9.1 Constrained autonomy of four groups of actors

	Four aspects of the holistic governance model			
	Loop 1 **Collapse of the rehabilitative ideal**	***Loop 2*** **Coping and crisis culture**	***Loop 3*** **Direct and benign resistance**	***Loop 4*** **Sustained obsolescence and redundancy**
Senior ministers in government *(Chapter 5)*	Some ministers have tried to reform the system but have seen their efforts unravel. Aware that prison reform is politically high risk for low returns. Ministers have 'default low' expectations on what is possible.	Benefit from presiding over a quiet and secure prison system. Tend to get involved during crisis periods and rely on their top officials to run the system otherwise. May benefit politically from dealing with crisis.	Ministers may struggle to sustain will for change at highest levels of government. They also encounter direct resistance, particularly from union, or benign resistance from operational actors in the system.	'Second-order' concern for top ministers. Off senior ministerial radar. Prisons minister likely to be involved. Argue that funds are limited and bemoan failure at operational level.
Senior officials in the Prison Service and NOMS *(Chapter 6)*	See their role as primarily responding to ministerial priorities and 'making the system work'. Benign scepticism towards idea that prison should be judged on rehabilitative outcomes, citing population pressures and difficulties in attributing causation.	See their priority as delivering quiet and secure system. Mediated through meeting targets. Seek to maintain flexibility of options to aid coping. Maintaining perception of coping also helps their cause politically.	Contend with political interference and uncertainty, particularly during crisis periods. Also contend with direct or benign resistance by staff and unions, and shaping behaviour by governors, in response to reform attempts.	Recognize obsolescence but tend to be fatalistic about the chances of securing funds for modernization. Interest in resisting professional 'voice' of governors. Signs of technology-averse culture at senior levels.

Governors and prison staff *(Chapter 7)*	Claim that there is much that can be done to improve rehabilitative role of prison. But that they are constrained by crowding, limited resources, and the disruptive effects of national coordination of prisoners.	Governors respond to command and control. Professional ethos that prisoners must be accommodated. They find ways to cope with ageing or inadequate facilities, and to stretch capacity.	Governors may attempt to resist command and control but often in vain. Also resist excessive managerialism and performance bureaucracy. They contend with resistance staff cultures.	Governors acknowledge their own beleaguered collective professional status vis-à-vis senior officials. Also fatalistic about their ability to affect obsolescence as it is seen as a system-wide issue.
Private sector firms *(Chapter 8)*	Claim there is room for innovation but that they are constrained by having to deliver equivalent standards as the public sector. Also constrained by tight profit margins in the contract.	Cope with the same population pressures, but have some protection through the contract. Maturing prisons now less likely to struggle with high staff turnover and inexperience.	Less constrained by union resistance and public-sector rules. But they claim that public-sector cultures impinge on their ability to innovate or find cost-efficiency savings.	Less visible obsolescence as prisons are newer and better designed. Cultures seem altogether more 'normal'. But claim that they absorb obsolescence as part of the public-sector system.

ministers, senior officials were inclined to point to the political difficulties of explaining the nuances such technical modelling to the public and tabloid media. It was a case of if the method of evidencing success has to be explained, then it is success not worth mentioning. A critical media would no doubt write off Ministry of Justice modelling as tricky civil servants cooking the books.

Such illustration highlights the difficulties for senior officials and their ministers on rehabilitation, and helps to explain how or why senior officials and their ministers may seek to tread a less ambitious and less potentially controversial path. Even if it can be shown that the rehabilitative work of prisons is moving in the right direction, the evidence of success is too technical for popular consumption. Indeed, the kind of success required for the system to publicly claim success would be too unrealistic in the first place. It may not be surprising therefore that we have found signs of latent scepticism towards rehabilitative goals amongst top officials. As well as the difficulties of demonstrating success, there are also difficulties associated with having to cope with system running at close-to-tolerance levels of capacity. Many have said that in an ideal world it would be nice to focus more on rehabilitation, but the pragmatic imperatives of running the system on a daily basis at close to 100 per cent capacity occupied most of their time.

Among governors and staff, we have found perhaps more inclination to talk up the rehabilitative role of prisons, and their responsibility in doing what they can locally to reduce reoffending. But again, arguments here emphasize the inherent limitations of this activity, due mainly to strained resources, continued churn of short-term prisoners, and the associated disruptive effects of national population management. Even two years after the declaration of the 'rehabilitation revolution' by the Conservative–Liberal coalition, we have seen signs that a shift in culture and emphasis in prisons towards rehabilitation has been partial at best. A joint report by the Prisons and Probation Inspectorate in July 2012, for example, highlighted a combination of capacity stress in the system as well as deep-seated cultural resistance in prisons towards prioritization of rehabilitative work (CJJI, 2012).

In the private sector, directors see themselves freer to experiment with rehabilitative outcomes, and have been inclined to see crowding and capacity stress as less of a constraint. This is perhaps part of the reason why private-sector prisons were selected as the first to pilot new 'payments by results' schemes as part of the coalition government plans for reform. As we have seen, however, there has been little in place contractually to incentivize private prisons to reduce reoffending for prisoners leaving their care. Hence there is little evidence that private prisons have been any more effective than public-sector prisons in this area despite a good line in compelling rhetoric about their positive impacts. Indeed, as Chapter 8 has emphasized, private prisons are very much part of the national prison system and face many of the same constraints. This does not mean that private-sector directors have deprioritized the importance of rehabilitative work. It is simply that they must manage their own constrained autonomy as any other actor in the system.

The second aspect of the schema relates to *coping and crisis culture*, and the role it plays in helping the system to retain some kind of operational stability. We have seen signs of this at all levels, both in the sense that actors are well aware of the imperative to find ways of making the system work, and in the sense that coping and (the threat of) crisis may be used instrumentally in order to defend the interests and demonstrate the valiant efforts of the system in general. As one former Prisons Minister put it: 'The Prison Service seems to be unable to cope with success. We cope [...] just. We acknowledge the objectives, and then say unfortunately we can't make them work. But at least we cope.' This insight also echoes the point made in the previous paragraphs about the inherent difficulties of demonstrating success (even if it can be evidenced).

From the high political perspective, ministers acknowledge as a basic minimal requirement the importance of presiding over a quiet and secure prison system. In doing so, they have relied heavily on the assurance from their top officials that the system is coping. We have seen how this reliance intensifies during periods of acute capacity stress, and how ministers have taken it upon themselves to venture out into the field to see for themselves what is happening in prisons (something which is often termed 'meddling' by officials, but seen by ministers as part of their ministerial prerogative). It is interesting that former ministers, perhaps sceptical of validity of information coming up through their officials, often reflected on how they relied on the views of trusted governors as their 'eyes and ears' in the field.

Clearly, top officials have borne the brunt of ongoing capacity stress over the years, and Chapter 6 conveys this culture of coping. Managing the relationship upwards with ministers has been difficult at times, according to many, and we have seen also how the relationship downwards has come to rely on command-and-control as a means of forcing the system to cope with population pressures. These top officials have also acknowledged that they would use whatever tools they had available to strengthen their case with ministers and the Treasury. Indeed, many pointed out that maintaining a perception of coping and crisis in the system has also helped their cause politically. As Chapter 4 has shown, an important part of coping has also involved maintaining flexibility in measures and standards, and this has allowed officials to rationalize and legitimate increments in capacity stress.

Coping with a rising short-term prison population has meant that the costs of capacity stress have been pushed down the system, and managers and staff in public and private prisons, not to mention prisoners themselves, are expected to absorb these costs. Governors have demonstrated a strong professional ethos geared towards finding a balance between accommodating requests from above, while doing their best for staff and prisoners. Governors' complaints about inadequate resourcing, ageing facilities, disruptive effects of national population management, and bureaucratic overload from performance management systems, all feed into their perception of coping. Many pointed out the 'feedback' dynamics, in that the capacity in the system to cope feeds into a tendency for senior ministers to rely on further ability of the system to cope. The counter-dynamic to this is a tendency for messages to feed up the system that it is near the brink of collapse, and this has presented a difficult 'moral hazard' dilemma for ministers.

Although coping culture is visible throughout the system, the idea that it is a pure coping culture seems excessive. Pure coping cultures do not tend to support performance improvements of the kind seen during the three decades. Also, actors at all levels do not see themselves as existing in a state of pure coping. Certainly, directors in the private sector and many public-sector governors have been critical of these prevalent cultures and have pointed out, quite legitimately one would assume, that they do not go into work in the morning in a chronic coping mode. Clearly, coping is part of the condition, but it is also continually challenged by actors' inclinations to want to change the system (or their bit of it) by design.

This leads to the third aspect, namely *direct and benign resistance* to change. We have seen numerous illustrations of direct resistance from all levels of the system, including explicitly risk-averse behaviour from ministers or threats of industrial action from the prison officers' union. Many interviewees have warned particularly against underestimating the political resonance of such threats by the POA, and the de facto power that this has had over ministers and governments, particularly Labour ones. We have also seen signs of direct resistance from the Prime Minister's office and from Treasury, in response to ministerial requests for funding investment in prison capacity. Top officials have reported resistance from above and below. They have had to contend with risk-averse attitudes from ministers, or political pressure to find ways of stretching existing capacity. We have seen how governors have sought to resist command-and-control dynamics, often less by direct resistance, and more often by shaping the use of capacity in their own establishments. Governors have also frequently talked about the problems of changing resistant staff cultures in their prisons, particularly large local prisons in which unionized influences have tended to be dominant.

It is, however, the concept of benign resistance that is equally if not more valuable in helping to explain why the system has lagged or been slow to change or reform. Benign resistance is the type that is much harder to discern or identify, as it is not usually explicitly manifest in the actions or behaviours of actors, but rather is a more subtle by-product of the actors attempting to manage their own predicaments in the system context. It may be that they perceive themselves as having to cope or make their bit of the system work that leads them to resist impetus for change in benign ways, in other words out of what they perceive to be practical necessity rather than out of their own pure self-interest. Top officials in the system, for example, may not explicitly resist the idea that prisons should rehabilitate offenders, but they may be inclined to resist benignly by making the seemingly reasonable argument there is a limit to what prisons can do in this respect with short-sentence prisoners who are only in custody for two or three weeks. It may be also that the system has been set up to focus more directly on the rehabilitative interventions with longer-sentence prisoners, an area in which they feel (perhaps legitimately) that they have more of an opportunity to work constructively with prisoners and intervene with more positive outcomes. Indeed, the data suggest that the longer the sentence, the less chance of reoffending, and in this respect, it may not be surprising that the system chooses to prioritize rehabilitation of longer-sentence prisoners, and in relative terms to deprioritize the rehabilitative work with shorter-sentence offenders. Such conventional wisdom, as we have seen, is visible throughout the system.

The final aspect relates to *sustained obsolescence and redundancy*. This is the fourth crucial element in the overall CCS heuristic, as it is both the product of continually coping and resisting systems, as well as an aggravating factor that sustains the need for coping and resisting. There have been many examples of this throughout. One striking example is the argument that the population management system (one that has been largely unautomated and run with pencil, paper, and telephone) is by nature too complicated to automate. This is despite the fact that many logistical and shipping companies, for example, appear to operate quite comfortably with automated systems for tracking freight and containers around the world. The perception of a coping or resisting system working valiantly is however strong, and feeds into the (entirely flawed) conventional wisdom that the system is too complex or sensitive to modernize in line with changes in wider society. Only relatively recently has the prison system implemented a system-wide database for prisoners, so this example is perhaps empirically a bit out of date. The basic idea of obsolescence and redundancy in the system, however, retains its relevance in other ways and illustrations.

At ministerial level, system obsolescence or redundancy tends to be seen as a 'second-order' concern, a 'matter of operation' rather than of high politics or policy. Manageable obsolescence does not tend to become a major priority for senior ministers unless it has acute crisis implications. Top officials have commonly acknowledged problems of obsolescence and redundancy over the years, and how this has led to privatization, market testing, performance-improvement plans, more managerialist targets, and so on. Yet one can argue that senior officials have helped to sustain aspects of redundancy and inefficiency, for example by tightening centralized command-and-control. Not surprisingly, governors share broadly fatalistic views about their own ability to impact on technological, infrastructural, and cultural forms of obsolescence in the system. Benign resistance to modernization has self-fulfilling characteristics, as systems naturally incur obsolescence over time, while at the same time being seen as too critical and complex to reform.

Obsolescence tends to be much less visible in the private sector, largely because these prisons are newer, designed for purpose, and are freer of many of the entrenched cultures and eccentricities found in the public sector. As Chapter 8 has illustrated, private prisons tend to reflect more 'normal' environments, much closer to current societal practices in terms of the look and feel of the physical environment, and the cultures of work and opportunity available for prisoners. Staff cultures also tend to be closer to what one might expect from modern firms or public bodies, in terms of a more equitable gender balance, positive incentives for staff to improve their skill levels, and negative sanctions for staff who serially underperform or engage in disruptive practices. As one private director put it: 'Normal is good in prisons, because you are always managing the abnormal. You are always trying to change the abnormal into normal.'

In each of these four loops, therefore, the overall equilibrium must be seen as contingent on the countervailing tensions across different levels of actors. We have seen how the characteristics at each level are largely determined by tensions and pressures from upwards and downwards in the principal–agent chain. This is in contrast to seeing the problem of crowding or CCS as a product of failure of instrumental will (or lack of it) in one particular group. To see the chronic problem as the failure of ministers, for example, is to overlook the fact that ministers must operate in conditions of constrained autonomy themselves, and are likely to adapt their efforts and commitments according to their own perceptions of where the limits of constraint and autonomy lie. In addition, characteristics of one part of the system can to a great extent be defined in opposition to the other parts with which it interacts. The conclusion is that these dimensions of chronicity must be looked at in relation to each other. They must also be looked at in terms of possibilities and limitations which constrained autonomy places on the individual actors involved.

9.2 Theoretical implications of the holistic approach

Theory has helped to build this schema and develop the concept of CCS. It has helped us understand the different aspects of the problem, both how they interact dialectically, and how through the predicaments and decisions of individual actors, we can bring these aspects to life. This theoretical treatment has allowed us to see a familiar and much discussed problem of prison crowding in a more sophisticated light, as an archetypal illustration of a more generic and widely applicable public-policy condition of CCS. In this next section, I turn the concept of CCS back onto the theory which founded it, and ask what are the implications of CCS for these main streams of theoretical approach?

Perhaps the most important characteristic of CCS has been one of countervailing dynamics. We have seen how it is possible for a system to incorporate simultaneously aspects of success and failure, aggravation and compensation, and signs of capacity shortage yet, at the same time, signs of capacity surplus and striking inefficiency. All of these dynamics are part of the same system, and are constituent in the same equilibria in the system. The implications of this analytical and empirical observation are potentially profound for existing theoretical approaches.

Let us return to the economistic theories discussed in the opening section of the first chapter. We have seen how public-choice theories such as rent-seeking and bureau-shaping have provided explanations for under-supply in public-policy systems. Such theories are often presented in opposition to 'budget-maximizing' explanations (Niskanen, 1998), namely that bureaucratic systems will tend towards situations of over-supply as a result of bureaucrats seeking to increase the size of their budgets. Such approaches therefore tend to see public-policy systems as either sustaining situations of under-supply or over-supply, defined by a single point on a continuum around a theoretical point of equilibrium. In other words, a bureaucratic system, in terms of its budget at least, is either running in a situation of stress or surplus; the implication being that both cannot apply simultaneously.

But the concept of CCS raises some tricky qualitative questions for this linear conception. CCS would clearly be associated with the position of under-supply given that capacity stress denotes stretch and shortfall in supply. We have seen much in this research to substantiate such a view. But there are some problems with this linear conception when talking about the equilibrium in the system as a whole. For countervailing dynamics tell us the system can sustain situations of relative under-supply and over-supply at the same time. In other words, both dynamics are part of the same condition of CCS. Given these two separate dynamics in the same system, it makes no logical sense to try to find a point of average or interaction between them. Such linear conception of supply is therefore not sufficient in a system which appears to incorporate chronic aspects of relative under-supply and over-supply at the same time and as part of one whole.

Constrained autonomy highlights a further potential fallacy at the heart of economistic explanations. The normative basis for these explanations is individual actors. But the problem is that these tend to be a particular abstracted type of individual actor, who is able to step back from and think strategically about their position in the system. In reality, however, actors are rarely if ever afforded the luxury of the economist's viewpoint. Horn's transaction-cost model, for example, has much in common with the concept of constrained autonomy, in the sense that he views strategic actors as attempting to engineer an optimal balance between decentralizing and centralizing measures. Where this comes apart from the concept of constrained autonomy, however, is in suggesting that this balance can be something which is engineered *by design*, rather than something which happens *by default* as an outcome of constrained autonomy of all actors in the system. Roberts and other management economists have argued that organizations can be 'efficiently fickle' (Nickerson and Zenger, 2002). By this, they mean that they can find long-term optimality by sustaining acceptable forms of short-term sub-optimality. This has intriguing implications for thinking about why a system sustains sub-optimal states over the long term. But again, this approach assumes that these actors have a sufficient degree of strategic instrumentality over the system in order to be able to engineer these outcomes. Constrained autonomy suggests that they do, but only to a limited degree.

The research highlights limitations of cultural explanations too. Culturally fatalist concepts such as 'impossible jobs' and 'permanently failing organizations' are shown to have general 'mood' value, not least because they provide high-impact concepts which are immediately evocative of particular syndromes of chronicity. We can recognize aspects of 'impossible jobs' and 'permanent failure' as part of CCS in the prison system. There is, however, much to suggest that this prison system has been anything but 'permanently failing', and has shown in fact how strategic and persistent instrumental action over an extended period can gradually bring about a great many improvements. Most top officials may be inclined to recognize elements of 'impossible jobs' in their work, but they would reject the systemic pessimism implicit in these two concepts. As I hope this research has shown, the system is more complicated and has shown aspects of improvement through instrumental design and managerialist reform, not to mention concerted effort.

The insightful comparative study of prison systems in Hood et al. (2004) examines the idea that 'cultural clumsiness' – i.e. cultural hybridity – is a key characteristic of successful control and accountability. They argue that a 'clumsiness deficit' in the prison system is caused by 'racking up of oversight without competition' leading to 'accountability overload without guaranteeing quality or robustness' (p. 204). As a summary of the key pathologies highlighted in this research, this cultural diagnosis is not bad at all. We have seen a stymied growth in competition, as well as complaints of bureaucratic and managerialist overload. Yet, from an empirical standpoint, there is much to suggest that hierarchical oversight has in fact had a strong impact on quality and robustness of the system. Strong emphasis on command-and-control, performance management, and beefed-up inspection[1] have also led to a much tighter and more disciplined system. Furthermore, constrained autonomy itself has demonstrated a high degree of intrinsic self-equilibrating 'clumsiness' of the kind thought to be showing 'deficit' in Hood et al.'s diagnosis.

The research has shown that there is a fine dividing line between strong command-and-control, which is able to get the system by the scruff of the neck and improve it, and excessive command-and-control, which ends up stifling and constraining the system's ability to realize its various goals. (This may be Horn's dilemma in a nutshell). In both cases, the hierarchical cultures may look the same, but they imply different outcomes (from the perspective of different actors in the system). In the opening chapter, we have discussed the trade-off between 'reliability' or 'resilience', on the one hand, and 'anticipation' or 'tightening' on the other, the implication being that public-sector systems have tended to move towards the latter of these two. This implies a shift towards excessively rule-based and nailed-down processes, rather than more 'loosely coupled' and agile arrangements. Again, the overall CCS schema and constrained autonomy raise questions for these dualistic conceptions of reality. The analysis in Chapter 3 and indeed in subsequent chapters has shown us that a prison system, or indeed any public-policy system, can incorporate all four of these aspects, all of which can have both positive and negative consequences. Hence, it is difficult in the context of the system to draw a line between one and the other, not to mention deciding whether one or the other is intrinsically good or bad.

It is also important to say something about the theoretical implications for systems theory. Clearly, some of the main ideas of systems theory have been important to the development of the concept of CCS, not least the importance of understanding the behaviours and actions of individual parts of the system in the context of the whole, and by consequence understanding adaptive and self-organizing characteristics of large and inherently complex systems. It is, however, clearly not enough to do the equivalent of throwing our hands up and saying that it is all too complex to really know (as systems theoretical approaches often tend to imply). As social and political scientists, it is, I would say, beholden on this kind of study that we at least attempt to get to some specifics about causal dynamics even if those dynamics are multifaceted and aggravating and undoubtedly complex. In these four dynamic aspects, the overall schema, and in the discussion of constrained autonomy of real-life actors in the system, I hope that I have done enough here to satisfy some basic requirements of specificity in causal explanation. Clearly, these dynamics require further work and refinement, and application in other public-policy contexts, but they are, I would argue, described specifically enough in these pages to count as a new theoretical and conceptual contribution to understanding the complex governance condition of CCS.

This brings us finally to the explanatory potential of paradigms of public policy and management, as discussed in the opening pages of the first chapter. Where does the concept of CCS, as developed here, leave us in terms of the explanatory value of dominant paradigms over recent decades, particularly New Public Management (NPM) and the 'post-NPM' era? I have shown NPM to be susceptible to countervailing and seemingly paradoxical dynamics, which, for want of a better expression, make life complicated. These dynamics remind us that we should be wary of attributing too much explanatory power, as it were, to the principles and predictions of established paradigms.

We have seen how the paradigm of NPM has been a crucial part of this story during the last thirty years, and how it has played a part as both aggravating and compensating factor at the heart of the concept of CCS. It has helped to tighten the system, impose order and management discipline. This has made it more able to manage and cope with capacity stress, yet at the same time it has imposed constraints, both perceived and actual, on realization of more ambitious value-based goals. Conclusions about NPM principles of efficiency and effectiveness seem far less clear cut in this light. There have been gradual improvements in quality-adjusted productivity. And we might also argue managerialist change has contributed to a more ordered and disciplined system, which itself has contributed to 7–20 per cent reductions in reconviction rates over ten years. NPM however has allowed the system to deprioritize other important goals, and normalize considerable obsolescence and redundancy beneath the surface. Changes which have allowed the system to become more efficient and effective have also apparently rendered it less efficient and effective in other ways.

We have seen the limitations of another key NPM principle, the introduction of competition into a public-sector system. Clearly, the private sector has grown, and these new markets have provided a basis for competition and innovation. Indeed, the allocation of relatively equal market share across three competing firms suggests that government has shaped the market to avoid severe imbalances or monopoly (although it is still oligopolistic). The system itself, however, has had constraining effects on competition. In many cases, this has played an important part in controlling private-sector rent-seeking, and in encouraging, as far as possible, a standardized service across public and private. Indeed, there is evidence that the need for some degree of parity of service between public and private has meant that private prisons have had to rein in their own outputs and performance (according to private directors at least).

Constrained autonomy has implications for the credibility of the NPM principle of separation of policy and operational functions. Looking at the system as a chain of principal–agent relationships, in which each actor must look after their own equilibrium, the idea that policy and operational functions can be meaningfully separated out seems far too simplistic. We have seen that the relationship is clearly more nuanced, how ministers have been inclined to get involved in the minutiae of capacity management during times of crisis. And we have also seen how operational actors have been able to maintain de facto power by being the deliverers of capacity equilibrium. The reliance on strong command-and-control mechanisms as part of the improvements identified in the prison system also suggest that decentralizing dynamics of NPM are only viable to a limited degree.

It is interesting that the NPM paradigm throughout the late 1970s and 1980s offered renewed optimism for transforming inefficiency and waste in the public sector. Yet, the prognosis at the end of the 2000s has been that NPM has been enigmatic to say the least and, in many ways, contradictory in its impact. As shown in Table 1.1, there have been clear signs of transition away from NPM in recent years, and some of its more constraining aspects. Dunleavy et al.'s (2006) 'digital era governance' paradigm provides a persuasive picture of what this transition has entailed – processes of 'reintegration, needs-based holism, and digitization' (see also Dunleavy and Margetts, 2012). These may be partly seen as an antidote to the constraining effects of NPM. They may also partly be seen as a reflection of public-management systems responding to fundamental changes in the way modern societies operate. Either way, the prison system has shown signs of change 'away from itself' in many of these respects.

New emergent paradigms such as 'digital era governance' are, however, likely to be integral and susceptible to the complexities of the system, and the predicaments facing actors of having to operate within. The scale of ambition to join up and re-engineer policy and services around individuals is often completely at odds with the capability and the capacity of the system. We have also seen how the prison system has had to drag itself into the digital era during the last ten years or so, and even now faces another ten years at least of real integration of new digital technologies into core business processes. Furthermore, obsolescence can actually be perpetuated by forcing dysfunctional systems to cope with more ambitious policy goals. Thirty-odd years of NPM may have brought the prison system to this point of apparent transition, but it is a fallacy to think that a brand new paradigm will come along and replace the old one, and make a condition like CCS go away. The challenge must be to interpret this chronic condition in its dynamic and changing light.

9.3 The future of chronic capacity stress: in prisons and beyond

It is hopefully clear by now that CCS is a multifaceted concept, one which incorporates a balance between aggravating and compensating dynamics, and which can be seen as a function of the way in which a whole public-policy system works. Functions are 'those observed consequences which make for the adaptation or adjustment of a given system' (Merton, 1957, p. 51). Prison crowding, it appears, has been exactly this kind of consequence, one which has 'made for' a degree of acceptable and manageable operation of the prison system over the decades – despite its unattractive consequences. The illusion is that nobody appears to will it or engineer it single-handedly, yet it has persisted in the system for a long period of time. For this reason, crowding has proven a classic archetype of CCS.

If there are not single identifiable causes or causal behaviours that explain CCS, then it is unlikely that we will be able to identify single remedies which will be able to alleviate it. Although single remedies can help to some extent, the approach in this book suggests that change would have to happen in balanced and complementary ways across all parts of the system for the chronic condition to be alleviated and or reversed. What therefore are the prospects for engineering this kind of complementarity or positive cycles of change? Basically, the answer would seem to lie in interventions in all four aspects of the CCS schema, in a balanced and sustained way.

Let us start with the prioritization of rehabilitative outcomes at high political level. What might be the systemic effects of this radical shift in policy? We can begin to trace through some of the system effects of this top-level emphasis on 'rehabilitative revolution'. This may encourage actors throughout the system to behave in ways which prioritize rehabilitative performance, and to challenge up the chain excessive command-and-control cultures that threaten to undermine the ability of actors below to do the things necessary to boost rehabilitation. Furthermore, as actors at all levels in the system become more directly incentivized to focus on rehabilitative goals, they may be likely to challenge other constraints. Governors, for example, may be more directly encouraged to stay in the same prisons for longer tenures, if they are more explicitly associated with and rewarded for being successful at rehabilitative outcomes. Indeed, many positive dynamic effects may result from a sustained shift in political discourse and commitment at the very top of the political system.

Political leadership also plays an important part in this respect, and we have seen over the years how shifts in top political personnel can scupper reform or take the system off on different policy trajectories. Since May 2010, the system had looked as if it may be given the chance to build up some of this complementarity towards rehabilitative change under the political leadership of the Minister of Justice, Kenneth Clarke. He had proven a skilful, pragmatic, and charismatic agent of political change, and in the twilight of his political career had little (arguably) to lose in pursuing reform. He had also presided over the prison system during a period of strong fiscal austerity, and consequently, had found it relatively easy to secure political support within the Conservative Party for policies that aimed to reduce the costs of prison – even if it was by committing to rehabilitative reform and a smaller prison population. The decision by the Prime Minister to replace Clarke with a new Secretary of State for Justice, Chris Grayling, in September 2012 was an example of this inherent political uncertainty that can potentially disrupt or dilute these complementarity effects. Political pressure on the reforming Clarke had built up from the right of his own party and his replacement reflected a desire for a return to a more authoritative and potentially less reformative policy on prisons. And so the political churn at the top rolls on.

What the fate of the 'rehabilitative revolution', however, is not clear. Its success is likely to depend on the extent to which demand-side measures can lead to some reduction (however, gradual) in the size of the prison population. Like many other governments before it, the Conservative–Liberal coalition has undertaken a consultation on sentencing guidelines, and ways to reduce the prison population through alternative non-custodial means. But the impact of these measures, of the kind which have become familiar over the decades, are still uncertain. It is not enough to will this change, or to make public pronouncements about it. There must, it seems, be some degree of actual reduction for positive complementarity to kick in. The fact that the prison population rose to around 88,000 by the end of 2011 did not reflect well. This was caused in large part by the government's and the judiciary's response to the outbreaks of rioting across the country during August 2011. During 2012, however, the prison population has seen marginal reduction back to around 85,000, illustrating the fact that the system has coped with the period of acute capacity pressure. Other signs suggest that demand-side pressures are being lessened, for example in the reduction in the number of young offenders committed to custody (PRT, 2012).

Running continually at close-to-tolerance should lead us towards more sceptical evaluation of the prospects for rehabilitative reform. Take, for example, the current pilot programmes in place to introduce 'payment by results' schemes into local prisons. Let us assume that these can be shown to work well in isolated prisons (although the pilots are set up so that we are not due to find out until 2014). Furthermore, let us assume that methods can be devised to attribute rehabilitative impact of these prisons on prisoners in such a way that 'results' can be remunerated. The problem is that once we begin to extend these schemes across the system, we must deal with the fact that the system as a whole has been run in such a way that it relies on the constant movement of prisoners from prison to prison in order to be able to function. If short-sentence prisoners are continually being moved around the estate, something that has been a major part of the system's coping mechanism for many years, then it is difficult to see how attribution of rehabilitative impact could be isolated in any meaningful way. Furthermore, the decision of which prisoners to move on overcrowding drafts has been left to individual prisons, and without central direction there would be even more incentive than there currently is for all prisons (public *and* private) to cream-skim the easiest prisoners and send on the more difficult to other local prisons. These things show how even the most lofty political aspirations can be constrained, partly or fully, by the realities of the day-of-day operations of making the system work.

Optimists may argue that it is entirely possible to re-engineer existing capacity in the system in order to balance up regional patterns of demand and supply, and this has undoubtedly been a preoccupation for NOMS strategic staff in recent years. Dealing with the lack of capacity in the London area has been key in this respect, and from 2010 new capacity in London and the south east has to some extent helped to redress this imbalance. However, in order to neutralize the need to move prisoners, more funds must be found to shape the prison estate. The bare fact of the matter for NOMS and the Ministry of Justice is that it has had to cut its budget by 25 per cent by 2014 as part of government spending commitments. It is therefore unlikely that funds will be found for new prison capacity,[2] and this will no doubt continue the pressure on the existing prison capacity to cope with any further rise in the prison population. Even maintaining a prison population at 85,000 will put pressure on the estate to cope, and further constrain the ability to renew physical capacity or take physical obsolescence out of the system.

The transfer of Birmingham prison, one of the largest and busiest prisons in the country, to private-sector management may be one important step towards ironing out some of the more obvious inefficiencies in the system. This is likely to be followed by transfer of further prisons from public to private management during 2013, although signs suggest that the government has scaled back its immediate plans in this respect. The breakdown of resistance to transferring a large local prison in particular into private-sector management throughout the 2000s may indeed go some way to radically modernizing important aspects of prison logistics nationally. As we have seen, Birmingham prison has been an important hub for distribution of prisoners, and it is conceivable that G4S, the new contractor, would want to use this hub position to look at more efficient ways of processing prisoners, their files, and their belongings, around the system. If a large London local prison is market tested and transferred, then this would increase pressure further on the system to modernize logistical and information systems for prisoner transfer. But it is far from clear that turning over the largest prison in the country to G4S will deliver a more effective prison system, particularly in the light of very public mismanagement of other major contracts with government in recent years (*The Times*, 2012).

We have also seen how prisoner information systems have been chronically behind the times throughout the 1990s and 2000s, still in many respects relying on manual paper-based processing of records. It was only since 2010 that the system as a whole has had a fully integrated online database system which, for the first time, has allowed administrators and prison staff access to information about all prisoners in the prison system at any one time. Practically all governors and staff acknowledged this would radically improve the way in which services can be delivered to individual prisoners. Again, we see how reduction in obsolescence can feed back positively into what managers and staff deem possible, which itself feeds into countering the coping mind-set. We should however be careful of painting too optimistic and deterministic picture of the effects of a new computer system. One experienced official described new constraints that emerge from new systems:

> The classic one is that the P-NOMIS system does not allow population management to know how many prisoners are serving what kind of sentences in prisons. It is impossible now to plan the population because it was never built into the spec. Every week I get prison population figures. I used to get them broken down by sentence. Up to

> twelve months, up to four years, etc. That is now blank and has been blank since last August (2010). And so research and development are spitting tacks. They are saying how on earth can we do population projections because we don't know the prison population.

In this quotation above, we are brought back to the countervailing ways in which systems function or only partly function. Ten years in development and implementation, the new P-NOMIS is clearly an improvement on the previous system, yet at the same time it illustrates how dynamic change introduces new aspects of dysfunction and coping. It is again part fallacy to think that brand new systems come along and replace old ones, and make chronic conditions go away.

Prisons may be sui generis institutions and, for the multiple reasons explored in this book, particularly suited to CCS analysis. It is, however, also the case that CCS, or variations of, can be seen in many other public-policy systems across UK government and potentially further afield. Indeed, it is quite often the case in the UK that we hear of public-sector agencies struggling against the tide or having to cope with large backlogs of caseloads or sudden surges of demand, and it is usually apparent that one does not have to dig too deeply to identify exactly the aspects of CCS that we have examined in this book, as well as the same kinds of constrained autonomy among the actors in the systems involved. We hear in the news and media how large public-policy systems quite regularly encounter periods of acute crisis that are symptomatic of more fundamental chronic conditions that stay with these agencies for longer periods of time. These variations of CCS can work both as symptoms and causes of dysfunction. They may also work their way into normalized cultures of the system and operate as justifications and rationale for sub-optimal outcomes. In all these senses, they may not be ideal. But they sustain because they are, for a whole host of reasons, sustainable.

There is not room here to examine at great length further comparable cases of CCS. It has been necessary to dig deeply into one area, prison crowding, in order to build the conceptual schema of CCS. As I have been researching and writing this book, however, there has rarely been a month when there has not been at least one major story in the news that has shown signs of aspects of CCS. Much like prisons, these have usually involved systems that process caseloads, for example immigration and border controls (Vine, 2012), child-welfare services (Munro, 2011), or regulatory systems overseeing healthcare professions (CHRE, 2012). We see aspects of CCS also in other core state activities that do not necessarily involve caseload processing, but involve obvious issues of capacity stress in supply of frontline public services, for example inadequacy of equipment or resources supplied to armed forces in combat situations (Ministry of Defence, 2010, p. 4) or complaints from frontline systems such as policing or public-sector transport workers that they have insufficient manpower or resources to fulfil the 'goals' expected of them. In other areas of the public sector, we also often see quite contradictory or even paradoxical situations in which systems appear to be under stretch and coping, yet at the same time, subject to considerable hikes in financial or intellectual investment. And it is also the case that many of these core public-sector systems have normalized often quite striking levels of obsolescence and redundancy in systems that are vital to their day-to-day operations. Beneath the modern managerial discourse and cultures of today's public sector, we find systems and processes that often seem to be grossly out-of-kilter with even quite modest expectations of what modern public services should look like.

Taking one of these major examples, the UK border-control system has showed clear signs of CCS in recent years. This is a large public-policy system that has had to find ways of balancing the demand for carrying out border checks against its available resources. Indeed, it has done so by relying on systematic suspension of certain aspects of these checks during times of peak inflow of passengers. These suspensions have usually been sanctioned by senior ministers, and justified by officials on a range of pragmatic grounds (Vine, 2012). Either way, they have allowed the border-control system to sustain a form of manageable and acceptable equilibrium between the demands made of it and the supply of capacity. Just as the prison system has normalized crowding over many years, the border-control system has normalized discretionary suspensions of certain checks in order to cope with fluctuations in passenger flows.

From mid-2009, however, the Labour government introduced the policy requirement that biometric data should be checked for incoming passengers to the UK. The technology and systems for this policy requirement were provided through an outsourced contract, and border-control staff were responsible for operating the new system. In July 2010, however, the contract ran into difficulty, and was terminated, hence putting pressure on border-control management and staff to continue to administer in line with policy requirements. Between July 2010 and July 2011, border-control management took the decision to suspend biometric checks during times of high demand. In the summer of 2011, the Home Secretary was informed about these discretionary suspensions, and banned any further suspensions. Despite this resistance from the top of the system, managers continued to sanction intermittent suspensions, albeit at a much reduced rate, with the result that the Home Secretary asked for the resignation of the chief of the Border Force and announced a root-and-branch reform of the border-control administration (Bastow, 2012).

In this brief example, we see many of the same conditions and predicaments which have faced actors at all levels in the prison system. For the senior ministers involved, the realization that senior officials were systematically suspending checks against explicit orders was unacceptable and, we might argue, understandably so. The political response to this acute realization came in the form of a declaration of sweeping reform and resignations of the senior staff involved. For the top officials involved, however, we can also view their predicament with equal amounts of empathy, in that they were being asked to make the whole system work in a context of reduced staffing, continued austerity measures, a failed contract for business-critical IT, and ever-growing numbers of incoming passengers who had to be subject to ever-growing range of risk-profiling and checks. On the frontline, border staff have found themselves having to integrate new risk-management approaches, at the same time as coping with partly functional biometric IT equipment, reliance on old-fashioned manual checking techniques, and dwindling numbers of staff on duty. As we have seen in the prisons case, actors at all levels are inclined to finesse their own equilibrium by resorting to particular arguments to support their case. And sure enough, we have seen border-staff unions and media in recent years highlighting the reduction in staffing and resources as a main reason for capacity stress (BBC, 2012). Clearly this is part of the problem, but as we have seen throughout the book CCS is more complicated than simple lack of resources, and such arguments are themselves as much a construct of the system as they are an objective reflection of the conditions at its heart.

This is admittedly an all-too-brief taster of how CCS can be applied to a great many public-policy systems. It is, however, illustration of how one needs a fairly in-depth qualitative approach to understand the countervailing dynamics involved, and how they sustain chronic conditions over time. I do not suggest here that there is one type of CCS, and that all aspects of it should be uniform. It is rather the case that the four aspects of CCS that we have covered throughout this book together provide a more integrated way of disentangling and understanding the dynamics of these common kinds of problems. All of these and many more are cases of large public-policy systems incorporating different types of CCS, operating in broadly manageable and acceptable ways, and somehow doing so despite themselves. All of these and many more can be analysed through exactly the same CCS lens. They would highlight similar countervailing dynamics which aggravate and compensate, and which allow systems to function in one way or another under stress. Furthermore, individual actors in all of those systems would experience similar types of constrained autonomy on their choices and actions, thus feeding into and sustaining CCS. The condition of prison crowding has provided the in-depth empirical substance for pulling apart and understanding the dynamics of this chronic condition, the likes of which, I would suggest, appear in many forms and guises across modern public policy and management.

Notes

1 Traditional Explanations of Capacity Stress and Their Limitations

1. Literature on 'policy disasters' (Dunleavy, 1995; Gray and t'hart, 1998; Birkland, 2009), 'service delivery disasters' (Dunleavy et al., 2010), and 'policy fiascos' (Bovens and t'Hart, 2005). There has been slightly less attention paid to the other end of the spectrum, i.e. policy successes, although there have been recent policy-focused exceptions (Cabinet Office, 2008; Rutter et al., 2012).
2. Goffman (1961) describes a 'total institution' as a 'place of residence and work where a large number of like-situated individuals, cut off from the wider society for an appreciable period of time, together lead an enclosed, formally administered round of life' (p. 11).
3. The fifth archetype, the 'hermit', denotes a worldview devoid of any conception of social solidarity.
4. Other critics have argued along similar lines, particularly in relation to 'high-reliability' public-policy systems (Landau, 1969; Landau and Chisholm, 1995; Frederickson and LaPorte, 2002). Landau points out that the push for economic efficiency over the years has the effect of tightening the system, thus reducing levels of redundancy which are often vital in ensuring reliability and adaptiveness to sudden environmental change (1969, p. 356).
5. Wilson (2000) characterizes prisons as 'coping institutions' because of the difficulties which society encounters in monitoring both outputs and outcomes of prison activities.
6. For an in-depth account of the concepts of complexity theory, see Kauffman (1995). Complexity theory becomes more prevalent in UK management journals throughout the 2000s, for example Houchin and MacLean (2005). In more recent years, public-administration theorists have began to apply complexity theory to public policy: see, for example, Van Buuren and Gerrits (2008); Teisman and Klijn (2008); Teisman et al. (2009).
7. Kauffman (1995) puts this idea eloquently: 'in such a poised world, we must give up the pretense of long-term prediction. We cannot know the true consequences of our own best actions. All we players can do is be locally wise, not globally wise. All we can do, all anyone can do, is hitch up our pants, put on our galoshes, and get on with it best we can' (p. 29).
8. See Warfield and Perino (1999) and Warfield (2003) for discussion on design and use of 'problematique'. Warfield and Perino (1999) explain that 'problematiques portray graphically how a set of problems is interrelated, in terms of influencing each other. In addition the relationship pictured is typically one of significant aggravation rather than the more commonly invoked causality' (p. 224).

2 A More Holistic Governance-Style Approach

1. I use the term 'holistic' here cautiously, as it has been the subject of scepticism over the years as an 'everything-or-nothing' term, which tends to lay claims towards a need for more expansive explanations, yet by definition cannot avoid falling victim to the practical need to limit the scope of its explanations in one way or another (Phillips, 1976).
2. See Ruggles-Brise (1921), Fox (1952), and McConville (1981, 1995) for extensive and detailed historical coverage of goal ambiguity in the England and Wales prison system over the last 300 years.
3. A senior member of the Prisons Board at the time, Ian Dunbar, also wrote in a much-cited report that 'a sense of futility has become pervasive and has led to what some observers have called a moral vacuum' (1985, p. 6).
4. A sense of perpetual failure is closely linked to the perception that governments and courts send too many people to prison. For versions of this argument, see Bottoms, 1980; King et al., 1980; Fitzgerald and Sim, 1982; Stern, 1993; Coyle, 1994, 2007; Dunbar and Langdon, 1998; Garland, 2001; Newell, 2003; Wilson, 2003; Hedderman, 2005, 2008; Faulkner, 2006; Blom-Cooper, 2008; Loader, 2007, 2008, 2009. Demand-side explanations for prison-capacity stress also tend to argue, explicitly or implicitly, for restrictive policies on building new prison capacity. For discussions over the years, see Blumstein and Cohen, 1973; Howard League, 1974, 1981, 1996, 2005; Downes, 1980; Blumstein et al., 1983; Funke, 1985; Blumstein, 1988; Mathieson, 1991; D'Alessio and Stolzenburg, 1997; Garside, 2005; Heddermann, 2008.
5. Although there is a large body of criminological literature on the prison system that argues that prison populations are excessively high, a small number of authors have argued the opposite, and characterize these demand-side interpretations as part of a 'misguided liberal consensus'. Fraser (2006) argues that demand-side arguments 'appear to wield considerable influence on our criminal justice policies because their anti-prison philosophy fits in with the government's own objectives, and Home Office and Treasury civil servants are happy on occasions to let them do the talking for them' (p. 71).
6. See for discussion, Evans, 1980; King et al., 1980; Downes, 1988; Mylotte, 1989; King and McDermott, 1989, 1995; and Casale, 1994.
7. The Woolf report, published in April 1991, refers to the major independent inquiry into the riots at Strangeways prison in Manchester in April 1990 and the series of disturbances across the prison system that led up to this major disturbance. This inquiry was led by Lord Justice Woolf, and is widely recognized as a key turning point for reform of the England and Wales prison system.
8. See for discussion, King and McDermott, 1995; Talbot, 1996, 2004; Cavadino and Dignan, 2003, 2006; Matthews and Young, 2003; Pollitt et al., 2004a, 2004b; Boin et al., 2006; and Lacey, 2008.
9. See for discussion, Faulkner, 2004, 2005, 2006; Gough, 2004; Padfield, 2004; Hedderman, 2005; Rumgay, 2005; and Cavadino and Dignan, 2006.

3 Performance and Capacity in a Managerialist Era

1. Positive productivity may result from increases in the prison population. For many observers this is a sign of wider 'failure' to avoid use of prison. In this sense, output-driven productivity improvement may be seen paradoxically as the 'wrong' kind of improvement, one which is in fact contributing to fuelling a problem of rising prison populations rather than remedying it.
2. Outputs consist of the total average size of the prison population, cost-weighted in terms of the average cost of running different types of prisons. Six types of prisons were included in this cost-weighting: local and remand, high security, closed adult, closed youth, open adult, and open youth. Inputs consisted of total current operating expenditure in real terms from 2011. Total factor productivity was calculated as a ratio of cost-weighted outputs over inputs.
3. Throughout the first half of the 2000s, local Primary Care Trusts (PCTs) began to take over responsibility for commissioning and provision of healthcare in prisons. By April 2006, responsibility for healthcare services was fully transferred to Department of Health, with local PCTs responsible for commissioning and provision of healthcare services, in conjunction with the Prison Service and Home Office.
4. Coyle (1994) writes that

   > by the mid-1980s, [overtime] had reached an impossible situation [...] accounting for almost one third of the salary bill. Officers were discontented that they had to work so many hours overtime to earn what they considered to be a decent wage. Management was frustrated by the demand-led nature of work and the rigid staffing levels which provided staff with a set of arcane working practices which guaranteed virtually unlimited overtime. (p. 139)

5. The Princeton project was a collaboration during the early 1990s between the Bureau of Justice Statistics in the US Department of Justice, and the Princeton University Study Group on Criminal Justice Performance Measures. For further details, see DiIulio (1993).
6. This has been acknowledged in interviews with a wide range of politicians, officials, and governors. It has also been referenced frequently in generalist academic literature on the development of the prison system. Cavadino and Dignan (2003) point out that 'although the effects have been experienced most intensely within the dispersal prisons themselves, the rest of the prison system has not been immune from the growing security syndrome' (p. 181).
7. In 2002, ten separate incidents were recorded from analysis of press and media. These were relatively low-level cases. Lincoln prison experienced large-scale rioting in October 2002. It was described as the worst rioting since the Manchester riots in April 1990.
8. Table 3.2 provides an overview of the intensity of performance management in the prison system over thirty years. It uses reporting of outputs data in annual reports as a proxy for performance-management intensity. From 1993 onwards, the Prison Service formally evaluated its activities against Key Performance Targets (KPTs), and these have been reported each year in the

annual report. Prior to 1993, the Prison Department did not have formalized KPTs, and hence I have coded any data tables featured in annual reports, also scoring any tables or graphs at 1 point each. Some KPTs have been discontinued due to responsibility for that moving to another jurisdiction.

9. See Goetz (2006), Pollitt (2008), and Pollitt and Bouckaert (2009) for useful discussions on the importance and relative neglect of the temporal dimension in public-policy research.
10. The crowding index is calculated as the mean of the percentage of crowding above the certified normal accommodation (CNA) in each local and remand prison. See Chapter 4 for more details on CNA. For each year, I calculated the mean percentage of crowding for that year in each local and remand prison, and then calculated an annual mean of these for each year. The index line is median smoothed.
11. Ministry of Justice data suggests that around one third of offenders sentenced to less than 12 months are moved on overcrowding drafts. For the period June 2008 to June 2009, 16,320 overcrowding drafts took place. This is equivalent to 16 per cent of all sentenced prisoners received into local prisons, and 30 per cent of all sentenced prisoners received into local prisons on sentences 12 months or less. Many of these drafts would involve the same individual prisoners being moved more than once.
12. Common abbreviation for the centralized 'Population Management' unit based at Prison Service headquarters, responsible for coordination and movement of the prison population.

4 Measuring and Setting Capacity Standards

1. Christensen and Lægreid (2002) identify a 'shift in accountability from the political to the managerial sphere and from input and processes to outputs and outcomes' (p. 308). Hood et al. (2004) identify a similar shift from inputs to outputs, from 'emphasis on detailed *ex ante* authorization to *ex post* appraisal and audit of activity and performance against general guidelines and principles' (p. 194).
2. CNA and Op Cap have evolved sub-categories over the years, for example, CNA has developed into more specific variations such as 'In-use CNA' or 'Baseline CNA', but for the purpose of this analysis, they are discussed in their generic form.
3. The actual term appears to have been introduced around the end of the 1970s, with first specific mention in official documentation in the 1980 Prison Department annual report.
4. The 1979 May Inquiry made recommendation that the Prisons Inspectorate should be made independent and that the Chief Inspector should be independent of the Prison Service. One interviewee reflected on the 'tremendous row' that went on between Lord Justice May and Robert Armstrong, former head of the civil service, about the constitutional status of the Inspectorate. It nevertheless remained part of the Home Office, and the Chief Inspector has reported to the Home Secretary (now Minister for Justice).
5. McConville (1981) identifies localized crowding in urban prisons throughout the nineteenth century. He writes about a period circa 1857, 'even when the authorities enlarged their prisons, committals overtook the new capacity, and

as at Liverpool prison, instead of being separated as was intended, prisoners were, within a couple of years, once more sleeping three to a cell' (p. 365). Fox (1952) explains how the 'separate system' in England was slowly eroded due to population pressures in the post-war years. He writes that the

> breach is due simply to overcrowding: before the war there had always been cells enough for all-comers, but post-war pressure on the available accommodation has led first, to the creation inside the prisons of small dormitories in whatever rooms could be made available, and next to the regrettable necessity, in the majority of local prisons of sleeping a proportion of prisoners three in a cell. (p.104)

6. Weiler (1992) writes that

   > there was no formal consideration by the Prisons Board, no Ministerial statement, no Parliamentary or press interest, and no comprehensive instructions to the Prison Service. Nor could I even establish the precise date on which the first location of three men in a cell took place. There was certainly no appreciation that this regrettable deterioration in prison conditions would be a long term one. (p. 24)

   He observes that

   > there had been no relevant comment in the extracts from governors' annual reports since 1952. It is not unreasonable to infer that the service and headquarters had come to accept 3-in as a normal and inevitable feature of post war life. (p. 40)

7. Silvia Casale and Joyce Plotnikoff have drawn attention to the resistance at ministerial and senior official level to developing objectifiable minimum standards for prison capacity. See PRT (1986, 1993b); Casale and Plotnikoff (1989, 1990); and Casale (1994).
8. A new Prison Rule that no establishments should hold more prisoners than is provided for in certified normal level of accommodation, with provisions for Parliament to be informed if exceptionally there is to be material departure' +/- 3 per cent for more than 7 days in a period of any 3 months. (Woolf, 2008, p. 247)
9. These data were based on my own analysis of prison population and CNA figures for year 1979 to 2011 from Prison Service and NOMS annual reports. Percentage crowding figures were calculated for each year, and then the thirty-year series was median smoothed. Three-year averages were calculated from the year listed. For example, for 1979, I took the mean average of smoothed data for years 1979, 1980, and 1981.
10. The first formal mention I found was in Prison Service Instruction 19 (HMPS, 1992a).
11. Reference to Sir David Ramsbotham, former Her Majesty's Chief Inspector of Prisons 1995–2001. See Ramsbotham (2005).

5 Senior Ministers and the Limits of Their Influence to Resolve the Capacity Problem

1. Figure 5.1 is based on near-comprehensive analysis of individual references to 'prison' and 'crowding' made by parliamentarians in both Houses of Parliament between 1980 and 2011.

2. Party-political conference platform speeches provide a reasonably standardized format for comparative analysis. I reviewed twenty-seven ministerial platform speeches out of a possible thirty-two, counting the number of words in each relating to prisons, penal policy, and sentencing. For each Home Secretary in each category, I recorded the average number of words across years in office. All Conservative Party speeches were sourced from the Conservative Party Archive held at the Bodleian library in Oxford. All Labour speeches were sourced online through Google search. The speeches included are as follows: Whitelaw (1979, 1980, 1981, 1982), Brittan (1983, 1984), Hurd (1985, 1986, 1987, 1988, 1989), Waddington (1990), Baker (1991), Clarke (1992), Howard (1993, 1994, 1995, 1996), Straw (1997, 1999), Blunkett (2002, 2003), Clarke (2005b), Reid (2006), Straw (2007, 2009), and Clarke (2010, 2011).
3. Balen (1994) records Kenneth Clarke's disbelief, on becoming Home Secretary in November 1992, that the Criminal Justice Act 1991 had gone so far to limit judges' sentencing power (p. 240). In the Criminal Justice Act 1993, Clarke reversed many of the key aspects of the 1991 Act. The irony here is that Clarke himself voted for this 1991 Act whilst Minister for Education, but in his own defence points out that 'like most people who voted for that Act I had not kept in adequate touch with the detail when it went through the House of Commons' (p. 241).
4. On 19 September 2005, Charles Clarke gave a very similar speech to the Prison Reform Trust entitled 'Where next for penal policy?', emphasizing strongly the rehabilitative goals of prison (Clarke, 2005).
5. For each mention of 'crowding', I read the context in which it had been mentioned, and recorded the implied sense of whether crowding was seen as a demand-side or a supply-side problem. If the speaker, for example, mentions the term 'crowding' in conjunction with arguments for building more capacity or not having enough capacity in the system, I coded this as a supply-side interpretation of crowding. If crowding is mentioned in conjunction with arguments about excessively large prison population or inability to reduce the size of the prison population, I coded this as a demand-side interpretation. Often, it was not possible to discern either way, in which case, I coded this as neither one nor the other. Sometimes, both senses were implied, in which case I coded this as both.
6. Section 127 of the 1994 Criminal Justice and Public Order Act.
7. As part of Regulatory Reform (Prison Officers) (Industrial Action) Order 2005, section 127 was removed in respect of prison officers in the England and Wales system. This followed the signing of the 'Joint Industrial Relations Partnership Agreement' (JIRPA) between the Prison Service and the POA which stated that the POA was not to 'induce, authorize or support any form of industrial action by any of its members employed in the Prison Service relating to a dispute concerning any matter, whether covered by this agreement or otherwise'. The POA subsequently gave notice of their withdrawal from the JIRPA which expired on 8 May 2008. Section 138 of the 2008 Criminal Justice and Immigration Act reintroduced a statutory prohibition on inducing prison officers in England and Wales to take industrial action or commit a breach of discipline (CJIA, 2008).
8. It is important to distinguish here between Permanent Secretaries of the department on the one hand, and the top officials in the Prison Service and

NOMS on the other. Interviews with Permanent Secretaries suggest that they have seen their own role as one of looking after the relationship of their ministers with the department and the top operational officials, and in this sense it is reasonable to see their interests as synonymous with the interests of their senior minister.

6 Top Officials and the Interface between Political and Operational

1. I use the term 'senior officials' to refer to the top layers of management in the Prison Service and NOMS. In the Prison Service, this includes the Director General (DG), Deputy Director General (DDG), Prisons Board members, and first tier regional directors or managers.
2. Jenkins (2008) reflects on the tendency across government for Ministers to 'ignore the civil service' and for civil servants to 'find themselves outside the centre' (p. 188). Such pessimism is echoed by critics writing on the prison system; for example, Lacey (2008) identifies the tendency for governments to 'ignore the advice of technically neutral civil servants whenever this is judged to interfere with the chances of electoral success or expediency' (p. 72).
3. The dates in parentheses indicate the years during which these individuals held key positions in the administration of prisons in England and Wales. Joshua Jebb was a Royal Engineer, who was appointed Surveyor-General of prisons in the late 1830s in order to advise the government on design and construction of new prisons built during the 1840s. He was appointed the first Chair of the newly created Board of Directors of Convict Prisons in 1850 and also served as Surveyor-General of convict prisons until his death in 1863. Edmund du Cane was the first Director of the Prison Commission, set up in 1877 to oversee prison system in England and Wales. Formerly a Royal Engineer, he was known for his 'autocratic and military manner' (Tibber, 1980, p. 12), distrust of the civil service (p. 13), and pragmatic focus on reform and deterrence aspects of prison. Evelyn Ruggles-Brise was his successor as Chair of the Commission in 1895 until 1921. Ruggles-Brise was an Eton- and Oxford-educated civil servant, former Principal Private Secretary to various Home Secretaries. He created the first penal facility for young offenders, and founded the regime known as the 'borstal' system.
4. Tibber (1980) writes:

   > In a private letter from the Treasury, WH Smith (Secretary to the Treasury) wrote to Cross warning him not to 'mention DuCane by name as he is a red flag to certain people here'. Unfortunately the incident was typical of the problems Du Cane had as he tried to make the new prison administration envisaged by the Act of 1877 a reality. More often than not opposition came from within the Home Office itself for Du Cane was trying to isolate a particular department traditionally the responsibility of the Home Office and to make it autonomous. Du Cane's principal opponent was the Permanent Under Secretary at the Home Office, Godfrey Lushington. (p. 11)

5. The creation of the Prison Commission as part of the 1877 Prisons Act marked what is widely seen as the beginning of a national prison system. This Act brought county and borough prisons under the administration of the Home

Office, in the form of a Board of Commissioners of Prisons. This performed parallel functions to the Board of Directors of Convict Prisons. The merger of the Prison Commission with the Board of Directors of Convict Prisons took place in 1898, and consolidated control of all prisons in England and Wales under central leadership under the direction of the Home Office. The Commission was then fully incorporated into the Home Office as the Prison Department in 1963.

6. Former senior civil servant David Faulkner describes a decision by Home Secretary Douglas Hurd to 'intensify efforts to control the prison population and place limitations on sentencing' (Faulkner, 2006, p. 114). A 1988 Green Paper 'Punishment, Custody and the Community' was published, followed by 1990 White Paper 'Crime, Justice and Protecting the Public'. Faulkner describes this as the 'subject of intensive consultation with the criminal justice services, voluntary organizations, academic criminologists, and tentatively but with increasing confidence, the judiciary' (p. 114).
7. Cleland House was Prison Service headquarters in Victoria, London, until summer of 2010.
8. The Weare prison was purchased from the US and towed across the Atlantic and moored in Portland Harbour. It formed part of the England and Wales prison system from 1997 for eight years. It operated as a closed training prison with CNA of around 400. It was decommissioned in March 2005, and sold to an oil firm for use in Nigeria.
9. See Table 3.4 and related discussion for further details on overcrowding drafts.
10. The 'core day' sets out a standardized schedule for all prisoners in local and closed training prisons. For weekdays, Fridays, weekends, schedules are coordinated across the estate so that regimes are as similar as possible across different prisons of similar types.

7 Governors, Staff, and Strategies of Local Adaptation

1. By 'governors', I refer mainly in this chapter to the highest grade of prison governors, known as 'governing-governors' or 'Number 1 governors'. I carried out sixty-two interviews with current or former governing-governors. I also conducted focus groups with deputy governors, and interviewed and met many other prison managers during my visits to twenty-nine prisons.
2. See Wilson and Bryans (1998) and Bryans (2000, 2007).
3. The Prison Service and NOMS over the years have developed what they call a 'closeness to home' agenda, a programme and strategy to reduce the extent to which prisoners are moved away from their homes or key support networks.
4. 'Operation Safeguard' is the name of a contingency measure introduced in October 2006 to sanction use of police and court cells to accommodate prisoners during periods of acute prison population pressure.
5. HDC stands for Home Detention Curfew. It is a scheme for release on licence of certain short-term prisoners usually weeks or months before the completion of their sentence. Prisoners are assessed for eligibility and suitability for release, and release is sanctioned by the governor of the prison. Prisoners are fitted with an electronic tag to ensure that they adhere to the restrictions of curfew. HDC was introduced in 1999 under the Crime and Disorder Act 1998.

8 Privately Contracted Prisons: New Setting, Same Condition

1. I use the term 'authority' to refer to the contracting party, i.e. government, in the form of the Prison Service, NOMS, or the Home Office or Ministry of Justice. The specific location of contracting authority staff has shifted over the last two decades, from inside the Prison Service to inside NOMS.
2. For brevity, I use the term 'private prison' to refer generally to prisons which are managed by the private sector under contract to the Home Office or Ministry of Justice.
3. Stephen Nathan at the Public Services International Research Unit (PSIRU) has published extensive financial and commercial information on private-sector prison markets in the UK. This has been a vital source of information to researchers. It has provided extensive background information for my own work in this chapter.
4. See Ryan and Ward (1989).
5. *On Rye Hill prison.* In April 2005, the Chief Inspector of Prisons reported on an unannounced inspection of Rye Hill 'very serious concerns about safety' and staff turnover at 'around 40% a year'. The report stated that

    > the situation we found at Rye Hill raises some important questions. They include: whether contractually agreed staffing levels are sufficient for a prison of this kind; what systems and pay structures need to be in place to support staff retention; and the effectiveness both of internal management systems within the prison, and of external monitoring and management. (HMCIP, 2005, p. 10)

    On Ashfield prison. In April 2002, PPRI stated that Ashfield has been 'plagued with staffing shortages and other problems since it opened'. In December 2001 the company was issued with an improvement notice for non-compliance with its contract. In May 2002, Ashfield was fined in excess of £250,000 and taken into Prison Service emergency management until the contractor could improve the situation (PPRI, 2002). Throughout 2003, Ashfield stabilized. A report by the Chief Inspector of Prisons in September 2003 wrote, 'No-one involved in overseeing, resourcing or monitoring Ashfield should imagine that the task is complete and support withdrawn' (HMCIP, 2003a, p. 3).

    On Dovegate prison. A report by the HM Inspectorate reported about Dovegate that there was also a worrying lack of experience and confidence amongst a young, locally recruited staff, few of whom had any previous prison experience, and who were operating with low staffing levels and high staff turnover (HMCIP, 2003b, p. 3). In 2012, the Chief Inspector found serious problems in behaviour and drug use amongst prisoners at Wolds prison, run by G4S. This report led to the cancellation of the Wolds contract and return of the prison back to the public sector (HMCIP, 2012).
6. In privately managed prisons, the equivalent role of 'governing governor' tends to be known as the 'contract director' or 'director'. In this chapter, I use the term 'director' to refer to the equivalent of governing-governor in private-sector prisons.
7. The extent to which private-sector closed training prisons are able to select particular types of prisoners depends on their admission criteria. Private prisons tend to have fewer discerning admission criteria compared with

public-sector prisons, and so are less able to determine which prisoners they receive. This is compared with many public-sector prisons which have built up often quite restrictive criteria over the years.

8. Indeterminate sentences for Public Protection (IPP) were introduced by the Labour government in 2005 as a measure to deal with the most dangerous offenders. In theory, these prisoners would not be released back into society until they had satisfactorily completed a range of accredited programmes. The problem has been, however, that the probation and prison system have lacked the necessary resources to provide these programmes to IPP prisoners, with the consequence that many have been left stranded in the system even after their maximum tariffs have passed.
9. Techniques have evolved for controlling gaming behaviour by the contractors. For example, threshold levels have increasingly been based on averaged capacity over an extended period of time to reduce the risk of gaming around the thresholds whereby one prisoner over a threshold triggers a whole new payment schedule.
10. In this quote, DOM and RCM both refer to senior levels of management in the hierarchy of the prison system under the Director and Deputy Director Generals. DOM stands for Director of Offender Management. Since 2007, DOMS have reported directly to the Deputy Director General of NOMS, and are responsible for commissioning offender management services at a regional level. RCM stands for Regional Custodial Manager. This role replaced the former area manager, and covers similar management of prisons at a regional level.
11. A study by the Home Office in 2000 found that, for the specific year 1998–99, selected private prisons provided around 11 per cent greater savings in terms of cost per prisoner costs compared to public sector comparators (Home Office, 2000).
12. Prisoner Escort and Custody Services (PECS). This is the range of regionally managed contracts for escorting prisoners under secure conditions in vans to and from courts, and between prisons.

9 Chronic Capacity Stress: A Complex Condition

1. Inspectorate reports are widely seen as influential on governors and their career prospects. And in the last ten years, the Inspectorate has increased its unannounced inspections to two in every three.
2. Justice Minister Crispin Blunt told the House of Commons on 23 November 2010 that 'we are not in a position to create enough prison places to be able to address the problem of overcrowding'. Hansard HC, 23 November 2010, c15530.

Bibliography

Aucoin, P. (1990). 'Administrative reform in public management – paradigms, principles, and pendulums', *Governance*, 3: 115–137.

Baker, K. (1993). *The Turbulent Years: My Life in Politics*. London: Faber and Faber.

Balen, M. (1994). *Kenneth Clarke*. London: Fourth Estate.

Barnett, J. (1982). *Inside the Treasury*. London: André Deutsch.

Barnett, M. and Finnemore, M. (1999). 'The politics, power, and pathologies of international organizations', *International Organization*, 53(4): 699–732.

Bastow, S. (2010). 'Can Clarke square the circle of reforming criminal justice while also cutting costs by a quarter, by getting 20,000 people out of jail?', *British Politics and Policy at LSE* (2 July) Blog Entry [Online].

—— (2012). 'Suspending UK border security checks – how chronic capacity stress becomes crisis. *British Politics and Policy at LSE* (27 February) Blog Entry. [Online].

—— (2012) Overcrowded as Normal: Governance, Adaptation, and Chronic Capacity Stress in the England and Wales Prison System, 1979 to 2009. PhD thesis, The London School of Economics and Political Science.

BAPG (British Association of Prison Governors) (1979). *British Association of Prison Governors: Submission to the Inquiry into the UK Prison Services*. London: British Association of Prison Governors.

BBC (British Broadcasting Corporation) (2009). 'Call to scrap short jail terms' [Online]. (Accessed 6 October 2009).

—— (2010). Radio 4 *Analysis*. 'Rehabilitation revolution' (14 November).

—— (2012). Radio 4 *The Report*. 'Border agency' (26 July).

Bennett, J., Crewe, B. and Wahidin, A. (eds) (2008). *Understanding Prison Staff*. Cullompton: Willan.

Bennett, J. and Wahidin, A. (2008). 'Industrial relations in prisons'. In Bennett, J., Crewe, B. and Wahidin, A. (eds) *Understanding Prison Staff*. Cullompton: Willan.

Besley, T. (2006). *Principled Agents? The Political Economy of Good Government*. London: Oxford University Press.

Birch, A.H. (1984). 'Overload, ungovernability and delegitimation: the theories and the British case', *British Journal of Political Science*, 14: 135–160.

Birkland, T. (2009). 'Disasters, catastrophes, and policy failure in the homeland security era', *Review of Policy Research*, 26(4): 423–438.

Black, J. (1995). 'Industrial relations in the UK Prison Service: the "Jurassic Park" of public sector industrial relations', *Employee Relations*, 17(2): 64–88.

Bleich, J. (1989). 'The politics of prison crowding', *California Law Review*, 77: 1125–1989.

Blom-Cooper, L. (2008). *The Penalty of Imprisonment: Why 60 Per Cent of the Prison Population Shouldn't Be There*. London: Continuum.

Blumstein, A. (1988). 'Prison populations – a system out of control?', *Crime and Justice*, 10: 231–266.

Blumstein, A. and Cohen, J. (1973). 'A theory of stability of punishment', *Journal of Criminal Law and Criminology*, 64: 198–207.

Blumstein, A., Cohen, J. and Gooding, W. (1983). 'The influence of capacity on prison population: A critical review of some recent evidence', *Crime and Delinquency*, 29: 1–51.

Blunkett, D. (2006). *The Blunkett Tapes: My Life in the Bear Pit*. London: Bloomsbury.

Boin, A., James, O. and Lodge, M. (2006). 'The new public management "revolution" in political control of the public sector: promises and outcomes in three European prison systems', *Public Policy and Administration*, 21(2): 81–100.

Bolton, E. and Savell, L. (2010). *Towards a New Social Economy: Blended Value Creation through Social Impact Bonds*. London: Social Finance Ltd.

Bottoms, A. (1980). 'An introduction to "the coming crisis"'. In Bottoms, A. and Preston, R. (eds) *The Coming Penal Crisis: A Criminological and Theological Exploration*. Edinburgh: Scottish Academic Press.

Bovens, M. (1990). 'The social steering of complex organizations', *British Journal of Political Science*, 20(1): 91–117.

Bovens, M. and t' Hart, P. (2005). *Understanding Policy Fiascos*. London: Transaction Publishers.

Braithwaite, J. (2008). *Regulatory Capitalism: How It Works, Ideas for Making It Better*. Cheltenham: Edward Elgar.

Brans, M. and Rossbach, S. (1997). 'The autopoiesis of administrative systems: Niklas Luhmann on public administration and public policy', *Public Administration*, 75: 417–439.

Bryans, S. (2000). 'Governing prisons: an analysis of who is governing prisons and the competencies which they require to govern effectively', *The Howard Journal*, 39(1): 14–29.

——. (2007). *Prison Governors: Managing Prisons in a Time of Change*. Cullompton: Willan.

Cabinet Office (2008). *Excellence and Fairness: Achieving World Class Public Services*. London: The Stationery Office.

Casale, S. (1984). *Minimum Standards for Prison Establishments*. London: NACRO.

—— (1994). Conditions and Standards. In Player, E. and Jenkins, M. (eds) *Prisons after Woolf: Reform through Riot*. London: Routledge.

Casale, S. and Plotnikoff, J. (1989). *Minimum Standards in Prisons: A Programme of Change*. London: NACRO.

—— (1990). *Regimes for Remand Prisoners*. London: Prison Reform Trust.

Cavadino, M. and Dignan, J. (2003). *The Penal System: An Introduction*. London: Sage.

—— (2006). *Penal Systems: A Comparative Approach*. London: Sage.

Chapman, L. (1982). *Waste Away*. London: Chatto and Windus.

CHRE (Council for Healthcare Regulatory Excellence) (2012). *Strategic Review of the Nursing and Midwifery Council. Interim Report*. 10 April. London: CHRE.

Christensen, T. and Lægreid, P. (eds) (2002). *New Public Management: The Transformation of Ideas and Practice*, Aldershot: Ashgate.

CJIA (Criminal Justice Immigration Act) (2008). 'Explanatory notes to the Criminal Justice and Immigration Act 2008' Chapter 4, p. 15. London: The Stationery Office.

CJJI (Criminal Justice Joint Inspection) (2012). *Second Aggregate Report on Offender Management in Prisons: Findings from a Series of Joint Inspections by HM*

Inspectorate of Probation and HM Inspectorate of Prisons. London: HM Inspectorate of Prisons.

Clarke, C. (2005). 'Where next for penal policy?' A speech by the Home Secretary Rt. Hon. Charles Clarke to the Prison Reform Trust, 19 September. London: Prison Reform Trust

Coleman, J. and Fararo, T. (eds) (1992). *Rational Choice Theory: Advocacy and Critique*. London: Sage.

Conservative Party (2008). *Prisons with a Purpose: Our Sentencing and Rehabilitation Revolution to Break the Cycle of Crime*. London: Conservative Party.

Coyle, A. (1994). *The Prisons We Deserve*. London: HarperCollins.

—— (2007). 'Does custodial sentencing work?', *Prison Service Journal*, 171: 13–15.

Crick, M. (2005). *In Search of Michael Howard*. London: Simon & Schuster.

Crozier, M. (1964). *The Bureaucratic Phenomenon*. Chicago: University of Chicago Press.

Cyert, R. and March, J. (2001). *A Behavioural Theory of the Firm*. Oxford: Blackwell Publishers.

Dahl, R. (1947). 'The science of public administration: three problems', *Public Administration Review*, 7(1): 1–11.

D'Alessio, J. S. and Stolzenberg, L. (1997). 'The effect of available capacity on jail incarceration: an empirical test of Parkinson's Law', *Journal of Criminal Justice*, 25(4): 279–288.

DiIulio, J. (1990). 'Managing a barbed-wire bureaucracy: the impossible job of corrections commissioner'. In Hargrove, E. and Glidewell, J. (eds) *Impossible Jobs in Public Management*. Lawrence, KS: University Press of Kansas.

—— (1993). *Rethinking the Criminal Justice System: Toward a New Paradigm*. Bureau of Justice Statistics – Princeton University Study Group on Criminal Justice Performance Measures.

Douglas, M. (1986). *How Institutions Think?* Syracuse, NY: Syracuse University Press.

Downes, D. (1980). 'Abolition: possibilities and pitfalls'. In Bottoms, A. and Preston, R. (eds) *The Coming Penal Crisis: A Criminological and Theological Exploration*. Edinburgh: Scottish Academic Press.

—— (1988). *Contrasts in Tolerance: Post-War Penal Policy in the Netherlands and England and Wales*. Oxford: Oxford University Press.

Downs, A. (1957). *An Economic Theory of Democracy*. New York: Harper & Row.

Dunbar, I. (1985). *A Sense of Direction*. London: Home Office.

Dunbar, I. and Langdon, A. (1998). *Tough Justice: Sentencing and Penal Policy in the 1990s*. London: Blackstone Press.

Dunleavy, P. (1991). *Democracy, Bureaucracy and Public Choice: Economic Explanations in Political Science*. Hemel Hempstead: Harvester-Wheatsheaf.

—— (1995). 'Policy disasters: explaining the UK's record', *Public Policy and Administration*, 10(2): 52–70.

Dunleavy, P. and Carrera, L. (2013). *Growing the Productivity of Government Services*. Chichester: Edward Elgar.

Dunleavy, P. and Hood, C. (1994). 'From old public administration to new public management', *Public Money and Management*, 14(3): 9–16.

Dunleavy, P. and Margetts, H. (2010). 'The second wave of digital-era governance'. Annual Meeting of the American Political Science Association, 2–5 September.

Dunleavy, P., Margetts, H., Bastow, S. and Tinkler, J. (2006). *Digital Era Governance: IT Corporations, the State, and e-Government*. Oxford: Oxford University Press.

Dunleavy, P., Tinkler, J., Gilson, C. and Towers, E. (2010). 'Understanding and preventing delivery disasters in public services'. Political Studies Association Conference, Edinburgh, 30 March.

Dunsire, A. (1990). 'Holistic governance', *Public Policy and Administration*, 5(1): 4–19.

Easton, D. (1965). *A Framework for Political Analysis*. Englewood Cliffs, NJ: Prentice Hall.

—— (1967). *A Systems Analysis of Political Life*. New York: John Wiley & Sons.

Evans, P. (1980). *Prison Crisis*. London: George Allen & Unwin.

Faulkner, D. (2004). 'NOMS and civil renewal', *Vista*, 9(2): 90–99.

—— (2005). 'Relationships, accountability and responsibility in the NOMS', *Public Money and Management*, 25(5): 299–305.

Faulkner, D. (2006). *Crime, State and the Citizen*. Hampshire, UK: Waterside Press.

Fitzgerald, M. and Sim, J. (1982). *British Prisons*. Oxford: Basil Blackwell.

Foster, C. and Plowden, F. (1996). *The State under Stress: Can the Hollow State be Good Government?* Open University Press: Buckingham.

Foucault, M. (1991). *Discipline and Punish: The Birth of the Prison*. London: Penguin.

Fox, L. (1936). *The Modern English Prison*. London: Routledge & Sons.

—— (1952). *The English Prison and Borstal Systems*. London: Routledge & Kegan Paul.

Fraser, D. (2006). *A Land Fit for Criminals: An Insider's View of Crime, Punishment and Justice in the UK*. Brighton: Book Guild Publishing.

Frederickson, H. and LaPorte, T. (2002). 'Airport security, high reliability, and the problem of rationality', *Public Administration Review*, 62: 33–43.

Funke, G. (1985). 'The economics of prison crowding', *Annals AAPSS*, 478(March): 86–99.

Gamble, A. and Thomas, R. (2010). 'The changing context of governance: implications for administration and justice'. In Adler, M. (ed.) *Administrative Justice in Context*. Oxford: Hart Publishing.

Garland, D. (2001). *The Culture of Control: Crime and Social Order in Contemporary Society*. Cambridge: Cambridge University Press.

Garside, R. (2005). 'Wrong question: wrong answer', *Prison Service Journal*, 161: 10–14.

Genders, E. (2002). 'Legitimacy, accountability, and private prisons', *Punishment and Society*, 4(3): 285–303.

—— (2003). 'Privatization and innovation – rhetoric and reality: the development of a therapeutic community prison', *Howard Journal*, 42(2): 137–157.

Goetz, K. (2006). 'Temporality and the European administrative space', Connex Thematic Conference 'Towards a European administrative space', London, 16–18 November.

—— (2008). 'Governance as a Path to Government', *West European Politics*, 31(1–2): 258–279.

Goffman, E. (1961). *Asylums: Essays on the Social Situation of Mental Patients and other Inmates*. London: Penguin

Gough, S. (2004). 'Carter and NOMS: the enemy at the door – a critical analysis', *Gatelodge* [Prison Officers Association magazine]: (December) 20–22. Bourne: Warner Group Publications.

Gray, P. and t'Hart, P. (eds) (1998). *Public Policy Disasters in Western Europe*. London: Routledge.

Harding, R. (2001). 'Private prisons', *Crime and Justice*, 28: 265–346.

Hargrove, E. and Glidewell, J. (eds) (1990). *Impossible Jobs in Public Management*: Lawrence, KS: University Press of Kansas.

Hedderman, C. (2005). 'NOMS and the prison population', *Prison Service Journal*, 162: 3–7.

—— (2008). 'Building on sand: why expanding the prison system is not the way to secure the future'. In Hough, M., Allen, R. and Solomon, E. (eds) *Tackling Prison Overcrowding: Build More Prisons? Sentence Fewer Offenders?* Bristol: Policy Press.

HMCIP (Her Majesty's Inspectorate of Prisons) (2003a). *Report on a Full announced Inspection of HMP/Young Offender Institution Ashfield, 22 September to 26 September 2003 by the Chief Inspector of Prisons*. HM London: HM Inspectorate of Prisons.

—— (2003b). *Report on a Full Announced Inspection of HMP Dovegate, 31 March to 4 April 2003, by HM Chief Inspector of Prisons*. HM London: HM Inspectorate of Prisons.

—— (2005). *Report on an Unannounced Inspection of HMP Rye Hill, 11–15 April, 2005, by HM Chief Inspector of Prisons*. HM London: HM Inspectorate of Prisons.

—— (2012). *Report on an Announced Full Follow-up Inspection of HMP Wolds, 23–27 April, 2012, by HM Chief Inspector of Prisons*. HM London: HM Inspectorate of Prisons.

HMPS (Her Majesty's Prison Service) (1992a). *Certified Normal Accommodation and the Monitoring of Capacity. Circular Instruction 19/1992*. London: HM Prison Service.

—— (1992b). *A Code of Standards for the Prison Service*. London: HM Prison Service.

—— (1996). *Prison Service Annual Report and Accounts 1996. HC 274*. London: HM Prison Service.

—— (2001). *Certified Normal Accommodation. Prison Service Order. August 2001*. London: HM Prison Service

—— (2003). *Prison Service Annual Report and Accounts 2003. HC 718*. London: The Stationery Office.

—— (2006). *Prison Service Annual Report and Accounts 2006. HC 717*. London: The Stationery Office.

Hobhouse, S. and Brockway, A. (1922). *English Prisons Today: Being the Report of the Prison System Enquiry Committee*. London: Longmans, Green & Co.

Hogwood, B. and Peters, B. (1985). *The Pathology of Public Policy*. Oxford: Clarendon.

Home Office (1991a). *Prison Disturbances April 1990. Report by an Inquiry by the Rt. Hon. Lord Justice Woolf and His Honour Judge Stephen Tumin. February 1991*. Cmnd 1456. ('The Woolf Report'). London: HM Stationery Office.

—— (1991b). *Custody, Care and Justice: the Way Ahead for the Prison Service in England and Wales (White Paper)*. London: HM Stationery Office.

—— (2000). *Review of Comparative Costs and Performance of Privately and Publicly Operated Prisons 1998–99*. London: Home Office.

Hood, C. (1998). *The Art of the State: Culture, Rhetoric and Public Management*. Oxford: Oxford University Press.

Hood, C., James, O., Peters, B. and Scott, C. (eds) (2004). *Controlling Modern Government: Variety, Commonality and Change*. Cheltenham: Edward Elgar.

Hood, C. and Peters, B. (2004). 'The middle aging of new public management: into the age of paradox', *Journal of Public Administration Research and Theory*, 14: 267–282.

Horn, M. (1995). *The Political Economy of Public Administration: Institutional choice in the Public Sector*. Cambridge: Cambridge University Press.

Houchin, K. and MacLean, D. (2005). 'Complexity theory and strategic change: an empirically informed critique', *British Journal of Management*, 16: 149–166.

Howard League (1974). *Ill-founded Premises: The Logic of Penal Policy and the Prison Building Programme*. London: Howard League for Penal Reform.

—— (1981). *No More Prison Building*. Howard League for Penal Reform (Andrew Rutherford and Rod Morgan). London: Howard League for Penal Reform.

—— (1996). *Bricks and Mortar: Prison Building Is Expensive and No Solution*. London: Howard League for Penal Reform.

—— (2005). *The Big Prison Squeeze: Prison Overcrowding*. London: Howard League for Penal Reform.

Human Rights Watch (1992). *Prison Conditions in the United Kingdom: A Helsinki Watch/Prison Project Report*. New York: Human Rights Watch.

Hurd, D. (2003). *Douglas Hurd: Memoirs*. London: Little Brown.

Jacobson, J., Roberts, J. and Hough, M. (2008). 'Towards more consistent and predictable sentencing in England and Wales'. In Hough, M., Allen, R. and Solomon, E. (eds) *Tackling Prison Overcrowding: Build More Prisons? Sentence Fewer Offenders?* Bristol: The Policy Press.

James, A., Bottomley, A., Liebling, A. and Clare, E. (1997). *Privatizing Prisons: Rhetoric and Reality*. London: Sage.

James, O. (2003). *The Executive Agency Revolution in Whitehall: Public Interest versus Bureau-shaping Perspectives*. Basingstoke: Palgrave Macmillan.

Jenkins, K. (2008). *Politicians and Public Services: Implementing Change in a Clash of Cultures*. Cheltenham: Edward Elgar.

Jenkins, R. (1991). *A Life at the Centre*. London: Macmillan.

Kauffman, S. (1995). *At Home in the Universe*. Oxford: Oxford University Press.

King, A. (1975). 'Overload: problems of governing in the 1970s', *Political Studies*, 23: 284–296.

King, R. and McDermott, K. (1989). 'British prisons 1970–1987: the ever-deepening crisis', *British Journal of Criminology*, 29(2): 107–128.

—— (1995). *The State of Our Prisons*. Oxford: Clarendon Press.

King, R., Morgan, R., Martin, J. and Thomas, J. (1980). *The Future of the Prison System*. Aldershot: Gower.

Klijn, E. and Snellen, I. (2009). 'Complexity theory and public administration: a critical appraisal'. In Teisman, G., Buuren, A. V. and Gerrits, L. (eds) *Managing Complex Governance Systems*. London: Routledge.

Lacey, N. (2008). *The Prisoners' Dilemma: Political Economy and Punishment in Contemporary Democracies*. Cambridge: Cambridge University Press.

Landau, M. (1969). 'Redundancy, rationality, and the problem of duplication and overlap', *Public Administration Review*, 29(4) (July–August): 346–358.

Landau, M. and Chisholm, D. (1995). 'The arrogance of optimism: notes on failure-avoidance management', *Journal of Contingencies and Crisis Management*, 3(2): 67–80.

Lewis, D. (1997). *Hidden Agendas: Politics, Law and Disorder*. London: Hamish Hamilton.

Liebling, A. (2004). *Prisons and Their Moral Performance: A Study of Values, Quality, and Prison Life*. Oxford: Oxford University Press.

Loader, I. (2007). 'We lock people up with no thought and to little effect: appetite for vengeance and political expediency has led to an overcrowded prison system which doesn't work', *Guardian*, 23 November.

—— (2008). 'The great victim of this get tough hyperactivity is Labour: the Casey report is an example of the rhetoric that suggests that total protection against crime can be a reasonable expectation', *Guardian*, 19 June.

—— (2009). 'How, and why, to stop banking on prisons (Perrie Lectures 2009)', *Prison Service Journal*, 186: 14–20.

Lodge, M. and Wegrich, K. (eds) (2012). *Executive Politics in Times of Crisis*. Basingstoke: Palgrave Macmillan.

Logan, C. (1993). *Criminal Justice Performance Measures for Prisons*. Bureau of Justice Statistics – Princeton University Study Group on Criminal Justice Performance Measures.

Low, D. (ed.) (2012). *Behavioural Economics and Policy Design*. Singapore: World Scientific Publishing Company.

Maor, M. (1999). 'The paradox of managerialism', *Public Administration Review*, 59: 5–18.

Margetts, HZ (1999). *Information Technology in Government: Britain and America* (Routledge Research in Information Technology and Society). London: Routledge.

Margetts, H., Perri 6 and Hood, C. (eds) (2010). *Paradoxes of Modernization: Unintended Consequences of Public Policy Reform*. Oxford: Oxford Scholarship Online.

Mathieson, T. (1991). 'The argument against building more prisons'. In Muncie, J. and Sparks, R. (eds) *Imprisonment: European Perspectives*. London: Harvester /Wheatsheaf.

Matthews, R. (ed.) (1989). *Privatizing Criminal Justice*. London: Sage

Matthews, R. (1999). *Doing Time: An Introduction to the Sociology of Imprisonment*. Basingstoke: Palgrave Macmillan.

Matthews, R. and Young, J. (eds) (2003). *The New Politics of Crime and Punishment*. Cullompton: Willan.

McConville, S. (1981). *A History of English Prison Administration: Volume 1 1750–1877*. London: Routledge & Kegan Paul.

—— (1995). 'The Victorian prison: England 1865–1965'. In Morris, N. and Rothman, D. (eds) *The Oxford History of the Prison: The Practice of Punishment in Western Society*. Oxford: Oxford University Press.

McLean, I. (2001). *Rational Choice and British Politics: An Analysis of Rhetoric and Manipulation from Peel to Blair*. Oxford: Oxford University Press.

—— (2002). 'Review Article: William H Riker and the Invention of Heresthetic(s)', *British Journal of Political Science*, 32: 535–558.

Merton, R. (1957). *Social Theory and Social Structure. Revised and Enlarged Edition*. London: The Free Press of Glencoe/Collier-Macmillan Limited.

Meyer, M. and Zucker, L. (1989). *Permanently Failing Organizations*. London: Sage.

Miller, G. (1992). *Managerial Dilemmas: The Political Economy of Hierarchy*. Cambridge: Cambridge University Press.

—— (2009). *Capacity and Competition Policy for Prisons and Probation*. London: Ministry of Justice.

—— (2010). *Breaking the Cycle: Effective Punishment, Rehabilitation, and Sentencing of Offenders*. London: Ministry of Justice.

—— (2011). 'Adult reconvictions: Results from the 2009 cohort, England and Wales'. *Ministry of Justice Statistics Bulletin*. March, London: Ministry of Justice.

Minkin, L. (1997). *Exits and Entrances: Political Research as a Creative Art*. Sheffield: Sheffield Hallam University.

MoD (Ministry of Defence) (2010). *Securing Britain in an Age of Uncertainty. Presented to Parliament by the Prime Minister. Cm 7948. October 2010*. London: The Stationery Office.

Moe, T. (1995). 'The politics of structural choice: toward a theory of public bureaucracy'. In Williamson, O. (ed.) *Organization Theory: From Chester Barnard to the Present and Beyond*. New York: Oxford University Press.

MoJ (Ministry of Justice) (2007). *Securing the Future: Proposals for the Efficient and Sustainable Use of Custody in England and Wales. A Report to the Prime Minister and the Minister for Justice by Lord Patrick Carter*. London: Ministry of Justice.

—— (2011). *Adult Re-convictions: Results from the 2009 Cohort England and Wales*. Ministry of Justice Statistics Bulletin London: Stationery Office.

Munro, E. (2011). *The Munro Review of Child Protection: A Child-centred System*. London: The Stationery Office.

Mylotte, M. (1989). *The Crisis of Prison Overcrowding*. Norwich: Social Work Monographs.

NAO (National Audit Office) (1985). *Home Office and Property Services Agency: Programme for the Provision of Prison Places*. HC 135. Report by the Comptroller and Auditor General. London: HM Stationery Office.

—— (2000). *The Refinancing of the Fazakerley PFI Prison Contract*. HC 584. Report by the Comptroller and Auditor General. London: The Stationery Office.

—— (2005). *National Offender Management Service: Dealing with Increased Numbers in Custody* HC 458. Report by the Comptroller and Auditor General. London: The Stationery Office.

—— (2006). *Update on PFI Debt Refinancing and the PFI Equity Market* HC 1040. Report by the Comptroller and Auditor General. London: The Stationery Office.

Nathan, S. (2003). 'Prison privatization in the United Kingdom'. In Coyle, A., Campbell, A. and Neufeld, R. (eds) *Capitalist Punishment: Prison Privatization and Human Rights*. London: Zed Books.

Newell, M. (2003). 'A new paradigm of decarceration', *Prison Service Journal*, 150: 2–8.

Nicholson, C. (2011). *Rehabilitation Works: Ensuring Payment by Results Cuts Reoffending*. London: Centre Forum.

Nickerson, J. and Zenger, T. (2002). 'Being efficiently fickle: a dynamic theory of organizational choice', *Organization Science*, 13 (5) (September–October): 547–566.

Niskanen, W. (1998). *Policy Analysis and Public Choice: Selected Papers of William A Niskanen*. Cheltenham: Edward Elgar.

NOMS (National Offender Management Service) (2006). *Improving Prison and Probation Services: Public Value Partnerships*. August. London: NOMS.

O'Friel, B. (1994). 'Overcrowding: past, present and future', *Prison Service Journal*, 92: 20–23.

Padfield, N. (2004). 'NOMS and Parliament', *Justice of the Peace*, 168: 214–216.

Page, E. (1992). *Political Authority and Bureaucratic Power: A Comparative Analysis*. London: Harvester Wheatsheaf.

Parker, M. (2002). *Against Managerialism: Organization in the Age of Managerialism*. Cambridge: Polity.

PD (Prison Department) (1984). *Management in the Prison Service. Circular Instruction 55/1984*. London: Home Office.

—— (1988). *Certified Normal Accommodation. Circular Instruction 3/1988*. London: Home Office.

—— (1991). *Management of the Prison Service. A Report by Admiral Sir Raymond Lygo KCB. December 1991 ('The Lygo Report')*. London: Home Office.

Peters, B. (2010). Governance as political theory. Jerusalem papers in regulation and governance. Working paper 22. August 2010.

Peters, B. and Savoie, D. (eds) (2000). *Governance in the Twenty-first Century: Revitalizing the Public Service*. Montreal: McGill-Queen's University Press.

Phillips, D. (1976). *Holistic Thought in Social Science*. Stanford, CA: Stanford University Press.

Pierre, J. and Peters, B. (2005). *Governing Complex Societies – Trajectories and Scenarios*. Basingstoke: Palgrave Macmillan.

Pollitt, C. (2008). *Time, Policy, Management: Governing with the Past*. Oxford: Oxford University Press.

—— (2009). 'Complexity theory and evolutionary public administration: a sceptical afterword'. In Teisman, G., Buuren, A. V. and Gerrits, L. (eds) *Managing Complex Governance Systems*. London: Routledge.

Pollitt, C. and Bouckaert, G. (2009). *Continuity and Change in Public Policy and Management*. Cheltenham: Edward Elgar.

Pollitt, C., Talbot, C., Caulfield, J. and Smullen, A. (2004a). *Agencies: How Government Do Things through Semi-Autonomous Organizations*. Basingstoke: Palgrave Macmillan.

—— (2004b). 'Prisons'. In Pollitt, C., Talbot, C., Caulfield, J., and Smullen, A., (eds) *Agencies: How Government Do Things through Semi- Autonomous Organizations*. Basingstoke: Palgrave Macmillan.

PPRI (Prison Privatisation Report International) (2002). *Prisons Report: Privatization Factfile published by Stephen Nathan at Public Services International Research Unit (PSIRU)*, October. London: PRIRU.

PRT (Prison Reform Trust) (1986). *Prison Rules: A Working Guide*. London: Prison Reform Trust.

—— (1993). *Prison Rules: A Working Guide*. London: Prison Reform Trust

—— (2012). 'Ken Clarke celebrates reduction in the number of children in custody'. *Prison Reform Trust Newsletter*, July. London: Prison Reform Trust.

Ramsbotham, D. (2005). *Prison Gate: The Shocking State of Britain's Prisons and the Need for Visionary Change*. London: Simon & Schuster.

Rhodes, R. (1994). 'The hollowing out of the state: the changing nature of the public service in Britain', *Political Quarterly*, 65: 138–151.

Rhodes, R. (1996). 'The new governance: governing without government', *Political Studies*, 44(4): 652–667.

Riker, W. (1986). *The Art of Political Manipulation*. New Haven, CT and London: Yale University Press.

Rittel, H. and Webber, M. (1973). 'Dilemmas in a general theory of planning', *Policy Sciences* 4: 155–169.

Roberts, J. (2004). *The Modern Firm*. Oxford: Oxford University Press.
Rose, R. (1979). 'Ungovernability: is there fire behind the smoke?', *Political Studies*, 27(3): 351–370.
Rose, R. (ed.) (1980). *Challenge to Governance: Studies in Overloaded Politics*. London: Sage.
Ruggles-Brise, E. (1921). *The English Prison System*. London: Macmillan & Co.
Rumgay, J. (2005). 'NOMS bombs?', *Howard Journal*, 44(2): 206–208.
Rutter, J., Marshall, E. and Sims, S. (2012). *The 'S' Factors: Lessons from IFG's policy success reunions. A report by the Institute for Government*. London: Institute for Government.
Ryan, M. and Ward, T. (1989). *Privatization and the Penal System: The American Experience and the Debate in Britain*. Buckingham: Open University.
Sachdev, S. (2008). 'Private punishment? An examination of the expansion, development and employment relations of private prisons'. In Hough, M., Allen, R. and Solomon, E. (eds) *Tackling Prison Overcrowding: Build More prisons? Sentence Fewer Offenders?* Bristol: Policy Press.
Scharpf, F. (1997). *Games Real Actors Play: Actor-centered Institutionalism in Policy Research*. Oxford: Westview Press.
—— (1999). *Governing in Europe: Effective or Democratic?* Oxford: Oxford University Press.
SCPS (Society of Civil and Public Servants) (1978). *Memorandum from the Prison and Borstal Governors Branch of the Society of Civil and Public Servants to the House of Commons Expenditure Committee's Inquiry into the Administration of the Prison Service*. London: SCPS.
Shefer, G. and Liebling, A. (2008). 'Prison privatization: in search of a business-like atmosphere', *Criminology and Criminal Justice*, 8: 261–278.
SI (Statutory Instrument) (1949). *The Prison Rules*. London: HM Stationery Office.
—— (1964). *The Prison Rules*. London: HM Stationery Office.
—— (1999). *The Prison Rules*. 728, 26. London: The Stationery Office.
Stern, V. (1993). *Bricks of Shame: Britain's Prisons*. London: Penguin.
Talbot, C. (1996). 'The Prison Service: a framework of irresponsibility?', *Public Money and Management*, 16(1): 5–7.
—— (2004). 'Executive agencies: have they improved management in government?', *Public Money and Management*, 24(2): 104–111.
Teisman, G., Buuren, A.v. and Gerrits, L. (eds) (2009). *Managing Complex Governance Systems*. London: Routledge.
Teisman, G. and Klijn, E. (2008). 'Complexity theory and public management: an introduction', *Public Management Review*, 10(3): 287–297.
Thompson, M., Grendstad, G. and Selle, P. (eds) (1999). *Cultural Theory as Political Science*. London: Routledge.
Thompson, M., Ellis, R. and Wildavsky, A. (1990). *Cultural Theory*. Boulder, CO: Westview Press.
Tibber, P. (1980). 'Edmund Du Cane and the Prison Act 1877', *The Howard Journal*, 19: 9–16.
Times, The (2012). 'We may avoid big events, says G4S chief', *The Times*, 6 October.
Tournier, P. (1994). 'The custodial crisis in Europe: inflated prison populations and possible alternatives', *European Journal on Criminal Policy and Research*, 2(4): 89–100.

Tropman, J. (1981). 'The constant crisis: social welfare and the American cultural structure'. In Tropman, J., Dluhy, M. and Lind, R. (eds) *New Strategic Perspectives on Social Policy* New York: Pergamon Press.

Tullock, G. (1967). *The Politics of Bureaucracy*. New York: Public Affairs Press.

—— (2005). *The Rent-Seeking Society*. Indianapolis, IN: Liberty Fund.

van Buuren, A. and Gerrits, L. (2008). 'Decisions as dynamic equlibriums in erratic policy processes', *Public Management Review*, 10(3): 381–399.

Vaughan, D. (1996). *The Challenger Launch Decision: Risky Technology, Culture, and Deviance at NASA*. Chicago: University of Chicago Press.

—— (2005). 'System effects: on slippery slopes, repeating negative patterns, and learning from mistakes'. In Starbuck, W. and Farjoun, M. (eds) *Organization at the Limit: NASA and the Columbia Disaster*. London: Blackwell.

Vine, J. (2012). *An Investigation into Border Security Checks by the Independent Chief Inspector of the UK Border Agency*. London: The Stationery Office

Walsh, K (1995). *Public Services and Market Mechanisms: Competition, Contracting and the New Public Management* (Basingstoke: Macmillan Press).

Warfield, J. (2003). 'A proposal for systems science', *Systems Research and Behavorial Science*, 20: 507–520.

Warfield, J. and Perino, G. (1999). 'Problematique: evolution of an idea', *Systems Research and Behavorial Science*, 16: 221–226.

Weiler, T. (1992). 'Coping with a crisis: the introduction of three and two in a cell', *Prison Service Journal*, (92): 24–50.

Whitelaw, W. (1989). *The Whitelaw Memoirs*. London: Aurum Press.

Widdecombe, A. (1999). *Inspired and Outspoken: The Collected Speeches of Ann Widdecombe*. London: Politico's Publishing.

Wildavsky, A. (1988). *Searching for Safety*. New Brunswick, NJ: Transaction Publishers.

Wilson, D. (2003). 'A different approach to prison numbers: creating the climate for decarceration and penal abolition', *Prison Service Journal*, 150: 12–15.

Wilson, D. and Bryans, S. (1998). *The Prison Governor: Theory and Practice*, Leyhill: *Prison Service Journal*.

Wilson, J.Q. (2000). *Bureaucracy: What Government Agencies Do and Why They Do It?* New York: Basic Books.

Woolf, H. (2008). *In Pursuit of Justice*. Oxford: Oxford University Press.

Index

adaptation
by governors and staff (Ch. 7), 178–99
in private sector market, 214
in the whole system, 29–33, 227–37, 243
Ashfield prison (private), 204, 216, 259
Association of Chief Police Officers (ACPO), 192
austerity, 53, 68, 128, 244, 249
autopoiesis, 31

Baker, Kenneth, 125–8, 132–6, 256, 261
Barnett, Michael, 28, 147
behavioural economics, 34
Birmingham prison, 110, 148, 181–2, 204, 208, 216, 246
Blair, Tony, 128, 133, 147
Bleich, Jeff, 50
Blunkett, David, 129, 133–5, 149, 191, 256
bossism, 25, 28, 189
Bottoms, Anthony, 42, 272
bounded rationality, 34
Bovens, Mark, 32
Bristol prison, 109, 204
British Association of Prison Governors, 191
Brittan, Leon, 127, 133–5, 256
Brixton prison, 1–4, 56, 62, 110, 128, 197, 208, 220
Brown, Gordon, 133, 147, 176
Bryans, Shane, 178, 184–5, 258
bureau-shaping, 21, 237

Cabinet Office, 20
Casale, Sylvia, 50, 252, 255
Cavadino, Mark, 42, 47, 252, 253
Certified Normal Accommodation (CNA), 9, 98, 101–22, 143, 162, 172, 199, 204, 213–17, 254, 255, 258
Chakrabarti, Suma, 167
Chancellor of the Exchequer, 132–3, 144
chronic capacity stress (CCS)
application to the prison system, 40–64
capacity standards, 96, 98, 121–3
definition of, 4
four aspects of, 7–8, 235–43
future of, 247–50
governors and staff, 178–9, 198
in privately managed prisons, 201, 210, 223–4
theoretical underpinning, 12–37,
churn, of prisoners, 50, 181, 199, 232, 244
Clarke, Charles, 129, 135–6, 150, 172–6, 256
Clarke, Kenneth, 55, 128–9, 134–5, 244, 256
Cleland House, 161, 258
coalition government, 42, 129, 136, 144, 208, 232, 244
complexity
of population management, 164
in public management paradigms, 14–17, 66, 94
of social problems, 57
theory of, 30–5, 251
Conservative Party, 1, 42, 58, 126, 129–46, 150–1, 208, 232, 244, 256
constrained autonomy, 6, 63, 123, 230, 233, 237–41, 247, 250
description of, 9–10
of governors and staff, 178–9
of private sector officials, 198–200, 224
of senior ministers, 150–2
of senior officials, 153–4, 175–7
and systems theory, 33

contracts, 16, 202–23, 231, 259–60
  in border control, 248–9
  prisoner escort, 163
  Private Finance Initiative (PFI), 90
  refinancing, 57
  Service Level Agreements, 121
control through counterbalance, 9, 98, 119, 121
coping
  consequences of, 94, 144
  cultures of, 7–8, 170
  fatalism, 25–8
  in the prison system, 13, 40–1, 47–52, 58–60, 65, 84, 116, 134–6, 164, 175, 182, 188–9, 199, 230–6, 245–51
core day, 165, 258
Coyle, Andrew, 46, 252–3
Criminal Justice Act, 55, 127–9, 136, 141, 256
crisis
  culture of, 8, 25–8, 58–60, 230, 242, 247
  of legitimacy, 42, 47
  political, 22, 127–9, 142, 145–6, 170–2
  prison population, 167, 175
  in the prison system, 48–52, 189, 234–6
  Whitemoor and Parkhurst, 73
crowding index, 82–3, 254
Crozier, Michel, 27
cultural theory, 7, 19, 24–9, 34–7
Cyert, Richard, 31

Dahl, Robert, 30, 33
Daily Mail, 143, 192
Dartmoor prison, 109, 209
deterrence, 24, 42, 128, 257
Dignan, James, 42, 47, 252, 253
Directors of Offender Management (DOMS), 260
disinvestment, 207
Doncaster prison (private), 224
doubling, of prisoners in cells, 57, 75, 103, 109, 115, 118, 167
Douglas, Mary, 25
Dovegate prison (private), 204–5, 216, 259
drugs
  addiction, 57, 259
  testing, 76, 78
  treatment, 92, 94, 186, 218, 222
Du Cane, Edmund, 154, 155, 257
Dunbar, Ian, 48, 252
Dunsire, Andrew, 18

Easton, David, 14, 30
education in prison, 43, 75–8, 85–6, 165, 186, 207, 222
Edwards, Helen, 157
effectiveness
  and managerialism, 15–16, 241
  of prisoner programmes, 77
  of privately managed prisons, 202, 218
  of rehabilitation, 85, 228
  of standards, 122
efficiency
  and managerialism, 3, 11, 15–16, 50, 65, 66
  and obsolescence, 56, 61
  of the prison system, 89, 91, 96, 131, 183, 231, 236–7, 241–2, 251
  of privately managed prisons, 202
egalitarian culture, 25–9, 48
End of Custody Licence (ECL), 129, 131, 171–2
escapes from custody, 73–84, 95, 126, 128, 143, 151, 156–7, 166, 193
European Standard Minimum Rules, 105
excellence, public sector, 13

failure
  and fatalism, 26–32, 45–56
  perceptions of, 1, 7, 40–7, 62, 72, 252–3
  permanently failing, 239
  of privately managed prisons, 204
  of reform, 23, 131, 146, 151
  success and, 11, 13, 65, 124–5, 165, 226–30
fatalist culture, 25–7, 36, 40–7, 85, 190, 199, 224–5, 230–1, 236, 239
Finnemore, Martha, 28

foreign national prisoners, 129, 146, 172, 194
Foucault, Michel, 29
Fresh Start, 69–70, 127

G4S (formerly Group 4), 202–4, 246, 259
Garland, David, 42, 45
GEO Group, 202
Glidewell, John, 27, 51
Goffman, Erving, 29, 251
governors, 5, 9, 20, 44, 62–3, 126
  as decision makers, 111, 117, 118, 155, 157, 161–9, 178–200
  performance evaluation, 100–4
  reflections of, 70, 83–4, 89–92, 95, 97, 110–23, 215–46, 253, 255, 258–60
Grayling, Chris, 129, 135, 136, 244
Group 4, 57, 203, 204

Harding, Richard, 53
Hargrove, Erwin, 26, 27, 51
Hatfield prison, 208
Her Majesty's Inspectorate of Prisons, 92–5, 115, 127, 183, 186, 254, 259, 260
Her Majesty's Prison Service (HMPS)
  culture, 189, 190
  humour, 188
  and managerialism, 53–5, 90, 164, 166, 174, 193, 221, 253–9
  and ministers, 171
  performance, 71, 76–8, 84, 94–5, 100, 103, 109–13, 153–60, 206–8, 225, 233
  and the Prison Officers' Association (POA), 149
hierarchist culture, 18, 25, 27–8, 48, 155, 218, 239–40
holistic governance, 18–19, 30–1, 36–7, 38–64, 101, 122, 125, 230, 237, 252
hollowing out, 15–17, 66, 94
Home Affairs Select Committee (HASC), 207
Home Detention Curfew (HDC), 128, 131, 191, 258
Home Office, 43–4, 55, 102, 145–58, 252–60
Home Secretary, 1, 55, 61, 102, 115, 124–36, 140–58, 171–3, 207, 248–9, 254–8
Hood, Chris, 48, 239, 254
Horn, Murray, 23, 238, 240
House of Commons, 44, 256
Howard League, 114
Howard, Michael, 128, 135, 150, 156–7, 176
human rights, 57, 105
humane containment, 48
Hurd, Douglas, 125, 127, 132–5, 256–8

iatrogenic control, 28
immigration, 57, 247, 256
impossible jobs, 26, 27, 239
incidents, 74–8, 253
indeterminate sentences, 131, 206, 260
Isle of Wight, 183

Jebb, Joshua, 154, 257
Jenkins, Roy, 126, 142, 147, 257

Kalyx (now Sodexho), 202–4
Key Performance Targets (KPT), 76, 78, 95, 253
King, Roy, 48, 50

Langdon, Anthony, 48
Lewis, Derek, 55, 128, 150, 156–7
Lincoln prison, 129, 253
Lindholme prison, 208
Liverpool prison, 110, 204, 209, 255
lock-outs, 117, 127
Logan, Charles, 72
Lord Chief Justice, 127, 140, 143
Lord Justice Woolf, 105, 127, 252
Luhmann, Niklas, 31
Lygo Report, 128, 185

managerialism, 4, 8–10, 14–17, 22
  countervailing dynamics, 82–96, 176–7, 193–4
  cultures of, 156
  as part of CCS, 44–53, 58–61, 66–7, 231

managerialism – *continued*
performance, 72, 183
and private sector, 202, 223
standards, 122
March, James, 31
market testing, 121, 149, 198, 208–9, 236
Matthews, Roger, 50–1
McConville, Sean, 42, 252, 254
McDermott, Kathleen, 48, 252
median-voter theory, 21
Merton, Robert, 29, 243
Meyer, Marshall, 26
Miller, Gary, 23
Ministry of Defence, 248
Ministry of Justice, 46, 53, 85, 87, 102, 142, 144, 167, 229, 232, 245, 254, 259
Minkin, Lewis, 62
modularized accommodation, 161
Moe, Terry, 23–4, 56
Moorland prison, 208
MQPL (Measuring the Quality of Prison Life), 165

Narey, Martin, 113, 143, 150, 157, 158, 165, 166, 176
National Audit Office, 57, 120
National Offender Management Service (NOMS), 62–4, 71–2, 94, 119–20
managing the prison population, 160, 230, 255–60
performance, 78–9, 92, 100, 164–74, 207–16, 229
reducing reoffending, 43, 46, 54–6, 84, 129, 150, 190
senior management, 157, 158, 245
standards, 113, 213
New Public Management (NPM)
governance paradigm, 15–22, 241, 242
as part of CCS, 47–55, 60–4
performance management, 98, 193
New Right doctrine, 15
Newell, Mike, 139, 252
normalizing deviance, 28, 49
Northumberland prison, 208

offender management, 56, 84, 95, 167, 169, 260
O'Friel, Brendan, 103
Operation Safeguard, 187, 258
Operational Capacity (Op Cap), 9, 91, 97–123, 165, 172, 180–8, 194, 204, 215, 217, 254
opportunity cost, 22
overcrowding drafts, 91–3, 118, 164, 180, 186, 245, 254, 258
overload, 14–17, 97, 105, 115, 198, 234, 239
overtime
abolition of, 69–71, 88, 127
culture of, 179, 193, 253

paradox, of managerialism, 17–18, 27, 29, 47, 67, 90–1, 122, 140, 180, 198, 199, 217, 223–9, 241, 248, 253
Parkhurst prison, 73, 83, 128, 156
pensions, cost of, 71, 89, 210, 248, 249
Pentonville prison, 102, 110, 221
permanently failing organizations, 26, 59, 94, 239
Peterborough prison, 224
Phillips, Denis, 30, 252
P-NOMIS, 246, 247
police cells, use of, 79, 81, 91, 100, 166, 171, 188
population management (Pop Man), 91–4, 115, 164–8, 175, 181–8, 227–35, 246, 254
Primary Care Trust, 186, 253
Princeton University, 67, 72, 253
principal-agent, 20–2, 149, 152, 227, 237, 241
Prison Act, 101–2
Prison Commission, 102–3, 155, 225, 257–8
Prison Department (PD), 54, 68, 69, 75, 78, 81, 106, 155–7, 170, 185, 254, 258
Prison Governors Association (PGA), 191, 192, 229

Prison Officers Association (POA), 22, 55, 70, 127–9, 139, 147–8, 174, 192, 209, 220, 221, 234, 256
prison population, 5–8, 17, 21, 44–71, 75, 82, 90–1, 100, 102, 112, 113, 119–25, 134–50, 159–73, 186, 191, 194, 205, 208, 214, 234, 244–7, 252–8
Prison Reform Trust, 114, 129, 256
Prison Rules, 102
prisoner and escort custody service (PECS), 1, 2, 78, 163, 201, 221, 260
Prisons Act, 103, 257
Prisons and Probation Inspectorate, 232
private finance initiative (PFI), 57, 90
privately managed prisons, cost of, 219
problematique, 36, 60–1, 251
productivity
  labour, 69–71
  quality-adjusted, 8, 67, 80–3, 241
  total factor, 67–72, 80–1, 253
profit, 144, 202–5, 210, 211, 212, 219
purposeful activity, 76, 78, 211–15
prison reception, 181, 187, 195, 197, 220, 221, 227

rational choice, 7, 14, 19, 30, 34, 36
reconviction rate, 46, 86–8
Rees, Mervyn, 147
refinancing, 57
Regional Custodial Managers (RCMs), 157, 169, 260
rehabilitation, 8, 45, 47, 72, 88, 95, 122, 143–4, 153, 169, 173, 224, 229, 232, 243
  revolution, 42, 61, 129, 134–6
Reid, John, 129, 133–6, 145–6, 150, 173, 176, 256
rent-seeking, 9, 21–9, 179, 205, 210, 224, 237, 241
resilience, 15, 28, 31, 66, 240
resistance
  benign, 7, 8, 41, 51–62, 94, 122, 154, 207, 208, 212, 230, 234–6
Riker, William, 23, 124
riots, 73, 74, 79, 81, 95, 105, 109, 127, 143, 151, 166, 252, 253
Roberts, John, 31, 238
Ruggles-Brise, Evelyn, 42, 154–5, 252, 257
Rye Hill, 204–5, 216, 259

self-organization, 33, 36, 240
separate system, 101, 102, 186, 203, 255
Serco, 1, 202–4
service level agreements (SLA), 121, 218
sex offender treatment, 77, 194
short-sentence prisoners
  increase in, 45, 129, 164
  movement of, 91, 92, 168, 186, 245
  reoffending amongst, 85, 87, 235
Society of Civil and Public Servants, 191
Spurr, Michael, 157, 167
stabilization period, 212
standards
  input, 9, 50, 97–121, 206, 254
  output, 53, 61, 98, 99, 104, 211, 217–18, 241, 251–4
Statutory Instrument (SI), 102
steering, 16, 18, 32, 51, 124
Strangeways prison (Manchester), 74, 103, 105, 109, 110, 127, 252
Straw, Jack, 115, 128–9, 134, 135, 143, 176
suicides in prison, 74–81, 142, 151
system theory, 7, 14, 30, 34, 35, 240

targets, 15, 28, 43, 47, 50, 61, 76–8, 83–5, 89, 92, 95, 99–100, 144, 164, 176, 177, 183–6, 194, 214, 218, 236, 253
Thatcher, Margaret, 133, 146, 199
Tilt, Richard, 157, 158
time out of cell, 78, 211
total institution, 22, 28, 251
Train, Chris, 155, 157
transcarceration, 50

Treasury, 57, 116, 129, 131, 139–55, 173, 176, 209, 233, 234, 252, 257
  Chief Secretary to, 144, 145
tripling (of prisoners in cells), 74, 103, 110, 128

ungovernability, 14, 15

value-based goals, 32, 38–47, 51–5, 241
varieties of capitalism, 17

Waddington, David, 127, 132, 135, 256
Wandsworth prison, 2, 110, 125, 209
(The) Weare prison, 161, 258
Weiler, Terry, 57, 103, 105, 255
Wheatley, Phil, 157, 158, 164–7, 176, 196
Whitelaw, Willie, 126–7, 133–5, 144
Whitemoor prison, 73, 83, 128, 156
whole-system, 6, 34, 38, 60–2
wicked problems, 13
Wildavsky, Aaron, 27, 28
(The) Wolds prison, 128, 204, 216, 259
workforce modernization, 89

young offender, 159, 160, 216, 244, 257

Zucker, Lynne, 26

CPSIA information can be obtained
at www.ICGtesting.com
Printed in the USA
LVOW04*1637140216
475067LV00005B/231/P

9 781137 289155